SEARCH FOR SIGNIFICANCE

LIFE Support Edition

ROBERT S. MCGEE

Learning Activities by Johnny and Sallie Jones

LifeWay Press
Nashville, Tennessee

ACKNOWLEDGMENTS

The *Search for Significance* was originally co-published by Word, Inc. and Rapha Resources, Inc. and is available in its original version in Christian bookstores. We want to thank Rapha Hospital Treatment Centers for making this book available to the LifeWay Press for its use.

Rapha Hospital Treatment Centers is an independent, nationwide provider of adult and adolescent in-hospital psychiatric care and substance abuse treatment from a Christian perspective. For information about Rapha Hospital Treatment Centers you may contact Rapha at 1-800-383-HOPE or write to Rapha, 12700 N. Featherwood, Suite 250, Houston, Texas 77034.

Search for Significance LIFE Support Edition
Copyright © 1992 by Rapha Publishing (Revised, 1993)

LifeWay Press books are published by The Sunday School Board, 127 Ninth Avenue, North, Nashville, Tennessee 37234

Item 7264-62
ISBN 0-8054-9990-3
Dewey Decimal Number 361.3
Subject Heading: COUNSELING // SELF-PERCEPTION

Sources for definitions in *Search for Significance* LIFE Support Edition:
Webster's Ninth New Collegiate Dictionary (Springfield, Mass.: Merriam-Webster Inc., Publishers, 1991).
W.E. Vine, *Vine's Expository Dictionary of New Testament Words*, (McLean, Virginia: MacDonald Publishing Company, n.d.).
Mercer Dictionary of the Bible, ed. Watson E. Mills, (Macon, Ga.: Mercer University Press, 1990).
Bob Hamblin and Bill Stephens, *The Doctrine of Lordship*, (Nashville: Convention Press, 1990).

Unless otherwise indicated, biblical quotations are from the *New American Standard Bible*. © The Lockman Foundation, 1960, 1962, 1963, 1968, 1971, 1972, 1973, 1975, 1977. Used by permission. Other versions used: From the Holy Bible, *New International Version*, copyright © 1973, 1978, 1984 by International Bible Society (NIV); and the *King James Version* (KJV).

Printed in the United States of America

Table of Contents

About the Author 4

Introduction...5

UNIT 1
Beginning the Search 9

UNIT 2
The Performance Trap 28

UNIT 3
Justification 47

UNIT 4
Approval Addict 71

UNIT 5
Reconciliation 88

UNIT 6
The Blame Game 104

UNIT 7
Propitiation 121

UNIT 8
Shame 142

UNIT 9
Major Obstacles to Growth...161

UNIT 10
Our Source of Change 181

UNIT 11
Renewing Our Minds...197

UNIT 12
The Trip In...212

My Identity in Christ..224

The Trip In, God's Truths/False Beliefs Chart ....Inside back cover

About the Author

Robert McGee is a professional counselor and lecturer who has helped thousands of people experience the love and acceptance of Jesus Christ. He also is the founder and president of Rapha, a nationally recognized health care organization that provides in-hospital care with a Christ-centered perspective for adults and adolescents suffering with psychiatric and substance abuse problems.

Johnny and Sallie Jones wrote the learning activities for *Search for Significance* LIFE Support Edition. Johnny is the LIFE Support project coordinator at the Baptist Sunday School Board in Nashville, Tennessee, and has been a pastor in Georgia. Sallie is a college instructor. They lead support groups to help individuals with personal issues.

LOOKING AHEAD TO THE SEARCH

INTRODUCTION

Case in point

> **WRETCHED AND WORTHLESS**
>
> Margie hung up the telephone and suddenly felt sick inside. She had called her mother to wish her a happy birthday. What started to be a pleasant conversation, however, suddenly turned sour. Instead of sounding happy that Margie called, Mom began to scold Margie for not visiting her often enough. Then when Margie related that her five-year-old son, Kevin, had a cough, Mom criticized Margie for not taking the child to the doctor sooner. She told Margie that if only she would insist that Kevin wear a sweater more often, he wouldn't get sick. As tension mounted between mother and daughter, Margie quickly ended the conversation and hung up, absolutely furious at her mother for this turn of events. Then Margie felt guilty about being angry at Mom. After all it was Mom's birthday. The whole incident made Margie feel wretched and worthless.

Have you ever known anyone in Margie's situation, or have you ever found yourself in a circumstance in which you felt utterly devastated as she did?

All of us have times when unpleasant life circumstances come along and knock the props out from under us, and we feel a sense of failure, rejection, guilt, shame, or all those emotions combined. These unpleasant circumstances can result from an everyday conversation between family members, such as in Margie's case, in which Margie received harsh criticism from another person, or from any number of other situations, such as—

- loss of a job
- failure to achieve a goal
- physical or emotional abuse
- a childhood home in which alcoholism or another addiction was present
- death of a spouse or other loved one
- living in impoverished circumstances

- imprisonment
- loneliness
- feeling too busy
- feeling misunderstood
- experiencing frequent anger
- experiencing hurt easily

If you can relate to any of these situations, and if you can relate to any of the negative feelings that stem from them, then *Search for Significance* LIFE Support Edition is for you.

Search for Significance LIFE Support Edition is designed to help you change your thinking about the circumstances you encounter. It is designed to do this by revealing God as the source of your self-worth and to help you experience love, acceptance, and forgiveness in your life.

Course goal

After you complete a study of *Search for Significance* LIFE Support Edition, you will be able to base your self-worth on the love, acceptance, and forgiveness of Jesus Christ and not on the world's standards, such as the approval of others or the ability to succeed at certain tasks.

To help you accomplish this goal, *Search for Significance* LIFE Support Edition will help you learn these things:

- **Four false beliefs** about yourself that result in painful emotions affecting your self-worth.
- **The painful emotions,** or consequences, resulting from the four false beliefs. These beliefs and their related emotions cause us to respond constructively or destructively to whatever situations we find ourselves in.
- **Truths from God's Word,** the Bible, that help you reject the false beliefs. We may not be able to change the situations we encounter, for these situations will occur in our lives day after day. What we can change is what we think or believe about those situations. When we change this, our emotions change as well. When our emotions change, our behavior also can change.
- **The Holy Spirit's renewing of your mind** to replace those false beliefs and harmful emotions.
- **Memorization of God's Word** so you can hide God's truths in your heart and make them a part of your everyday life.
- **An affirmation,** or positive statement, based on God's truths. You can memorize this affirmation and use it to reject the false beliefs as they arise.
- **How to take a Trip In,** a process in which you get in touch with what you really feel about a situation at times when you sense that your emotions could lead to destructive behavior. By identifying the emotion you feel, you learn to reject the false belief and then replace it with God's truths.

On page 224 and the inside back cover you will find the four false beliefs, God's truths, and the affirmation, "My Identity in Christ," described above. You will find them in a form you easily can memorize. Start now to memorize them (you'll review them more thoroughly at other points in the book and will be asked to focus on them in sections) so that by the end of the 12 weeks of study, they become a part of your everyday thought processes.

Search for Significance LIFE Support Edition is part of the LIFE Support Series. The LIFE Support Series is an educational system of discovery-group and support-group resources for providing Christian ministry and emotional support to individuals in the areas of social, emotional, and physical need. These resources deal with such life issues as chemical dependency, codependency, abuse recovery, eating disorders, divorce recovery, and grief. Persons using LIFE Support courses will be led through recovery to discipleship and ministry by using courses in the LIFE learning system. LIFE stands for Lay Institute for Equipping, an advanced approach for equipping Christians for discipleship, leadership, and ministry.

Search for Significance LIFE Support Edition is a discovery-group course designed to be basic to any church's support-group ministry. A discovery group studies dysfunctional family issues and other problem areas that individuals might face. A group leader guides discussion of the topics and helps group members consider applications to life. *Search for Significance* LIFE Support Edition is an ideal resource to help orient a church to support-group ministries because it does not deal with intense life issues that require heavy probing into painful past events. Therefore, it does not require a trained facilitator and is an easy entry point for small- and medium-sized churches that may not have access to persons who are trained. Because of its versatility and subject matter, however, *Search for Significance* LIFE Support Edition also can be used by ongoing support groups desiring to take a break from their regular course of study.

Who can benefit?

A wide variety of people will profit from studying *Search for Significance* LIFE Support Edition. The average individual can use its helps in day-to-day dealings with people. Likewise, people suffering from addictions and whose addictions mask underlying emotional pain will benefit from the material's efforts to help them understand their pain. People who have gone through failure or rejection can benefit from the course to help them develop a healthy identity based on Christ's unconditional love and acceptance.

Here is a sampling of other groups that can benefit.
- **College students**—*Search for Significance* LIFE Support Edition can help students with self-worth issues as they encounter such college-life situations as dating, academic pressures, and comparisons with other persons.
- **Parents**—Parents can study this resource to help understand the source of their own self-worth as well as to help them pass along a proper understanding of this to their children.
- **Depressed individuals**—This resource will help uncover causes of repressed hurt and anger which contribute to depression and will give skills for dealing with present wounds.
- **Prisoners**—Incarcerated individuals can use these helps to reject the false belief of *I am what I am. I cannot change. I am hopeless.*
- **Divorced individuals**—*Search for Significance* LIFE Support Edition will help divorced individuals understand their feelings of resentment, failure, and shame and will help them develop healthy thought processes for the future.
- **Church-staff members**—*Search for Significance* LIFE Support Edition will help church leaders understand and minister to individuals in their congregations suffering from emotional pain.
- **Businessmen/businesswomen**—Individuals in the workplace will benefit from learning how to avoid falling victim to the performance trap and will learn that their personal significance is not determined by achieving promotions, sales, or other business-related achievements.
- **Other persons** such as those participating in neighborhood Bible studies or other study groups in church settings.

The principles behind *Search for Significance* LIFE Support Edition represent a lifelong learning process; therefore, individuals and groups may benefit from studying the course more than one time. The first time of study introduces concepts and begins helping you incorporate them into your thinking. Subsequent times help you apply these principles to your life over and over again until you master the process.

Getting the most from the course

Search for Significance LIFE Support Edition is an integrated course of study. To achieve the full benefit of the educational design, prepare your individual assignments, and participate in the group sessions.

Study Tips. Five days a week (which compose a unit) you will be expected to study a segment of content material. You may need from 30 to 60 minutes of study time each day. Even if you find that you can study the material in less time, spread out the study over five days. This will give you more time to apply the truths to your life. Study at your own pace.

This book has been written as a tutorial text. Study it as if Robert McGee is sitting at your side helping you learn. When he asks you a question or gives you an assignment, respond immediately. Each assignment is indented and appears in **boldface type**. When you are to respond in writing, a pencil appears beside the assignment. For example, an assignment will look like this:

✎ **Read Psalm 139:13. Write what the verse tells about God's care for you.**

Of course, in an actual activity, a line would appear here and below each assignment. You would write your answer on this line. Then, when you are asked to respond in a nonwriting manner—for example, by thinking about or praying about a matter—an arrow appears beside the assignment. This type of assignment will look like this:

➡ **Think about an individual to whom you turn when you need encouragement. Stop and thank God for this person's role in your life.**

In most cases your "personal tutor" will give you some feedback about your response—for example, a suggestion about what you might have written. This process is designed to help you learn the material more effectively. Do not deny yourself valuable learning by skipping the learning activities.

You'll also noted a shaded, dotted line as you read through the material. The line, which looks like this– • is called a "thought stopper." It signals that the material at that point is switching from the subject you just studied and is moving to another topic.

Set a definite time and select a quiet place where you can study with little interruption. Keep a Bible handy for times when the material asks you to look up Scripture. Memorizing Scripture and other elements such as the false beliefs, God's truths, and the affirmation is an important part of your work. Set aside a portion of your study period for memory work. Make notes of problems, questions, or concerns that arise as you study. You will discuss many of these during your discovery-group sessions. Write these matters in the margins of this textbook so you can find them easily.

Discovery-Group Session. Once each week you should attend a *Search for Significance* LIFE Support Edition discovery-group session. These groups consist of up to 10 persons. A group session is designed to help you discuss the content you studied the previous week, practice your memory work, share insights gained, look for answers to problems encountered, and consider practical application of what you've learned to real-life situations.

The discovery group adds a needed dimension to your learning. If you have started a study of *Search for Significance* LIFE Support Edition and you are not involved in a group study, try to enlist some friends or associates who will work through this course with you. A husband and wife can go through the material together. Older youth could join the study alongside their parents. *Search for Significance Leader's Guide* provides guidance and learning activities for these sessions. (Send orders or inquiries to Customer Service Center; 127 Ninth Avenue, North; Nashville, TN 37234; call 1-800-458-2772; or visit your local book store. Ask for item 7269-62, ISBN 0-8054-9989-X.)

A key decision

A key decision to this study is the decision to trust Jesus as your Savior. If you have not done this already, we encourage you to make this decision as the study begins. Within the first pages of unit 1 are helps in making that decision. You will benefit more from this course if you go through this material already having committed your life to Christ. But if you're not ready to make that decision just now, be aware that the need for this decision will be an ongoing emphasis. The material gives you opportunity to look at your relationship with Christ and to determine your need to commit your life to Him.

BEGINNING THE SEARCH

TROUBLED RELATIONSHIPS

An ambitious father neglects his son, who grows up to be a **business executive**. The very day he started working for the company that executive thinks, *If I just can get the promotion I want, then I'll be happy. Success is what really counts in life!* The man receives many promotions and raises because he is driven to perform well, but happiness seems to elude him. A **homemaker** painfully wonders, *Why don't I feel close to my husband?* Having grown up with an alcoholic father and a demanding mother, this woman never has felt lovable and therefore is unable to receive her husband's love. (Read these and similar situations on page 13.) What do these persons need in their lives?

This week you'll–

- learn how the world influences us to believe harmful things about ourselves;
- learn that failure won't destroy a person who has a healthy self-concept;
- look at some things people do when they continually seek others' approval;
- study how God showed how highly He thought of human beings and learn what happened when Satan entered the picture;
- look at your personal relationship with Christ and have an opportunity to accept Him as your Savior and Lord if you have not done this already.

The First Step	Turning on the Light	Our Search for Significance	The Origin of the Search	Saving Solution vs. Satan's Snare
DAY 1	DAY 2	DAY 3	DAY 4	DAY 5

A key verse to memorize this week

And do not be conformed to this world, but be transformed by the renewing of your mind, that you may prove what the will of God is, that which is good and acceptable and perfect.

–Romans 12:2

Words to help you understand this week's lessons

redemption–n. pertains to the redemptive work of Christ, in which He brought deliverance for sinners through His death from the guilt and power of sin. (*Example: Because of Christ's **redemption** I am a new creature of infinite worth.*)

unconditional–adj. without limitation, absolute. (*Example: This week we study about God's **unconditional** love.*)

The First Step

And do not be conformed to this world, but be transformed by the renewing of your mind, that you may prove what the will of God is, that which is good and acceptable and perfect.

–Romans 12:2

In the introduction you read about the four false beliefs that you have developed about yourself over the years. We have these beliefs firmly fixed in our minds because of all the things we have experienced in life. In the Scripture at left, the apostle Paul urged us to avoid the world's influence. This belief system is conformed to the pattern of this world because it shows us the way the world would have us look at ourselves.

These false beliefs (remember–you'll find them on the inside back cover) are so much a part of our thinking, they cause us to react to certain life situations in harmful ways. Have you ever found yourself asking or commenting, "Why in the world did I do that?" or "Wow, that just goes to show what a dummy I am," or "I feel like a real loser," or "I'll *never* be able to do that correctly," or "Nothing in my life ever turns out right"? You probably made these remarks in response to an unpleasant situation you found yourself confronting.

In the introduction you read about an unpleasant situation in which Margie felt like a loser because her mother criticized her during a telephone conversation. Now it's your turn to write about your own experience.

When I felt like a loser

✎ **Try to remember an unpleasant situation you found yourself in the middle of recently. What did you feel? Describe the situation briefly.**

_____

_____

_____

Which of these statements describes how you felt at that time?

❏ I felt as if I were a failure.
❏ I felt as if someone were rejecting me.
❏ I felt guilty about what I said or did.
❏ I felt shame because nothing changes in my life.
❏ Other _____

The four false beliefs

✎ **Before we move on and study further how these false beliefs affect us, let's review them. By now you already may have started memorizing the four false beliefs. Feel free to peek at the list on the inside back cover if you need a little help.**

1. I must meet certain _____ to feel good about myself.

2. I must have the _____ of certain others to feel good about myself.

3. Those who _____ (including myself) are unworthy of love

   and deserve to be _____.

4. I am what I am. I cannot _____. I am _____.

In the introduction you also read that what you believe about a situation creates certain emotions. We have listed those painful emotions, or consequences, for you here.

The painful emotions

FALSE BELIEFS	PAINFUL EMOTIONS
The Performance Trap	❑ The fear of failure
Approval Addict	❑ The fear of rejection
The Blame Game	❑ Guilt
Shame	❑ Feelings of shame

✎ **In the boxes beside the painful emotions listed above, go back and check the emotions you feel you are most likely to get caught up in.**

As the introduction mentioned, *Search for Significance* LIFE Support Edition is designed to help you become transformed, or changed, by the renewing of your mind. We can allow God to transform our thinking from the pattern of this world (the false beliefs) to His truths about us in His Word, the Bible. (Read the Scripture at left to learn more about this kind of truth.)

If you abide in My word, then you are truly disciples of Mine; and you shall know the truth, and the truth shall make you free.

–John 8:31-32

✎ **In the list below match the false beliefs with the truths from God's Word that will help us reject the false beliefs about ourselves. These false beliefs and truths will be explained fully later in the book. Again, you likely will be starting to memorize these, but feel free to peek at the chart on the back pages until you have memorized them.**

God's truths

FALSE BELIEFS	GOD'S TRUTHS
I must meet certain standards to feel good about myself.	Because of *propitiation* I am deeply loved by God. I no longer have to fear punishment or punish others.
I must have the approval of certain others to feel good about myself.	Because of *justification* I am completely forgiven by and fully pleasing to God. I no longer have to fear failure.
Those who fail (including myself) are unworthy of love and deserve to be punished.	Because of *regeneration* I have been made brand-new, complete in Christ. I no longer need to experience the pain of shame.
I am what I am. I cannot change. I am hopeless.	Because of *reconciliation* I am totally accepted by God. I no longer have to fear rejection.

At this point a person can ask one of the following questions.

A major decision

❏ *Will my thinking be conformed to the pattern of this world?*
or
❏ *Will I renew my mind by accepting what God says through His Word about me?*

How you decide to answer these questions will determine whether the pattern of this world will control you or whether you will be transformed by the renewing of your mind.

As we discussed in the introduction, you will study in an in-depth manner during the next 12 weeks the four false beliefs, the painful emotions arising from these beliefs, and the truths of God's Word you can use to reject these beliefs. As you go through these weeks of study, everything will begin to fall in place. You will begin to understand the process of transforming your mind.

Finally, brethren, whatever is true, whatever is honorable, whatever is right, whatever is pure, whatever is lovely, whatever is of good repute, if there is any excellence and if anything worthy of praise, let your mind dwell on these things.

–Philippians 4:8-9

Changing our beliefs from the false beliefs to the truths of God's Word will assist us in experiencing more appropriate emotions and thereby will change the way we respond. However, if we do not begin to think good thoughts about ourselves, we will accomplish nothing lasting. The Scripture in the left margin tells us to dwell on positive thoughts instead of negative ones.

The affirmation, or positive statement about ourselves, that we read about in the introduction will aid us in this process of changing our thinking. This affirmation, "My Identity in Christ," focuses on God's truths and rejects the false beliefs that often control our minds. Remember, it's easier to meditate on something—whether it's a verse or a belief or a statement—if you can repeat it again and again in your mind. Memorizing this affirmation will help you recall it when you need to remember how much God cares about you.

Memorize just the first part of the affirmation here. (Memorization often is easier if you attack it in portions rather than trying to memorize the entire statement all at one time.) In later sessions you'll memorize other parts of the affirmation.

 Look on page 224 to get the affirmation fixed in your mind. Then fill in the blanks.

My Identity in Christ

MY IDENTITY IN CHRIST

Because of Christ's _____ I am a new crea-

tion of infinite _____ .

---

redemption–n. pertains to the redemptive work of Christ, in which He brought deliverance through His death from the guilt and power of sin. (Vine's)

Redemption, which appears in this part of the affirmation, may be new to your vocabulary. We'll spend more time explaining it in later chapters, but for now read the definition in the left margin.

Make these three items—the false beliefs, God's truths, and the affirmation "My Identity in Christ"—a part of your everyday thought processes. The psalmist said, "Thy word have I treasured in my heart, that I may not sin against Thee" (Psalm 119:11). Place these truths in your heart and let God speak to you through them so you will discover God's gracious, effective, and permanent solution to your search for significance. The journey you are about to begin will change your life forever and will lead you to a closer walk with Jesus Christ and to the freedom He has promised.

The journey you are about to begin will change your life forever!

➥ **Stop and pray as you begin this 12-week journey. Ask God to give you an open mind and a willing heart as you study these materials and as you listen for Him to speak to you as you read His Word.**

SUMMARY STATEMENTS

- Our reactions to life situations depend on an ingrained belief system about ourselves.
- We may not be able to change life situations we encounter; we can change what we think or believe about those situations.
- Memorizing God's Word will help us reject false beliefs about ourselves.

DAY 2

Three troubled relationships

unconditional–adj. without limitation, absolute. God loves us completely without requiring us to meet certain conditions. (Vine's)

We are hurt—emotionally, relationally, and spiritually.

Turning on the Light

An ambitious father neglects his son, who grows up to be a **business executive.** The very day he starts working for the company that executive thinks, *If I just can get the promotion I want, then I'll be happy. Success is what really counts in life!* The man receives many promotions and raises because he is driven to perform well, but happiness always seems to elude him.

A **homemaker** with three children painfully wonders, *Why don't I feel close to my husband?* Having grown up with an alcoholic father and a demanding mother, this woman never has felt lovable and therefore is unable to receive her husband's love.

A **pastor** speaks powerfully about God's **unconditional** love, yet guilt plagues him. He feels he must succeed in his public ministry but is withdrawn around his family. He never has understood how to apply his own teaching to *his* life and relationships.

 **Check the statement below that you think is most appropriate.**

    ❑ 1. The truths of God's Word control the people in these stories.
    ❑ 2. A false belief system about themselves controls the people in these stories. This false belief system distorts their understanding of who they truly are in Jesus Christ.

These stories illustrate a fact that is a reality in many of our lives: We are hurt—emotionally, relationally, and spiritually. Because we aren't aware of how wounded we actually are, we can't take steps toward healing and health. Our problem is not stupidity. It's a lack of objectivity—the ability to look at ourselves without letting our perceptions about life based on parental messages, past experiences, and the way we interpreted life in the past color our thinking. Because we lack this ability, we fail to see how real our pain, hurt, and anger are. Why do some of us lack objectivity? Why are we afraid to "turn on the lights" and experience the truth?

Numerous answers exist to these questions, and these answers are different for each person. Perhaps we think that our situations are normal. We may think that enduring loneliness, hurt, and anger represent a normal experience for all persons. Sometimes we think that "*good* Christians" don't have problems or feelings like ours. When we believe this, we deny that our painful emotions exist.

We think that "good Christians" don't have feelings like ours.

Human beings develop fancy ways to block pain and to gain significance. We suppress our painful emotions; we are perfectionists; we drive ourselves to succeed; we withdraw; we say hurtful things to people who hurt us; we punish ourselves when we fail; we try to make clever statements so people will accept us; we help people so they will appreciate us; and we say and do countless other things. A sense of need usually prompts us to look for another choice. We may have the courage to examine ourselves and desperately may want to change, but we also may be unsure about how and where to start.

We may not want to look honestly within ourselves for fear of what we'll find, or we may be afraid that if we discover what's wrong, nothing can help us.

We Need Help

Another person can assist

It is difficult—if not impossible—to turn on the light of objectivity by ourselves. We need the Holy Spirit's guidance. We also need the honesty, love, and encouragement of at least one other person who is willing to help us. Even then, we become depressed easily because of the extent of our wounds.

 Stop now and pray. Ask the Holy Spirit to help you look objectively at your life and to lead you to a person who can help you in the weeks ahead.

 When God directs you to that "someone," write his or her name in the blank below.

_____

dysfunctional family-n. a family in which alcoholism, drug abuse, divorce, absent father or mother, excessive anger, verbal and/or physical abuse exists

Some of us have deep emotional and spiritual scars resulting from the neglect, abuse, and manipulation that often accompany living in a **dysfunctional family** (see definition at left). However, despite the family in which we were reared, all of us suffer from the effects of our own sinful nature and from the imperfections of others. Whether our hurts are deep or whether they are relatively mild, we act wisely when we can be honest about them in the context of affirming relationships. That way, healing can begin.

Ask for God's guidance in the following areas

1. To help me be honest with myself
2. To help me in the healing process
3. To help me deal with my feelings
4. To know and apply God's truths to my life
5. To find a person with whom I can share and who will pray for me

Behold, Thou dost desire truth in the innermost being, and in the hidden part Thou wilt make me know wisdom.
–Psalm 51:6

Many of us mistakenly believe that God doesn't want us to be honest about our lives. We think He will be upset with us if we tell Him how we really feel. But God tells us through the Scriptures that He does not want us to be shallow—in our relationship with Him, with others, or in our own lives. The verse at left expresses the depths to which God wants us to go in our relationship with Him.

God Wants Us to Be Real

The Lord wants us to experience His love in all areas of our lives.

The Lord desires truth and honesty at the deepest level and wants us to experience His love, forgiveness, and power in *all* areas of our lives. Experiencing His love does not mean that all of our thoughts, emotions, and behaviors will be pleasant and pure. It means that we can be *real* as we feel pain and joy, love and anger, confidence and confusion.

Self-worth, often called self-esteem or personal significance, is characterized by a quiet sense of self-respect and a feeling of satisfaction with who we are. True self-worth, unlike pride, is not based on how we evaluate our performance.

✎ **Now write your own definition of *self-worth* or *self-esteem*.**

_____

_____

Name three things you like about yourself

1._____

2._____

3._____

Name three things you dislike about yourself

1._____

2._____

3._____

If you could change anything about yourself, what would you change?

_____

A quick look at who I am

✎ **What is your opinion about yourself? Mark the following statements as *T* (true) or *F* (false).**

_____ 1. I am glad I am who I am.
_____ 2. I love the way I am.
_____ 3. I like being who I am.
_____ 4. I have a healthy sense of self-worth.
_____ 5. I see changes which I need to make in my life, and I am eager to trust God for wisdom and discipline to make these changes.

If you answered false to any of these questions, your sense of self-worth is lower than is the self-worth God wants you to have. This is not a neutral feeling about yourself but a prevailing sense of value that is not related to your performance.

A healthy self-concept develops when a person recognizes his or her value and worth. It involves understanding that a person, as a unique human being, has certain gifts and abilities unlike those anyone else has. It is an understanding that one can contribute to the world in a special way.

Failure won't destroy a person who has a healthy self-concept.

A person who has a healthy self-concept will experience the pain of failure and defeat, but that failure won't destroy that person. A person with a positive sense of self-esteem can enjoy personal strengths and can accept the fact that she has weaknesses. This represents a wholesome love for oneself.

Blessed be the God and Father of our Lord Jesus Christ, who has blessed us with every spiritual blessing in the heavenly places in Christ, just as He chose us in Him before the foundation of the world, that we should be holy and blameless before Him. . . . In Him we have redemption through His blood, the forgiveness of our trespasses, according to the riches of His grace. . . . In Him, you also, after listening to the message of truth, the gospel of your salvation––having also believed, you were sealed in Him with the Holy Spirit of promise, who is given as a pledge of our inheritance, with a view to the redemption of God's own possession, to the praise of His glory.
–Ephesians 1:3-14

✎ **Read Ephesians 1:3-14 (some key verses as well as a definition from the verses appear in the margin at left) and check the statements that correctly describe what God already has done for you.**

❑ 1. God has blessed you with every spiritual blessing.
❑ 2. God has punished you because of your failures.
❑ 3. God has declared you holy and blameless.
❑ 4. God has forgiven you.
❑ 5. God at times has condemned and rejected you.
❑ 6. God has sealed you with the Holy Spirit.

The thoughts in the box below are helpful to remember.

seal–v. to make something secure and permanent

> **YOU ARE BLESSED IN EVERY WAY!**
>
> Because you are a child of God, God has blessed you with every spiritual blessing, chosen you, declared you holy and blameless, adopted you, redeemed you, forgiven you, made known to you the mystery of His will, and **sealed** you with the Holy Spirit.

✎ **Read Ephesians 1:3-14 once again and write below your thoughts about these truths.**

_____

_____

_____

You may feel very happy and thankful; you may be overwhelmed with the great extent of God's love; or you may be thinking, *This can't be true. I don't feel any of these things at all.* That's OK. It's better to be honest and to feel pain than to deny your discomfort and to try to convince yourself that you *are* happy. Remember, your feelings are not the basis of truth. God's Word is our authority. What it says is true, whether we *feel* it or not. The more we understand God's Word and live by it, the more our feelings will reflect His character and love.

From this point forward I am going to assume that I am speaking to people who are Christians—persons who have turned from their sins and who have placed their faith in Jesus Christ as Lord and Savior. If you have not made this key decision in your life, God's invitation always is open for you to come to Him. For help in making that decision, see pages 23-24.

➡ **By now you likely will have started earnestly on your memory work on the false beliefs, God's truths, and the affirmation "My Identity in Christ." Today look on the inside back cover and begin memorizing the first false belief. By the end of this week's study, you likely will have memorized this false belief.**

SUMMARY STATEMENTS

- We need the Holy Spirit to help us see ourselves objectively.
- The Lord wants us to be honest with Him and ourselves.
- Failure won't destroy a person who has a healthy self-concept.
- God has blessed you with every spiritual blessing, chosen you, declared you holy and blameless, adopted you, redeemed you, forgiven you, made known to you the mystery of His will, and sealed you with the Holy Spirit.

DAY 3

We never will find lasting, fulfilling peace if we continually must prove ourselves to others.

Our Search for Significance

God wants all people to achieve a balance between striving for excellence and being content with themselves, but relatively few of us experience that balance. From the beginning of life, we find ourselves on the prowl, searching to satisfy some inner, unexplained yearning. This yearning causes us to seek people who will love us. We strive for success as we drive our minds and bodies harder and farther. We hope that because of our sweat and sacrifice, others will appreciate us more.

But the man or woman who lives only for the love of others' attention never is satisfied—at least not for long. Despite our efforts, we never will find lasting, fulfilling significance if we feel we always must prove ourselves to others. Our desire to be loved and accepted is the symptom of a deeper need—the need that often determines our behavior and is the primary source of our emotional pain. Often unrecognized, this desire represents our need for self-worth.

✎ **Write in the blanks below some ways that people strive for personal significance. I have written in one example for you.**

1. *Making money*
2. _____
3. _____
4. _____

Discovering Our True Worth

In the Scriptures God tells us what we need to discover our true significance and worth. The first two chapters of Genesis tell about the creation of humankind. These chapters reveal the intended purpose for human beings (to honor God) and reveal how valuable people are (men and women are special creations of God).

> The thief comes only to steal, and kill, and destroy; I came that they might have life, and might have it abundantly.
>
> –John 10:10

John 10:10, which appears at left, also reminds us of how much God treasures His creation. It reminds us that Christ came to earth so that people might experience life "abundantly," or fully. However, as Christians, we can realize that we live this abundant life in a real world filled with pain, rejection, and failure. Therefore, experiencing the abundant life God intends for us does not mean that our lives will be problem-free.

On the contrary, life itself is a series of problems that often act as obstacles to our search for significance. The abundant life is the experience of God's love, forgiveness, and power in the midst of these problems. The Scriptures warn us that we experience a **warfare** that can weaken our faith, lower our self-esteem, and lead us into depression. In his letter to the Ephesians, Paul instructs us to put on the armor of God (Godlike qualities that make us spiritually strong) so that we can be equipped for this type of spiritual battle.

warfare–n. a spiritual conflict, as with a mighty army (Vine's)

However, it often seems that unsuspecting believers are the last to know that this battle is occurring and are the last to know that Christ in the end has won the war. They are surprised and confused by difficulties. They think that the Christian life is a playground, not a battlefield.

> Therefore, take up the full armor of God, that you may be able to resist in the evil day, and having done everything, to stand firm. Stand firm therefore, having girded your loins with truth, and having put on the breastplate of righteousness, and having shod your feet with the preparation of the gospel of peace; in addition to all, taking up the shield of faith with which you will be able to extinguish all the flaming missiles of the evil one. And take the helmet of salvation, and the sword of the Spirit, which is the word of God.
>
> –Ephesians 6:13-17

Read Ephesians 6:13-17 at left and complete the list below to learn what makes up this full armor of God:

1. Belt of _____

2. Breastplate of _____

3. Shod your feet with _____

4. Shield of _____

5. Helmet of _____

6. Sword of the _____

As Christians, our fulfillment in this life depends not on how skillfully we avoid life's problems but on how skillfully we apply God's specific solutions to those problems. A correct understanding of God's truths is the first step toward discovering our significance and worth. Unfortunately, many of us have been exposed to incorrect teaching both from religious and secular sources concerning our self-worth. As a result, we may have a distorted self-perception. We may be experiencing hopelessness rather than experiencing the rich and meaningful life God intends for us. Some psychologists say the goal of self-worth is that of simply feeling good about ourselves. A biblical self-concept, however, goes far beyond that limited perspective. It is an accurate perception of ourselves, God, and others, based on the truths of God's Word.

> An accurate, biblical self-concept contains both strength and humility, both sorrow over sin and joy about forgiveness, a deep sense of our need for God's **grace**, and a deep sense of the reality of God's grace.

grace–n.God's favor which is freely given and undeserved (Vine's)

If we confess our sins, He is faithful and righteous to forgive us our sins and to cleanse us from all unrighteousness.
–1 John 1:9

✎ **Rewrite 1 John 1:9, found in the left margin, in your own words. Make what you rewrite personal. Use *I*, *me*, and *my*.**

_____

_____

Whether we call it self-esteem or self-worth, the feeling of significance is crucial to humankind's emotional, spiritual, and social stability and is the driving element within the human spirit. Understanding this single need opens the door to understanding our actions and attitudes.

What a waste to attempt to change behavior without truly understanding the driving needs causing such behavior! Yet millions of people spend a lifetime searching for love, acceptance, and success without understanding the need that causes them to do this. We can understand that this hunger for self-worth is God-given and that only He can satisfy it. Our value does not depend on our ability to earn people's acceptance, which is subject to change. Instead, its true source is God's love and acceptance, which are unchanging. He created us. He alone knows how to fulfill *all* of our needs.

Our value does not depend on our ability to earn people's acceptance.

Do you do this sometimes?

✎ **Listed below are some examples of typical approval-seeking actions. Check the ones you can identify in your behavior.**

❏ I sometimes change my position on something or alter what I believe because someone shows signs that they disapprove of me.
❏ In order to avoid someone's displeased reaction, I sometimes don't say what I mean.
❏ I sometimes flatter people in order to make someone like me.
❏ I sometimes feel depressed or anxious when someone disagrees with me.
❏ I sometimes apologize for myself at every turn—the excessive "I'm sorry" designed to have others forgive me and approve of me all the time.

✎ **Why do we have a basic desire for personal significance? Why do people wrestle with the basic questions, Who am I? and, Why am I here? Write here your thoughts on this subject.**

_____

_____

When God created human beings, He gave them a sense of purpose. When people rebelled against God, they lost that sense of significance. Since then, people have tried to find purpose and meaning apart from God. But God has made us in such a way that He is the only One who can meet our needs.

Money, fame, fine houses, sports cars, and success are only counterfeits of the true worth we have in Christ.

Money, fame, fine houses, sports cars, and success in a job are only counterfeits of the true worth we have in Christ. Though these promise to meet our need for fulfillment, the things they provide are short-lived. God and His purposes alone can give us a profound, lasting sense of significance.

✎ **Look below at each pair of statements. Check which one in each pair indicates a self-worth based on God's acceptance.**

❏ 1. I am recognized as one of the best in my field.
❏ 2. I am recognized as a child of God.

❏ 1. My boss at work really appreciates me.
❏ 2. My Lord totally accepts me.

❏ 1. I almost always am successful in any endeavor I undertake.
❏ 2. I am deeply loved by God.

❏ 1. Everyone at work has noticed the change in me.
❏ 2. I am completely forgiven by the Father.

Realizing that your worth does not depend on meeting some condition will free you from the fears of failure and rejection and will give you joy, thankfulness, and a desire to honor the One who loves you so much.

Going against God's system

Does the world's system of evaluating ourselves govern how we act? The world's system goes against God's system, no matter what our standard of performance is and no matter whose approval we seek.

SUMMARY STATEMENTS

- The abundant life is the experience of God's love, forgiveness, and power in the midst of our problems.
- God has made us in such a way that He is the only One who can meet our needs for significance.
- An accurate, biblical self-concept contains both strength and humility, both sorrow over sin and joy about forgiveness, both a deep sense of our need for God's grace and a deep sense of the reality of God's grace.

DAY 4

The Origin of the Search

The Old Testament tells about the original incident of sin and the fall of human beings into sin:

When the woman saw that the tree was good for food, and that it was a delight to the eyes, and that the tree was desirable to make one wise, she took from its fruit and ate; and she gave also to her husband with her, and he ate. Then the eyes of both of them were opened, and they knew that they were naked; and they sewed fig leaves together and made themselves loin coverings (Genesis 3:6-7).

To understand properly the devastating effects of this event, we need to examine the nature of human beings before sin caused them to lose their sense of security and significance. The first created persons lived in unclouded, intimate fellowship with God. They were secure and free. In all of God's creation, no creature compared to them. Indeed, Adam and Eve, the first persons, were magnificent creations, complete and perfect in the image of God, designed to reign over all the earth (Genesis 1:26-28). Humankind's purpose was to reflect the glory of God. Through humankind God wanted to demonstrate His holiness (Psalm 99:3-5), love and patience (1 Corinthians 13:4), forbearance (1 Corinthians 13:7), wisdom (James 3:13,17), comfort (2 Corinthians 1:3-4), forgiveness (Hebrews 10:17), faithfulness (Psalm 89:1,2,5,8), and grace (Psalm 111:4). Through intellect, free will, and emotions, humankind was to be the showcase for God's glorious character.

✎ **Read Genesis 1:25-31 at left and answer the following questions.**

1. How do these verses show that God thought highly of people He created? (v. 26)

   _____

   _____

2. _____ and _____ are the two responsibilities God gave humankind

3. What was God's evaluation of creation before He created people?

   _____

4. What was His evaluation of it after He created people? _____

   _____

And God made the beasts of the earth after their kind, and the cattle after their kind, and everything that creeps on the ground after its kind; and God saw that it was good. Then God said, "Let Us make man in Our image, according to Our likeness; and let them rule over the fish of the sea and over the birds of the sky and over the cattle and over all the earth, and over every creeping thing that creeps on the earth." And God created man in His own image, in the image of God He created him; male and female He created them. And God blessed them; and God said to them, "Be fruitful and multiply, and fill the earth, and subdue it; and rule over the fish of the sea and over the birds of the sky, and over every living thing that moves on the earth." . . . And God saw all that He had made, and behold it was very good.

–Genesis 1:25-28, 31

(Answers)
1. That fact that God made in His image the people he created shows how highly He regarded them.
2. God created people to bear God's image and to exhibit His glory. In that role, He gave humans two responsibilities—dominion over the earth and procreation, filling the earth with people who also bore God's image.
3-4. Genesis 1:31 reveals that God's view of creation changed from "good" to "very good" after He created the first human beings.

> Before the first persons did a single deed, God said they were very good; therefore, the basis of God's evaluation could not have been their performance. The first persons were acceptable because God said they were.

Satan Enters the Picture

God also created Satan in perfection, just as He did Adam and his wife Eve. At the time God created him, Satan's name was Lucifer, which means "morning star." Lucifer was an angel of the highest rank, created to glorify God. He was clothed with beauty and power and was allowed to serve in the presence of God.

Sadly, Lucifer's pride caused him to rebel against God. He and a third of the angels were cast from heaven (Isaiah 14:12-15). When he appeared to Adam and Eve in the garden, he did so in the form of a serpent, "more crafty than any beast of the field which the Lord God had made" (Genesis 3:1).

✎ **Mark the following statements as *T* (true) or *F* (false).**

_____ 1. God evaluated Adam based on Adam's performance.
_____ 2. God evaluated Eve based on her acceptability.
_____ 3. Adam was acceptable because God said he was.

God gave humans authority over the earth, but if they, like Lucifer, rebelled against God, they would lose both their authority and perfection. They would become a slave to Satan and to sin (Romans 6:17) and subject to God's wrath (Ephesians 2:3). Therefore, destroying human beings was Satan's way to reign on earth. Satan apparently thought it also would overthrow God's glorious plan for humanity. In the above exercise, statements 1 and 2 are false, 3 is true.

Now the deeds of the flesh are evident, which are: immorality, impurity, sensuality, idolatry, sorcery, enmities, strife, jealousy, outbursts of anger, disputes, dissensions, factions, envying, drunkenness, carousing, and things like these, of which I forewarn you just as I have forewarned you that those who practice such things shall not inherit the kingdom of God.

–Galatians 5:19-21

✎ **Read Galatians 5:19-21 at left and list the sins that Satan has used to overthrow God's glorious plan for human beings.**

_____ _____ _____

_____ _____ _____

_____ _____ _____

_____ _____ _____

Sin--as close as the latest news

✎ **What effects of people's falling to temptation were evident in this morning's newspaper stories or in last night's TV news programs? List specific events.**

_____

_____

_____

_____

To accomplish his goal, Satan tempted Eve, who fell to temptation. Eve ate of the tree of the knowledge of good and evil. She believed it would make her wise and like God. Then Adam chose to forsake the love and security of God and to sin also.

In doing this, Adam and Eve not only lost the glory God had intended for humankind, but they also forfeited their close relationship and fellowship with God. Their deliberate rebellion also aided Satan's purpose. It gave Satan power and authority on earth.

And these will go away into eternal punishment, but the righteous into eternal life.

–Matthew 25:46

✎ **Read Matthew 25:46 in the left margin. According to this verse, what is the final outcome of fallen humanity?**

_____

_____

From that moment on after humanity fell, all history led to a single hill outside Jerusalem, where God appointed a Savior to pay the penalty for people's sin of rebellion. Though we justly deserve God's anger because of that deliberate rebellion (our attempts to find security and purpose apart from Him), His Son became our substitute, experienced the wrath our rebellion deserves, and paid the penalty for our sins. Christ's death represents the most overwhelming evidence of God's love for us. Because Christ paid for our sins, our relationship with God is restored. We can experience His nature and character, to commune with Him, and to reflect His love to all the world.

Christ's death represents the most overwhelming evidence of God's love for us.

Today we see effects of the fall in personal problems: sickness, loneliness, suicide; disputes between people, murder, rape, war; or natural disasters such as drought, famine, earthquakes.

What Is Your Relationship with Christ?

We cannot understand with human wisdom alone the truths of God's Word We are able to understand them with the help of the Holy Spirit. God the Father has given us the Holy Spirit as a free gift when we accept Jesus Christ as our Lord and Savior.

Ask yourself the question, Have I made Jesus my Lord and my Savior?

Stop for a moment and decide in your own heart and mind about your relationship with Jesus Christ. Ask yourself the question, *Have I made Jesus my Lord and my Savior?* Before you go any further in this search for significance, settle this question. Without the free gift of salvation that is found only in Jesus Christ, you do not possess the Holy Spirit. Without the Holy Spirit you do not possess spiritual understanding, and you never will be able to accept what God's Word says about you.

✎ **Read Titus 3:4-7 at left. On the basis of what are we saved?**

But when the kindness of God our Savior and His love for mankind appeared, He saved us, not on the basis of deeds which we have done in righteousness, but according to His mercy, by the washing of regeneration and renewing by the Holy Spirit, whom He poured out upon us richly through Jesus Christ our Savior, that being justified by His grace we might be made heirs according to the hope of eternal life.

–Titus 3:4-7

_____

_____

_____

We do not gain acceptance into God's eternal kingdom based on our good works. We can do no amount of good deeds—religious or otherwise—that will obligate God to save us. Salvation is a gift from God that comes to us when we accept in our hearts and minds that Jesus Christ died for all our sins on the cross of Calvary, when we confess that He is the Lord of our lives, and when we believe that He is alive and has conquered sin and death for us.

Call on the Lord in repentance, faith, and surrender, sincerely using the words in the box on the next page or using similar words of your own, and Jesus will become your Savior and Lord.

> Dear God, I know that Jesus is Your Son and that He died on the cross and was raised from the dead. I know that I have sinned and need forgiveness. I am willing to turn from my sins and receive Jesus as my Savior and Lord. Thank You for saving me. In Jesus' name. Amen.

If you prayed that prayer just now, welcome to the family of God. You have just made the most important decision of your life. You can be sure you are saved and have eternal life.

that if you confess with your mouth Jesus as Lord, and believe in your heart that God raised Him from the dead, you shall be saved; for with the heart man believes, resulting in righteousness, and with the mouth he confesses, resulting in salvation.
–Romans 10:9-10

✎ **Read Romans 10:9-10 at left. Which statements below are necessary for salvation to be ours?**

❏ 1. Confess that Jesus is Lord over your life.
❏ 2. Believe that He is a living Savior.
❏ 3. Believe that He has forgiven all your sins.
❏ 4. Believe that He has given the Holy Spirit to counsel you.

Wonderful things happen!

The moment you trust Christ, many wonderful things happen to you:

- All your sins—past, present, and future—are forgiven (Colossians 2:13-14).
- You become a child of God (John 1:12; Romans 8:15).
- You receive eternal life (John 5:24).
- You are delivered from Satan to the kingdom of Christ (Colossians 1:13).
- Christ comes to dwell in you (Revelation 3:20).
- You become a new creation (2 Corinthians 5:17).
- You are declared righteous by God (2 Corinthians 5:21).
- You enter a love relationship with God (1 John 4:9-11).
- God accepts you (Colossians 1:19-22).

...and to know the love of Christ which surpasses knowledge, that you may be filled up to all the fullness of God.
–Ephesians 3:19

✎ **Think of how these truths apply to your life. Then write a prayer thanking God for His wonderful grace. As you write your prayer, experience the love of Christ that surpasses knowledge, as the verse at left promises.**

_____

_____

_____

_____

_____

_____

 It's time to review again your memory work on the first false belief. Read it (turn to the inside back cover if you need to refer to the chart) until you can repeat this false belief from memory.

Saving Solution vs. Satan's Snare

DAY 5

We all have strong, God-given needs for love, acceptance, and purpose. Most of us go virtually to any lengths to meet those needs. Many of us have become masters at "playing the game" to be successful and to win others' approval. Some of us, however, have failed and have experienced the pain of disapproval so often that we have given up and have withdrawn into a shell of hurt, numbness, or depression. In both cases we are living by the deception that our worth is based on our performance and on others' opinions—some of us are simply more adept than others are at playing this game.

Our attempts to meet our needs for success and approval fall into two broad categories: compulsiveness and withdrawal.

Compulsiveness

Some people use extra effort, work extra hours, and try to say just the right things to achieve success and to please those around them. These people may have an overwhelming desire to be in control of every situation. They are perfectionists. If a job isn't done perfectly, if they aren't dressed just right, if their peers don't consider them the best, then they work harder until they achieve that coveted status. And pity the poor soul who gets in their way! Whoever doesn't contribute to their success is a threat to their self-esteem—an unacceptable threat.

This driven individual may be very personable and may have a lot of "friends," but the goal of any friendships this individual makes may not be to give encouragement and love. The goal may be to control others so others may contribute to the driven individual's success. That may sound harsh, but people who are driven to succeed often will use practically everything and everybody to meet that need.

 Check the correct boxes that describe characteristics of a person who is driven to succeed.

- ❏ 1. This person must be in control of every situation.
- ❏ 2. This person accepts herself with her imperfections.
- ❏ 3. This person will use practically everything and everybody to meet his need to succeed.
- ❏ 4. This person will work harder and harder until her peers consider her the best.
- ❏ 5. This person doesn't worry about how he dresses.

Withdrawal

The other broad category is withdrawal. Those who show this behavior usually sidestep risks by trying to avoid failure and disapproval. They won't volunteer for the jobs that offer much risk of failure. They move toward people who are comforting and kind. They skirt relationships that might demand that they will be vulnerable and that consequently might cause them to risk rejection. They may appear to be easygoing, but inside they usually are running from every possible situation or relationship that might not succeed.

✎ **Check the box beside the words or phrases below that characterize a person exhibiting withdrawal.**

❑ Avoidance
❑ Risk taker
❑ Fears disapproval
❑ Fears rejection

❑ Willing to be vulnerable
❑ Skirts demanding relationships
❑ Volunteers
❑ Runs from situations that may not be successful

Obviously, these are two broad categories. Most of us exhibit some combination of the two behaviors. We are willing to take risks and to work hard in the areas in which we feel sure of success, but we avoid the people and situations that may bring rejection and failure.

We develop a have-to mentality.

When we base our security on success and on others' opinions, we become dependent on our abilities to perform and to please others. We develop a have-to mentality: I have to do well on this exam (or my security as a good student will be threatened). I have to make that deal (or it will mean that my boss will think I am a failure). My father (or mother, spouse, friend) has to appreciate me and be happy with my decisions (because I cannot cope with his disapproval).

Only Christ Never Fails

God freely has given us our worth. Failure and/or others' disapproval can't take it away!

We do not *have to* be successful or *have to* please others to have a healthy sense of self-esteem and worth. God freely has given us our worth. Failure and/or others' disapproval can't take it away! Therefore, we can conclude, *It would be nice for my parents* (or whomever) *to approve of me, but if they don't approve of me, God still loves and accepts me.*

Do you see the difference? The *have-to* mentality is sheer slavery to performance and to the opinions of others, but we are secure and free in Christ. We don't *have to* have success or anyone else's approval. Of course, it would be nice to have success and approval, but the point is clear: Christ is the source of our security; Christ is the basis of our worth; Christ is the only One who promises and never fails.

We can choose two possible options to determine our self-worth:

The world's system

God's system

> The world's system: Self-worth=Performance (what you do) + Others' Opinions (what others think or say about you).
>
> God's system: Self-worth = God's Truth About You

The World's Self-worth System Versus God's System

✎ **The following are the four false beliefs that many of us apply daily in our relationships and circumstances. Estimate to what degree, from 0 to 100 percent, you live by each of these beliefs.**

_____% I must meet certain standards to feel good about myself.

_____% I must have the approval of certain others to feel good about myself. (Without their approval I cannot feel good about myself.)

_____% Those who fail (including myself) are unworthy of love and deserve to be punished.

_____% I am what I am. I cannot change. I am hopeless. (In other words, I am the sum total of all my successes and failures, and I'll never be significantly different.)

When we first begin to examine and confront these lies, the percentage to which these lies affect us may seem high. This is normal. It represents the beginning of change. In time this percentage should go down. To the extent that you believe these lies, the world's system influences your life. Each belief stems from the concept that your *self-worth = performance + others' opinions*.

The process of hope and healing

This book is dedicated to the process of understanding, applying, and experiencing the basic truths of God's Word. In its chapters we will examine the process of hope and healing. We also will identify four specific false beliefs Satan's deception generates. We also will discover God's gracious, effective, and permanent solution to our search for significance.

✎ **Review this week's lessons. Pray and ask God to identify one positive statement that had an impact on your understanding of who you are.**

Write that statement in your own words.

_____

_____

_____

Rewrite your thoughts as a prayer of thankfulness to God.

_____

_____

_____

You probably gained many insights as you worked through this week's lessons. Which insight stands out to you? Write it here.

_____

_____

_____

THE PERFORMANCE TRAP

Case in point

NEVER GOOD ENOUGH

Brent made a daily list of things he could accomplish if everything went perfectly in his world that day. He became angry if things didn't go well or if someone took too much of his time. He felt fulfilled if he was using his hours efficiently and effectively. Yet even when this happened, Brent was miserable. He constantly was driven to do more, but his best never was enough to satisfy him. Brent believed that accomplishing goals and making efficient use of his time represented what the Lord wanted him to do. When he experienced stress, he occasionally thought something wasn't quite right, but his solution was to try harder, make even better use of his time, and be even more regimented. (Read more about Brent's story on page 37.) What does Brent need in his life?

What you'll learn this week

This week you'll–

- learn what factors must exist before a person's emotional healing can occur;
- study about how perfectionism and despair—two side effects of the fear of failure—have a devastating impact on our lives;
- learn exactly how we are affected by the belief that we must meet certain standards to feel good about ourselves;
- learn some other ways—such as perfectionism, avoiding risks, anxiety, and anger—that the fear of failure impacts us;
- learn how God can use our painful failures to get our attention at times.

What you'll study each day

The Process of Hope, Healing	The Fear of Failure	A Rules-Dominated Life	Effects of the Fear of Failure	Getting Our Attention
DAY 1	DAY 2	DAY 3	DAY 4	DAY 5

Memory verse

A key verse to memorize this week

Behold, Thou dost desire truth in the innermost being, And in the hidden part Thou wilt make me know wisdom.

–Psalm 51:6

WordWatch

Words to help you understand this week's lessons

depressant–n. an agent that reduces a bodily functional activity or an instinctive desire. (*Example: Alcohol is a **depressant**.*)

stimulant–n. an agent that produces a temporary increase of the functional activity or efficiency of an organism. (*Example: Some drugs are **stimulants**.*)

<table>
<tr><td>

DAY

1

</td><td>

The Process of Hope, Healing

</td></tr>
</table>

Several factors must exist in a person's life before emotional healing can occur. These factors are not steps we can accomplish one right after the other. They are ingredients that promote healing when they all work at the same time and over a period of time. The box below lists these factors.

- honesty
- relationships that affirm me, or make me feel good about myself
- right thinking
- the Holy Spirit's power, strength, and wisdom
- time

If any of these is missing in a person's life, then her healing process will be slowed down, if not stopped completely.

 Which of the factors listed in the box above seems to be missing in your life? Why do you think this is true of you?

_____

_____

_____

Let's examine these five ingredients.

Honesty

Aware of our need

We can experience healing only to the degree that we are aware we need it. If we are completely unaware of our need, we won't seek a solution. If we have only a surface awareness of our need and are honest about it, we may seek (and find) only remedies that scratch the surface of our need.

But if someone encourages us to be honest at a deeper level about our painful needs, then we can experience the power of healing and comfort at that particular level.

 Read Psalm 51:6, which appears in the margin at left. From this passage and the above paragraph, why do you think the Lord wants us to be honest with Him? with others? with ourselves?

Behold, Thou dost desire truth in the innermost being, And in the hidden part Thou wilt make me know wisdom.
–Psalm 51:6

❏ Honesty is the best policy.
❏ The Bible tells us not to lie to one another.
❏ Honesty is the first crucial step toward healing and maturity.
❏ Honesty helps us go beyond a surface awareness of our need and to deal with our need for healing at a deeper level.

The Lord wants us to be honest with ourselves, with Him, and with at least one other person. We need honesty in our lives because it is the first important step toward healing and maturity and helps us go beyond surface awareness.

✎ **Check the statement you feel best describes how honest you are about your needs.**

❑ I am completely honest and objective about myself all the time.
❑ I feel that most of the time I am honest and objective about myself.
❑ I feel that I seldom am honest or objective about myself.
❑ I feel that I never am honest or objective about myself.

We need to ask God for increased understanding in order to determine what parts of our lives need change.

Because none of the people around us tell us otherwise, most of us believe that we are completely honest about ourselves and that we are objective (able to look at ourselves with an open mind). We can ask God for increased understanding in order to determine what parts of our lives need change.

Those of us from relatively stable backgrounds usually find it easy to be honest about the joys and pain in our lives. Some of us, however, come from dysfunctional families and have experienced tragedies that have caused deep wounds. These experiences prompt us to put up defenses designed to block pain. Defensive barriers often keep us from seeing problem areas in our lives.

Affirming Relationships

Without some affirmation from others, people seldom have the objectivity and the courage to be honest about their lives. The love, strength, and honesty we find in other people truly are Godlike traits.

A friend, a small group, a pastor, or a counselor who won't be frustrated by our slow progress—and who won't give us quick and easy solutions—is a valuable find! This person can listen to us reflectively instead of lecturing us and making judgmental statements about what we say. (Of course, we must use good judgment about what and with whom we share!)

Pray that God will provide a person or group of persons with whom you can be open and honest, who objectively can listen to you and share with you, and who will encourage you to make real, rather than surface, progress. This type of person truly is a treasure!

Fill in the first three blanks in the left margin. You probably have felt that your parents, a friend, a teacher, your spouse, or a group loved and valued you.

Name three persons who in past times affirmed or encouraged you:

_____

_____

_____

Name three persons who now are affirming and encouraging you.

_____

_____

_____

✎ **Check the statement(s) that best expresses how these persons' affirmation affected you.**

❑ I gained a sense of confidence.
❑ I felt encouraged.
❑ I withdrew from the person.
❑ I did not feel I deserved the affirmation.
❑ I felt that this person cared about me.

Now fill in the last three blanks in the left margin. Perhaps you now are receiving positive reinforcement from your parents, a counselor, a pastor, a close friend, or a group. Perhaps one of your children is among your major supporters. Perhaps you named a neighbor. Perhaps you named someone you see often or only occasionally.

✎ **Check the statement(s) below that best describes the effect this person (or group) has on you.**

❏ This person or group listens to me appreciatively.
❏ This person or group encourages my honesty.
❏ This person or group accepts my strengths and weaknesses.
❏ This person or group gives me respect and support.

Name the one person you have selected to assist you during this course.

_____

➡ **If you have not yet found someone who will encourage and affirm you, stop now and pray for God's leadership in this decision. You may want to consider someone in your discovery group.**

Right Thinking

We have structured many elaborate defenses to protect ourselves.

Many of us don't know what we really believe about God and about ourselves. We often say what we don't mean and mean what we don't say. God's Word is our guide. It is truly "a lamp to our feet and a light to our path" (Psalm 119:105). And yet we often have trouble applying scriptural concepts because over the years we have structured so many elaborate defenses to protect ourselves.

We must realize that we can use Scripture, as God speaks to us through it, to identify and attack these defensive barriers. This will enable us to experience an open and honest relationship with God. The verse below describes just how powerful Scripture can be in our lives.

> For the word of God is living and active and sharper than any two-edged sword, and piercing as far as the division of soul and spirit, of both joints and marrow, and to judge the thoughts and intentions of the heart. And there is no creature hidden from His sight, but all things are open and laid bare to the eyes of Him with whom we have to do.
>
> –Hebrews 4:12-13

What influences you most?

✎ **Think of how you have developed your thoughts and beliefs. In the list below give a score to each item (10 high, 0 low) to indicate what effect it has on your thoughts and beliefs.**

_____ Books		_____ Television programs	
_____ Movies		_____ Friends	
_____ Family		_____ God	
_____ Neighbors		_____ Pastor	

All of the above have influenced our lives and profoundly have affected our thoughts and beliefs. All of them have made a difference in our lives. But our family background probably has had the most impact on how our belief system developed.

Read 2 Timothy 3:16-17 in the left margin. Describe below in your own words what this verse tells you about how the Scriptures can help you.

_____

_____

All Scripture is inspired by God and profitable for teaching, for reproof, for correction, for training in righteousness; that the man of God may be adequate, equipped for every good work.
–2 Timothy 3:16-17

As God speaks to us through the Scriptures, they will teach us about life, show us where our views are in error, and correct our faulty perceptions so that we continually can experience the process of growth as well as experience God's love, forgiveness, and power.

The Holy Spirit

God gives us the Holy Spirit to communicate God's love, light, forgiveness, and power to our deepest needs.

Deep, spiritual healing requires giving attention to the whole person. It requires giving attention to a person's emotional, relational, physical, and spiritual needs. God gives us the Holy Spirit to communicate God's love, light, forgiveness, and power to our deepest needs. This spiritual aspect of healing perhaps is the most basic aspect of healing, because our view of God (and our relationship with Him) can determine the quality and degree of health we experience in every other area of our lives.

What a miracle!

Some of us believe that only positive, pleasant emotions like love and joy characterize the Holy Spirit's ministry. However, the Holy Spirit produces honesty and courage in our lives as we grapple with the reality of pain. This is one of the miracles of the Holy Spirit's work! He is the Spirit of truth, not of denial. He enables us to experience each element of the healing process as He gives us wisdom, strength, and encouragement through God's Word and through other people.

The Holy Spirit is the source of spiritual wisdom, insight, and power. He uses the Word of God and the people of God to instruct us and to model the character of Christ to us.

Read John 14:16-17 at left. How does it make you feel when you realize that the Holy Spirit is the Spirit of truth in your life as the verse and the paragraphs you just read above describe?

_____

_____

And I will ask the Father, and He will give you another Helper, that He may be with you forever; that is the Spirit of truth, whom the world cannot receive, because it does not behold Him or know Him, but you know Him because He abides with you, and will be in you.
–John 14:16-17

Time

Don't we sometimes wish we were computers so that solutions to our problems would occur in microseconds? People, however, don't change that quickly.

In the Scriptures we see many references to agriculture. The Scriptures depict seasons of planting, weeding, watering, growing, and harvesting. Farmers don't expect to plant seeds in the morning and harvest their crops that afternoon. Seeds must go through a complete cycle of growth before they mature. They receive plenty of attention in the process. In this age of instant coffee, microwave dinners, and instant banking, we assume that spiritual, emotional, and relational health will be rapid also. These unrealistic expectations only cause discouragement and disappointment.

No quick fixes

> Our growth will be stunted and superficial if we don't emphasize properly the essential five elements: honesty about our emotions, affirming relationships, right thinking promoted through Bible study and applying the Bible to our lives, the ministry of the Holy Spirit, and time.

We can remember that all of these elements are required to produce growth and health.

Why we get impatient

✎ Check the sentences below that best express the reasons we tend to get impatient and to expect fast results.

❑ We don't want to experience hurt.
❑ Others say something like a seminar or a book helped them instantly.
❑ Technological advances in society encourage us to expect dramatic results at the push of a button.
❑ When we experience a spurt of insight and healing, we conclude that the rest of the process should be quick and easy.

Our growth toward wholeness and maturity is a journey which we can't complete fully until we join the Lord in heaven. The apostle Paul understood this and saw himself as being in the middle of this process. In the verse in the left margin, read what he wrote about this to the Philippian believers.

Not that I have already obtained it, or have already become perfect, but I press on in order that I may lay hold of that for which also I was laid hold of by Christ Jesus. Brethren, I do not regard myself as having laid hold of it yet; but one thing I do: forgetting what lies behind and reaching forward to what lies ahead. I press on toward the goal for the prize of the upward call of God in Christ Jesus.

–Philippians 3:12-14

✎ Read Philippians 3:12-14 and indicate whether the following statements are *T* (true) or *F* (false).

_____ Paul felt he already had obtained his goal.
_____ Paul felt he was not perfect.
_____ Paul was in the process of obtaining his goal.
_____ Paul forgot what had been and was looking to the future.

If Paul, the foremost missionary and writer of much of the New Testament, saw himself as being "in the process," we can feel encouraged to continue in the process toward change as well. All statements but the first are true.

SUMMARY STATEMENTS

• Our growth toward wholeness and maturity is a journey that can't be completed fully until we join the Lord in heaven.
• God gives us the Holy Spirit to communicate God's love, light, and power to our deepest needs.

The Fear of Failure

Most of us do not realize how completely Satan has tricked us. He has led us blindly down a path of destruction, made us captives because we feel unable to meet our standards consistently, and made us slaves of our low self-esteem. Satan holds us in chains that keep us from experiencing Christ's love, freedom, and purposes.

Testing Our Thoughts

See to it that no one takes you captive through philosophy and empty deception, according to the tradition of men, according to the elementary principles of the world, rather than according to Christ.
—Colossians 2:8

For who has known the mind of the Lord, that he should instruct Him? But we have the mind of Christ.
—1 Corinthians 2:16

Read the first verse in the left margin to see what Paul warns about being held captive by wrong thoughts. We truly have become mature when we begin testing our minds' deceitful thoughts against the Word of God. We no longer have to live by our incorrect thoughts; we can have the mind of Christ (see the second verse at left). Through His Spirit we can challenge the long-held ideas and traditions that keep us feeling guilty and condemned. We then can replace those deceptions with the powerful truths of the Scriptures.

 Read the following Scriptures and after each one write the powerful truth of God's Word that you find there.

"There is therefore now no condemnation for those who are in Christ Jesus" (Romans 8:1).

_____

"Who shall separate us from the love of Christ? Shall tribulation, or distress, or persecution, or famine, or nakedness, or peril, or sword?" (Romans 8:35).

_____

"It was for freedom that Christ set us free: therefore keep standing firm and do not be subject again to a yoke of slavery" (Galatians 5:1).

_____

"yet He has now reconciled you in His fleshly body through death, in order to present you before Him holy and blameless and beyond reproach" (Colossians 1:22).

_____

"I am writing to you, little children, because your sins are forgiven you for His name's sake" (1 John 2:12).

_____

Success—No Road to Happiness

Many of us are deceived into believing that success will bring fulfillment and happiness. Again and again, we've tried to measure up, thinking that if we

Occasional failure may be so devastating that it dominates how we perceive ourselves.

could meet certain standards, we would feel good about ourselves. But again and again, we've failed and have felt miserable. Even if we succeed on a fairly regular basis, occasional failure may be so devastating that it dominates how we perceive ourselves.

 Think about a time you thought you would feel happy if you could succeed at a task. Write here why you believed this.

_____

_____

A threat to our significance

Consciously or unconsciously, all of us have experienced the feeling that we must meet certain arbitrary standards to attain self-worth. Failure to meet them threatens our security and significance. Such a threat, real or perceived, results in a fear of failure.

At that point we are accepting the false belief: I must meet certain standards in order to feel good about myself. When we believe this about ourselves, our attitudes and behavior reflect Satan's distortion of truth.

What standards do you set?

 Think for a moment about certain standards you have set for yourself. List one standard for each category identified.

Job: _____

Parent: _____

Christian: _____

Spouse: _____

Friend: _____

How We React to Satan's Deception

Because of our unique personalities, we each react very differently to deception. Some of us respond by becoming slaves to perfectionism. We drive ourselves over and over toward reaching goals. Others of us go into a tailspin of despair. Let's look at how these two reactions affect us.

Two ways to respond

As you read below about perfectionism, underline key words or phrases describing the behavior. I have underlined one for you.

Perfectionism. Perfectionists often may experience serious mood disorders. They often feel rejection is coming when they believe they haven't met standards they try hard to reach. Perfectionists tend to <u>react defensively to criticism.</u> They demand to be in control of most situations they encounter.

Because they usually are more competent than most, perfectionists see nothing wrong with their compulsions. "I just like to see things done well," they claim.

Nothing really is wrong with doing things well; the problem is that perfectionists usually base their self-worth on their ability to accomplish a goal. Therefore, failure is a threat and is totally unacceptable to them.

Karen's example

Karen, a wife, mother, and civic leader, seemed ideal to everyone who knew her. She was a perfectionist. Her house looked perfect; her children were spotless; and her skills as president of the Ladies' Auxiliary were superb. In each area of her life Karen always was successful. However, one step out of the pattern she had set could lead to a tremendous uproar. When others failed to comply with her every demand, she condemned them quickly and cruelly.

One day her husband decided that he couldn't stand any more of Karen's overly critical behavior. He wanted an understanding wife with whom he could talk and share. He didn't want a self-driven perfectionist. He wanted someone who supported him and did not condemn him when he made some inevitable mistake. Friends later could not understand why this husband chose to leave his wife, who seemed to be perfect. Like Karen, many high achievers are driven beyond healthy limitations. They rarely are able to relax and enjoy life because they're constantly striving toward some accomplishment. Their families and relationships suffer as they try to achieve often unrealistic goals.

Many high achievers are driven beyond healthy limitations. Their families and relationships suffer as they try to achieve goals.

Despair and Passivity. On the other hand, the same false belief (I must meet certain standards to feel good about myself) that drives many to perfectionism drives others to despair. They rarely expect to achieve anything or to feel good about themselves. Because they have failed in the past, they are quick to feel that their present failures only show how worthless they really are. They often become extremely sad and stop trying because they fear more failure.

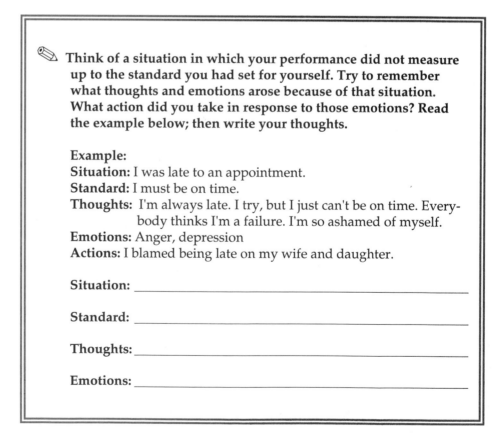

✎ **Think of a situation in which your performance did not measure up to the standard you had set for yourself. Try to remember what thoughts and emotions arose because of that situation. What action did you take in response to those emotions? Read the example below; then write your thoughts.**

Example:
Situation: I was late to an appointment.
Standard: I must be on time.
Thoughts: I'm always late. I try, but I just can't be on time. Everybody thinks I'm a failure. I'm so ashamed of myself.
Emotions: Anger, depression
Actions: I blamed being late on my wife and daughter.

Situation: _____

Standard: _____

Thoughts: _____

Emotions: _____

How we act when we fail

In almost any activity or relationship, we likely will experience the fear of failure. When we fail, we usually experience:

anger
resentment
worry

fear
anxiety
depression

In turn, these emotions express themselves through actions like:

withdrawal
hostility

rudeness
blaming others

➡️ **By now you likely will have started earnestly on your memory work on the affirmation "My Identity in Christ." Today look at the inside back cover and begin memorizing the first two lines of the affirmation. By the end of this week's study, you likely will have memorized this part.**

SUMMARY STATEMENTS

- We truly have become mature when we begin testing the deceitful thoughts of our minds against the Word of God.
- When we believe we must meet certain standards to feel good about ourselves, our attitudes and behaviors reflect Satan's distortion of the truth.
- Many high achievers are driven beyond healthy limitations. Their families and relationships suffer as they try to achieve goals.

DAY 3

A Rules-Dominated Life

The pressure of having to meet self-imposed standards to feel good about ourselves can cause a person to live a rules-dominated life. Individuals caught in this trap often have a set of rules for most of life's situations. They continually focus their attention on their performance and on their ability to stick to their schedule.

Brent, for example, made a daily list of what he could accomplish if everything went perfectly. He became angry if things didn't go well or if someone took too much of his time. He felt fulfilled if he was using his time efficiently and effectively. Yet even when this happened, Brent was miserable. He constantly was driven to do more, but his best never was enough to satisfy him.

Brent believed that accomplishing goals and making efficient use of his time represented what the Lord wanted him to do. When he experienced stress, he occasionally thought that something wasn't quite right, but his solution was to try harder, make even better use of his time, and be even more regimented.

Brent's example

Brent was right. Something wasn't quite right in his life. His focus was misdirected because his focus was not truly on Christ.

lordship–n. authority or power over (*The Doctrine of Lordship*)

> The focus of the Christian life should be on Christ, not on self-imposed regulations. Our experience of Christ's **lordship** depends on our moment-by-moment attention to His instruction, not on our own regimented schedule.

As these cases demonstrate, the false belief—I must meet certain standards to feel good about myself—results in a fear of failure. How much does this belief affect you? Take the following test on this page and the next to determine how strongly you fear failure.

✎ **Read each of the following statements; then, from the top of the test, choose the term that best describes your response. Put in the blank beside each statement the number above the term you choose.**

1	2	3	4	5	6	7
Always	Very Often	Often	Sometimes	Seldom	Very Seldom	Never

_____ 1. I often avoid participating in certain activities because of fear.

_____ 2. I become nervous and anxious when I sense that I might experience failure in some important area.

_____ 3. I worry.

_____ 4. I have unexplained anxiety.

_____ 5. I am a perfectionist.

_____ 6. I am compelled to justify my mistakes.

_____ 7. Certain areas exist in which I feel I must succeed.

_____ 8. I become depressed when I fail.

_____ 9. I become angry with people who interfere with my attempts to succeed and, as a result, make me appear incompetent.

_____ 10. I am self-critical.

_____ Total (Add the numbers you have placed in the blanks.)

What your score says about you

Did your test show that God's unconditional love guides your thinking or that a fear of failure is in the driver's seat of your life?

Interpreting Your Score

If your score is…

57-70

God apparently has given you a very strong appreciation for His love and unconditional acceptance. You seem to be free from the fear of failure that plagues most people. (Some exceptions, however: some people who score this high either are greatly deceived or have blocked their emotions as a way to suppress pain.)

47-56

The fear of failure rarely controls your responses or does so only in certain situations. Again, people who are not honest with themselves represent the major exceptions to this statement.

37-46

When you experience emotional problems, they may relate to a sense of failure or to some form of criticism. As you reflect on many of your previous decisions, you probably will find that you can relate many of them to this fear. The fear of failure also will affect many of your future decisions unless you act directly to overcome this fear.

27-36

The fear of failure forms a general backdrop to your life. Probably, few days exist in which this fear does not affect you in some way. Unfortunately, this fear robs you of the joy and peace your salvation is meant to bring.

0-26

Experiences of failure dominate your memory. They probably have caused you to be depressed a great deal. These problems will remain until you take definite action. In other words, this condition will not simply disappear; time alone cannot heal your pain. You need to experience deep healing in your self-concept, in your relationship with God, and in your relationships with others.

Cutting Yourself Off

When our performance meets our standard, it can give a sense of pride that we might mistake for self-worth. We feel good; we feel significant. We then strive to meet another standard and then another so we can feel good about ourselves again. We use performance to evaluate our self-worth because the system reinforces itself: when we perform well, we feel good. This "success" makes us feel that the system works, so we keep using it. (Please note: it isn't wrong to be glad we succeeded at something. The issue is whether we base our self-worth on succeeding. Either our performance leads us to pride, or God's truth leads us to true joy and the desire to honor Him in all things.)

It is not wrong to be glad we succeeded at something. The issue is whether we base our self-worth on our succeeding.

If you reject God's provision for self-worth and instead embrace the world's false promises, your performance is your only alternative for meeting this deep, almost all-encompassing need. You usually act according to your beliefs. If you believe you are a failure, you may cut yourself off from a worthwhile activity because you fear you will fail at it. In the box at left, describe a time you have done this. Another way you might have coped with this fear of failure was to drive yourself to succeed to prove that you're not a failure. Again, your performance often reflects your belief system. If your belief system is based on false beliefs, then your thoughts, emotions, and actions usually will reflect those false beliefs. See the chart below.

Think about a time you withdrew from an activity because you feared failing at it. Describe the activity.

_____

_____

_____

_____

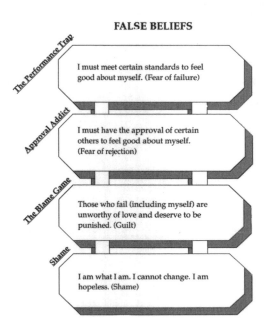

FALSE BELIEFS

The Performance Trap — I must meet certain standards to feel good about myself. (Fear of failure)

Approval Addict — I must have the approval of certain others to feel good about myself. (Fear of rejection)

The Blame Game — Those who fail (including myself) are unworthy of love and deserve to be punished. (Guilt)

Shame — I am what I am. I cannot change. I am hopeless. (Shame)

✎ **Write here the four false beliefs. By now you likely will have memorized the first false belief and probably are beginning to learn the others. Review by turning to the inside back cover for help.**

I must meet certain _____

_____

I must have _____

_____

Are you memorizing these?

Those who _____

_____

I am what _____

_____

SUMMARY STATEMENTS

- The focus of the Christian life should be on Christ, not on self-imposed regulations. Our experience of Christ's lordship depends on our moment-by-moment attention to His instruction.
- The false belief—I must meet certain standards to feel good about myself—results in a fear of failure.
- It is not wrong to be glad we succeeded at something. The issue is whether we base our self-worth on our succeeding.

DAY 4

Effects of the Fear of Failure

How the Fear of Failure Affects Our Lives

- Perfectionism
- Avoiding Risks
- Anger, Resentment
- Sexual Dysfunction
- Chemical Dependency

- Anxiety and fear
- Depression
- Low Motivation
- Pride

The fear of failure affects our lives in many ways. The above list does not represent all of the problems that result from the fear of failure. The fear of failure does not explain why all of these problems occur, either. However, recognizing and confronting the fear of failure in each of these experiences could result in dramatic changes.

Perfectionism

Perfectionism suffocates joy and creativity.

Again, one of the most common symptoms of the fear of failure is perfectionism. This unwillingness to fail suffocates joy and creativity. We tend to focus our attention on the area in which we failed rather than on those in which we did well because we consider any failure as a threat to our self-esteem. Some areas in which we tend to be perfectionists include work, being on time, house cleaning, our appearance, hobbies, and skills. Perfectionists often appear to be highly motivated, or driven, but their motivations usually come from a desperate attempt to avoid low self-esteem when they fail.

Avoiding Risks

Limiting our service to God

Another way fear of failure affects us is that we are willing to be involved in only those activities that we can do well. These individuals avoid challenging activities. Avoiding risks may seem comfortable, but it severely limits the scope of our creativity, self-expression, and service to God.

Anger, Resentment

Be angry, and yet do not sin; do not let the sun go down on your anger.
–Ephesians 4:26

Anger is a normal response when we fail, when others contribute to our failure, or when we are injured or insulted in some way. Feeling angry isn't wrong. In fact, the apostle Paul encouraged the Ephesians to be angry, but he also quickly warned them not to express anger in a sinful, hurtful way, as the verse at left shows. Unfortunately, rather than using our anger constructively, many of us either vent our fury without thinking about how it affects people or hold in anger. Anger that is held in eventually leads to outbursts in which we "get back" at people, deep and seething resentment, and/or depression.

✎ **Describe below a time in which one of these three problems resulting from the fear of failure has affected your life. How did you react to it?**

_____

_____

Anxiety and Fear

Failure can harden into a negative self-concept in which we expect to fail at almost everything we try.

Failure often causes us to condemn ourselves and causes others to disapprove of us. These actions are severe blows to a self-worth based on personal success and approval. If failure is great enough or occurs often enough, it can harden into a negative self-concept in which we expect to fail at almost everything we try. This negative self-concept goes on continually and leads to a downward spiral of anxiety about our performance and fear of disapproval from others.

Pride

When we base our self-worth on our performance and when we succeed in that performance, we often develop an inflated view of ourselves. This inflated view of ourselves is pride. Some of us may keep up this wrongful pride through any and all circumstances. For most of us, however, this sense of self-esteem lasts only until our next failure (or risk of failure). The self-confidence that most of us try to portray is only a false front to hide our fear of failure and insecurity.

Self-confidence or false front?

✎ **List below some activities that make you feel good about yourself because you usually succeed at completing these tasks.**

1. _____ 2. _____

Depression

Depression generally results when a person turns anger inward and/or has a deep sense of loss. Experiencing failure and fearing failing again can lead to deep depression. Once depressed, many people become emotionally numb or unfeeling. Their actions are passive, lacking energy or will. They believe they have no hope for change. Generally, depression is the body's way of blocking the mind's pain. It does this by numbing physical and emotional functions.

✎ **Describe a time in which you feel you reacted to fear of failure by one of these three ways just mentioned.**

_____

_____

_____

Low Motivation

If people believe they will fail, they feel they have no reason to put forth any effort.

Much of the time, people who seem lazy or who have low motivation actually feel hopeless. If people believe they will fail, they feel they have no reason to put forth any effort. The pain they endure for their passivity seems relatively minor and acceptable, compared to the agony of genuinely trying and failing.

Sexual Dysfunction

The emotional trauma failure causes can disturb sexual activity in marriage. Then, rather than experience the pain of failing sexually, many people tend to avoid sexual activity altogether.

Chemical Dependency

Many people attempt to ease their pain and fear of failure by using drugs or alcohol. Those who abuse alcohol often do so with the false idea that alcohol will make them perform at a greater level and will make them more likely to succeed. Alcohol, however, is a **depressant**. It actually makes the person who uses it less likely to perform well.

depressant–n. an agent that reduces a bodily functional activity or an instinctive desire (Webster's)

stimulant–n. an agent that produces a temporary increase of the functional activity or efficiency of an organism or any of its parts (Webster's)

People often use other drugs, which are **stimulants**, because they feel these will make them more productive. People who use these drugs likely consume larger doses more and more often until the users are addicted. Drug binges cause bodily resources to be depleted, so that when users come down from the chemical's "high" effect, they crash and can do very little without that "high."

Taking a drink can be a means of temporary escape. The problem is that chemical substances are addictive and are easily abused.

Individuals may have started using these substances as a way to escape from their troubles temporarily. They also may have thought using these substances would remove pressures to perform, as well.

However, when the substance's effect wears off these individuals, these people realize in despair that they are unable to cope without the substance. This pain-pleasure cycle continues, slowly draining the life from its victim.

Because they create such a false sense of well-being, alcohol or drugs may cause us to feel we actually are quite successful. But regardless of how it is achieved, success, or the idea of success, cannot dictate to us our sense of self-esteem.

Isn't their success enough?

Cocaine users represent a clear example of this truth. One reason cocaine is popular is that it produces feelings of greater self-esteem. However, we often note that many people who succeed by the world's standards use cocaine. If success truly provided a greater sense of self-esteem, these people probably would not be in the market in the first place for a drug that produces feelings of greater and greater self-esteem. The self-esteem they already feel from their success would be quite enough for them, and they would not be seeking more.

✎ **How do you think your life would be different if you did not experience the fear of failure? Write about this below.**

_____

_____

_____

Looking at Why We Do Christian Activities

Some people even try to obtain a more positive sense of self-worth through activities they perform as an outgrowth of being Christians. They may be doing what they believe the Bible instructs them to do, but they think doing so makes them more successful as a person. They may be doing the proverbial "right thing for the wrong reason."

✎ **List below some activities you perform as an outgrowth of being a Christian that you do in order to have increased self-worth.**

1. _____   3. _____

2. _____   4. _____

Any standard of performance—even a Christian standard—used to obtain a more positive sense of self-worth is contrary to God's truth and is, therefore, an ungodly means to fulfill your need for significance. If this is the case, then you still are trapped in the world's system.

Once we realize that our self-worth is secure in Christ, we want to do things that bring honor to Him. Coming from that motivation, our efforts, then, please God.

✎ **In light of what you just learned, read 1 Corinthians 10:31 in the left margin and write the verse in your own words.**

Whether, then, you eat, or drink or whatever you do, do all to the glory of God.
    –1 Corinthians 10:31

_____

_____

_____

Manipulating others

You might enter some relationships with selfish personal goals, which could cause you to manipulate others in an effort to reach those goals. Sometimes we even use kind and encouraging remarks to get others to do what we want them to. Sooner or later, these people usually realize that we actually are using kind remarks as manipulative devices. This causes them to be bitter and to stay away from us. If people prevent you from meeting your standards, you might become angry, enraged, or resentful; you might blame them, reject them, or withdraw from them. They have kept you from meeting one of your deepest needs!

➡ **It's time to review again your memory work on the affirmation "My Identity in Christ." Review the first two lines (turn to the inside back cover if you need to refer to the affirmation) until you can repeat them from memory. By the end of this week you likely will have memorized this part.**

SUMMARY STATEMENTS

- Avoiding risks may seem comfortable, but it severely limits the scope of our creativity, self-expression, and service to God.
- Failure can harden into a negative self-concept in which we expect to fail at almost everything we try.
- Even a Christian standard of performance used to obtain a more positive sense of self-worth is contrary to God's truth.

DAY 5

God often allows us to experience circumstances that will enable us to see how blindly we stick to Satan's deceptions.

Getting Our Attention

As long as we operate according to Satan's lies, we likely will fear failure. Although we all will continue to experience the fear of failure to some degree, we must realize that as Christians, we have the Holy Spirit's power provided to lay aside deceptive ways of thinking and to renew our minds by the truth of God's Word. For our benefit God often allows us to experience circumstances that will enable us to see how blindly we stick to Satan's deceptions. Many times these circumstances seem very negative; but through them we can learn valuable, life-changing truths.

In Psalm 107:33-36 we see a poetic example of this:

He changes rivers into a wilderness, and springs of water into a thirsty ground; A fruitful land into a salt waste, because of the wickedness of those who dwell in it. He changes a wilderness into a pool of water, and a dry land into springs of water; And there He makes the hungry to dwell, so that they may establish an inhabited city.

What a Way to Learn!

An important lesson

Has your fruitful land become a salt waste? Maybe God is trying to get your attention to teach you a tremendously important lesson—that success or failure is not the basis of your self-worth. Maybe the only way you can learn this lesson is by experiencing the pain of failure. In His great love God leads us through experiences that are difficult but important to our growth.

✎ **List below some ways you think God might be trying to get your attention on this matter.**

_____

_____

_____

The more sensitive you become to the fear of failure and the problems it may cause, the more you can understand your own behavior as well as that of others.

Overcoming the fear of failure is like stacking marbles—a difficult task but not any more difficult than trying to win the performance game.

The fear of failure is like stacking marbles—a difficult task but not any more difficult than trying to win the performance game. When we evaluate ourselves by our performance, we're ultimately going to lose, no matter how successful we are at the moment.

A rat placed in a box and shocked until it huddles in one particular corner soon learns to run to that corner as soon as it is placed in the box. How much of our energy do we expend in order to avoid the disapproving "shocks" of those around us? Even though God means for us to experience the freedom of His love and eternal purpose, how much time do we spend huddled in a corner like a laboratory rat?

✎ **Write below three rules you presently use in your life that regulate the way you go about your day.**

1. _____

_____

2. _____

_____

3. _____

_____

Relationships, not rules

Another consequence of having to meet certain standards to feel good about ourselves is that we lead a rules-dominated life. Many of us know persons who have a set of rules for everything and who always place their attention on their performance. However, the focus of the gospel is on relationships, not regulations. Christ's exercise of His lordship in our lives depends on our listening to His moment-by-moment instruction. Looking only at rules will keep us in a mental prison because we always have to examine ourselves.

On the other hand, we may feel very good about ourselves because we are winning the performance game. We may be so talented that we are reaching virtually every goal we have set for ourselves. We can't afford to mistake for positive self-worth the pride that we feel when we accomplish this. We must

Sometimes He will allow us to fail miserably so we will look to Him instead of to ourselves for our significance.

realize that God is able to bring about whatever circumstances are necessary to cause us to stop trusting in ourselves. God intends to bring us to Himself through prayer and through the study of His Word so that we can know, love, and serve Him. Sometimes He will allow us to fail miserably so we will look to Him instead of to ourselves for our security and significance.

> Before you become upset that God would allow you to experience failure, remember that any life less than God intended is a second-class existence. He loves you too much to let you continue to obtain your self-esteem from the empty promise of success.

And we know that God causes all things to work together for good to those who love God, to those who are called according to His purpose.
–Romans 8:28

✎ **Read Romans 8:28 at left. In your own words write the way God wants to use things that happen in your life.**

_____

_____

_____

As you become less influenced by the fear of failure, you can be happier, more loving, more spontaneous, and more thankful to God for His love.

✎ **Review this week's lessons. Pray and ask God to identify one positive statement that had an impact on your understanding of who you are.**

Write that statement in your own words.

_____

_____

_____

Rewrite your thoughts as a prayer of thankfulness to God.

_____

_____

_____

You probably gained many insights as you worked through this week's lessons. Which insight stands out to you? Write it here.

_____

_____

_____

JUSTIFICATION

> ### WRONG REASONING
>
> Brian attended church because he thought doing so would cause God to bless his business, not because he wanted to worship God. Cheryl chose not to gossip about Diane. Cheryl had told God she wouldn't spread bad news about Diane if He would get her the raise she wanted. (Read about these two situations on page 68.) What is wrong with Brian's and Cheryl's reasoning? What do Brian and Cheryl need in their lives?

What you'll learn this week

This week you'll–

- learn how God has given us a secure self-worth totally apart from our ability to perform;
- study about how Satan tricks us into wrongly believing that reliving sin to punish ourselves for it keep us from sinning again;
- look at six correct reasons to obey God;
- look at six incorrect reasons to obey God;
- learn the reason God sometimes disciplines us.

What you'll study each day

Right Standing with God	Forgiven, Fully Pleasing	Motivations for Obedience	More Reasons for Obedience	Poor Reasons for Obedience
DAY 1	DAY 2	DAY 3	DAY 4	DAY 5

Memory verse

A key verse to memorize this week

Therefore having been justified by faith, we have peace with God through our Lord Jesus Christ.

–Romans 5:1

WordWatch

Words to help you understand this week's lessons

justified–v. placed in right standing before God through Christ's death on the cross, which paid for our sins. (*Example: We have been **justified** freely through the death of Jesus Christ.*)

righteousness–n. an attribute of God, meaning essentially the same as His faithfulness or truthfulness, that which is consistent with His own nature and promises. (*Example: God didn't stop with just forgiving us; He credited to us the very **righteousness** of Christ.*)

repentance–n. a change of mind that involves both a turning from sin and a turning to God. (*Example: Satan tries to make us believe that reliving sin to punish ourselves for it is part of **repentance**.*)

Right Standing with God

If we base our self-worth on our ability to meet standards, we will try to compensate, either by avoiding risks or by trying to succeed no matter what the cost. Either way, failure looms as a constant enemy.

 Recall a time in your life when you were more than prepared to do something, but because you feared failure, you did not attempt the thing you had worked so hard to do. Describe this situation below.

_____

_____

When I Was a Teenager . . .

Fear on the basketball court

As I reflect on my life, I recall that I especially feared failure during my teenage years. This fear was apparent particularly in athletics.

During those years I practiced basketball a lot and became a good player. In the process I learned that I could attempt many maneuvers while I practiced on the court or while I played basketball with friends, but during a game when I felt intense pressure, I was afraid to do those same maneuvers. I now realize that same fear has prevented me from attempting things in several other areas of my life. Although God has enabled me on many occasions to conquer this fear, I still struggle with the risk of failing. This story may surprise some people who know me and who think of me as a successful person. Yet people who have experienced success know that they also often fear losing an achievement after they have done something important.

justified–v. placed in right standing before God through Christ's death on the cross, which paid for our sins. (Vine's)

Success truly does not reduce the amount of fear we experience in our lives. In fact, success often causes us to have even more fear because we feel that we have more to lose.

righteousness–n. an attribute of God, meaning essentially the same as His faithfulness or truthfulness, that which is consistent with His own nature and promises. (Vine's)

God's Solution

Thankfully, God has a solution for the fear of failure! He has given us a secure self-worth totally apart from our ability to perform. We have been **justified** (read in the left margin that what that means). But God didn't stop with our forgiveness; He also credited to us the very **righteousness** (that definition is at left also) of Christ (2 Corinthians 5:21).

being justified as a gift by His grace through the redemption which is in Christ Jesus;

–Romans 3:24

 Read Romans 3:24 and Titus 3:7, both at left, to find out how God accomplished justification with us. Answer the following questions yes or no, based on the above Scriptures.

that being justified by His grace we might be made heirs, according to the hope of eternal life.

–Titus 3:7

_____ I am justified by my actions.
_____ I am justified because people love me.
_____ I am justified by His grace and have the hope for eternal life.
_____ I am justified freely by His grace through the redemption that came by Jesus Christ.

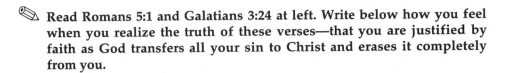

Just imagine! God transfers all our sin to Christ and erases it completely from us. Then He credits to us Christ's righteousness. That is what happens in justification.

Therefore having been justified by faith, we have peace with God through our Lord Jesus Christ.

–Romans 5:1

Therefore the Law has become our tutor to lead us to Christ, that we may be justified by faith.

–Galatians 3:24

✎ **Read Romans 5:1 and Galatians 3:24 at left. Write below how you feel when you realize the truth of these verses—that you are justified by faith as God transfers all your sin to Christ and erases it completely from you.**

_____

_____

The fact that you are justified is one of the truths of God's Word that you can use as you reject the false beliefs you have about yourself. As you reject these beliefs you can replace them with God's truths. See the chart below.

GOD'S TRUTHS

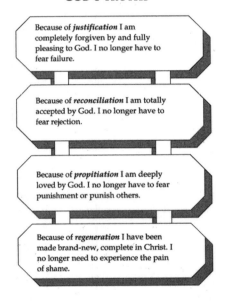

Because of *justification* I am completely forgiven by and fully pleasing to God. I no longer have to fear failure.

Because of *reconciliation* I am totally accepted by God. I no longer have to fear rejection.

Because of *propitiation* I am deeply loved by God. I no longer have to fear punishment or punish others.

Because of *regeneration* I have been made brand-new, complete in Christ. I no longer need to experience the pain of shame.

I once heard a radio preacher criticize members of his congregation for their hidden sins. He exclaimed, "Don't you know that someday you're going to die and God is going to flash all your sins upon a giant screen in heaven for all the world to see?" This minister misunderstood God's gracious gift of justification!

Much more then, having now been justified by His blood, we shall be saved from the wrath of God through Him.

–Romans 5:9

And according to the Law, one may almost say, all things are cleansed with blood, and without shedding of blood there is no forgiveness.

–Hebrews 9:22

And their sins and their lawless deeds I will remember no more.

–Hebrews 10:17

✎ **Read Romans 5:9 and Hebrews 9:22, at left. Complete the statement below:**

The justification of humankind was accomplished by the shedding of His

_____ .

Justification carries with it no guilt. If you need to be reassured about this, read Hebrews 10:17 at left. By dying on the cross, Christ paid for all of our sins—past, present, and future. God forgives us completely!

Blessed are those whose lawless deeds have been forgiven, and whose sins have been covered. Blessed is the man whose sin the Lord will not take into account.

Romans 4:7-8

Therefore having been justified by faith, we have peace with God through our Lord Jesus Christ. Much more, then, having now been justified by His blood, we shall be saved from the wrath of God through Him.

Romans 5:1-9

There is therefore now no condemnation for those who are in Christ Jesus. Who will bring a charge against God's elect? God is the one who justifies, who is the one who condemns? Christ Jesus is He who died, yes, rather who was raised, who is at the right hand of God, who also intercedes for us.

Romans 8:1,33-34

For the love of Christ controls us, having concluded this, that one died for all, therefore all died; and He died for all, that they who live should no longer live for themselves, but for Him who died and rose again on their behalf. He made Him who knew no sin to be sin on our behalf, that we might become the righteousness of God in Him.

2 Corinthians 5:14-15, 21

✎ **Read the verses that appear in the left margin. Now, based on the verses you just read, put a check by the statements below that indicate the results of justification.**

❏ Because of justification God forgives your sin and does not hold it against you.
❏ You have peace with God. You no longer are considered His enemy.
❏ You are saved from His wrath.
❏ You do not have to fear condemnation.
❏ You now can live to honor Him and to reflect His image.
❏ You are declared righteous.
❏ You are an heir of His eternal kingdom.

More than Forgiveness

As marvelous as justification is, it means more than forgiveness of sins. In the same act of love through which God forgave us, He also provided for our righteousness: the worthiness to stand in God's presence. By declaring us righteous, God attributes Christ's worth to us.

> The moment we accept Christ, God no longer sees us as condemned sinners. Instead, we are forgiven; we are declared righteous; and God sees us as people who are fully pleasing to Him.

Read the following verses:

Now we know that whatever the Law says, it speaks to those who are under the Law, that every mouth may be closed, and all the world may become accountable to God; because by the works of the Law no flesh will be justified in His sight; for through the Law comes the knowledge of sin. But now apart from the Law the righteousness of God has been manifested, being witnessed by the Law and the Prophets, even the righteousness of God through faith in Jesus Christ for all those who believe; for there is no distinction; for all have sinned and fall short of the glory of God.

–Romans 3:19-23

But God demonstrates His own love toward us, in that while we were yet sinners, Christ died for us. Much more then, having now been justified by His blood, we shall be saved from the wrath of God through Him. For if while we were enemies, we were reconciled to God through the death of His Son, much more, having been reconciled, we shall be saved by His life.

–Romans 5:8-10

And you were dead in your trespasses and sins, in which you formerly walked according to the course of this world, according to the prince of the power of the air, of the spirit that is now working in the sons of disobedience. Among them we too all formerly lived in the lusts of our flesh, indulging the desires of the flesh and of the mind, and were by nature children of wrath, even as the rest.

–Ephesians 2:1-3

✏️ **Now that you've read these verses, mark as _T_ (true) or _F_ (false) the statements that represent God's view of you before you were justified.**

_____ God loves and accepts me only when I do good deeds.
_____ God sees my sinfulness.
_____ God cares about me only when I say the right things.
_____ God views me as an enemy before I am reconciled to Him.
_____ God sees my unrighteousness.

How God viewed you before you were justified:
- **Unrighteous**
- **Sinful**
- **An enemy**
- **Dead in your sins**
- **Separated from God**
- **Disobedient in nature**
- **An object of God's wrath**

yet He has now reconciled you in His fleshly body through death, in order to present you before Him holy and blameless and beyond reproach.
–Colossians 1:22

holy–adj. separated from sin and therefore consecrated to God; sacred (Vine's)

Without Christ's righteousness, you would have no basis on which to stand before God. Before you were justified, God viewed you as being unrighteous, sinful, and an enemy. You were dead in your sins, separated from God, disobedient in nature, and an object of God's wrath. Romans 3:9-20 is how God describes people who are unjustified. You may be thinking, _I never really was that bad._ But to God even your best attempts at righteousness were as filthy rags (Isaiah 64:6). Romans 14:23 and Hebrews 11:6 also state that anything not done in faith is sin and displeases God. But take heart! The living God has seen your helplessness and has extended justification to you through Christ's death and resurrection.

✏️ **Read Colossians 1:22 at left. Are you beyond reproach, holy (the definition of this word is at left), and blameless before Christ?**

❏ Yes   ❏ No Why or why not?_____

_____

If you have trusted in Christ's death on the cross for the forgiveness of your sins, God has declared you to be righteous in His sight! If you were anything less than that, you would not be pleasing enough to be His companion for eternity. We sometimes seem to say to God, "In heaven I guess we are perfect in His sight; but down here in the real world, we just aren't that way." We may respond like this because we are convinced that our worth depends on our performance. To God our worth does not depend on our performance at all! Our worth is established and secure to God because He has credited to us the righteousness of Christ.

If God had to choose favorites

Suppose you and Christ were seated next to each other, and someone asked God, the Father, "Which of these two persons do You love the most? Which person is more acceptable to You? Which person is holy and blameless before You?" God, the Father, would respond: "They are equally loved in my sight."

➡️ **By now you likely will be in the process of memorizing God's four truths. Look at the inside back cover and begin memorizing the first one. By the end of this week you likely will have memorized this truth.**

SUMMARY STATEMENTS

- If you have trusted in Christ's death on the cross for the forgiveness of your sins, God has declared you to be righteous in His sight.
- God has a solution for the fear of failure! He has given us a secure self-worth totally apart from our ability to perform. We have been justified and have had credited to us the very righteousness of Christ.

<table>
<tr>
<td>

DAY

2

</td>
<td>

Forgiven, Fully Pleasing

God intended for Adam and his descendants to be righteous people. He intended for them to experience fully His love and His purposes for them. But sin short-circuited that relationship. God's perfect payment for sin—the death of His Son—since has satisfied the righteous wrath of God. This again has allowed us to have that status of righteousness and to delight in knowing and honoring the Lord.

</td>
</tr>
</table>

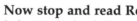 **Mark the following statements as *T* (true) or *F* (false).**

_____ Reliving past sin to punish myself is part of **repentance** (see left margin).
_____ Reliving past sin to punish myself is a way of paying for sin.
_____ Reliving past sin to punish myself is a way to control my actions.

repentance–n. a change of mind that involves both a turning from sin and a turning to God (Vine's)

The Realities of Redemption

God desires for those of us who have been redeemed to experience the realities of His redemption. We are forgiven and righteous because of Christ's sacrifice; therefore, because we are His children we are pleasing to God in spite of our failures.

This fact can replace our fear of failure with peace, hope, and joy.

The fact that we are pleasing to God can replace our fear of failure with peace, hope, and joy.

> Failure need not be a millstone around our necks. Neither success nor failure is the proper basis of our self-worth. Christ is the source of our forgiveness, freedom, joy, and purpose.

Blessed are those whose lawless deeds have been forgiven, and whose sins have been covered. Blessed is the man whose sin the Lord will not take into account.
–Romans 4:6-8

Now stop and read Romans 4:6-8 and Hebrews 10:17, which both are at left. Mark the following statements as *T* (true) or *F* (false).

_____ Satan tricks us into thinking that reliving sin in order to punish ourselves for sin is part of repentance.
_____ Reliving sin in order to punish ourselves represent the flesh's way of trying to pay for sin and control our actions.

And their sins and their lawless deeds I will remember no more.
–Hebrews 10:17

Being aware of sin is a crucial element of repentance. However, it's simply not true that reliving sin in order to punish ourselves somehow represents a part of repentance! Satan tricks us into believing these untruths.

Our wrongful thinking goes like this: *By reliving this sin in order to punish myself, I inflict pain upon myself. That pain will become associated with these sins so I never will do them again. Therefore, remembering sin is helpful and good.*

Why does recalling these sins cause pain? Each time you remember them, you judge yourself according to your poor past performance. The evaluation always comes out negative, and the pain of self-hatred follows. If you were not evaluating yourself by your past performance, you probably would not dredge up the painful memory of these sins.

✎ **Stop now and pray. Carefully consider the following questions and answer them honestly to yourself and to God.**

Do you relive past sins? ❏ Yes ❏ No

If so, how does reliving past sins motivate you? _____

_____

➥ **Reliving sin is a destructive way of trying to produce a godly life. God's method is to forgive our sins (Hebrews 10:17). Ask God to enable you to accept His forgiveness.**

condemn-v. to give judgment against, pass sentence upon. (Vine's)

Therefore having been justified by faith, we have peace with God through our Lord Jesus Christ.

-Romans 5:1

In the same way, we were **condemned** (see definition at left), but now we are declared righteous! Romans 5:1 at left refers to us as having been justified by faith, a statement in the past perfect tense. Therefore, if we have trusted in Christ for our salvation, we each can say with certainty this statement:

> I am deeply loved. I am completely forgiven. I am fully pleasing. I am totally accepted by God. I am absolutely complete in Christ.

➥ **Think for a minute about what you just read. From your study of justification, how do being justified and having Christ's righteousness help you believe this statement?**

Because God has credited to you the righteousness of Christ, you are just as pleasing to the Father as Christ is! You can do nothing to add to or to take away from what Christ did for you on the cross. As a result of your justification, you are completely forgiven and fully pleasing to God. Although you may try to justify yourself by doing good deeds to show God that you deserve your justification, it is a vain attempt to gain what you already have. Your new life is a product of God's workmanship in which He is very pleased. As this truth renews your mind, you increasingly will reflect this in your attitudes and behavior.

Your new life is a product of God's workmanship in which He is very pleased.

Am I Really Pleasing to God?

Some people have difficulty thinking of themselves as being pleasing to God because they link pleasing so strongly with performance. They tend to be displeased with anything short of perfection in themselves, and they suspect that God has the same standard. In the box at left describe a time when you thought this.

> **Describe a time when you thought you were not pleasing to God because of your poor performance.**
>
> _____
>
> _____
>
> _____
>
> _____

The point of justification is that we never can achieve perfection on this earth; even our best efforts at self-righteousness are as filthy garments to God (Isaiah 64:6). Yet He loves us so much that He appointed His Son to pay for our sins. God credited to us His own righteousness, His perfect status before God.

Right Motivations

Or do you not know that your body is a temple of the Holy Spirit who is in you, whom you have from God, and that you are not your own? For you have been bought with a price: therefore glorify God in your body.

–1 Corinthians 6:19-20

This doesn't mean that our actions don't matter and that we can sin all we want. Our sinful actions, words, and attitudes make the Lord sad, but our status as beloved children remains intact. In His love He disciplines and encourages us to live godly lives—both for our good and for His honor. The apostle Paul was so awed by the fact that he was forgiven and righteous in Christ that he was determined to please God by his actions and his deeds. In 1 Corinthians 6:19-20 (see left margin), 2 Corinthians 5:9, Philippians 3:8-11, and other passages Paul strongly stated his desire to please, honor, and glorify the One who had credited to him Christ's righteousness.

Some people may read these statements and become uneasy, believing that I am not considering sin as serious. As you will see, I am not minimizing the destructive nature of sin, but I simply am trying to make sure we see Christ's payment on the cross as very, very important.

Understanding our complete forgiveness and acceptance before God does not mean we should have a casual attitude toward sin. On the contrary, understanding this gives us a greater desire to serve the One who died to free us from sin. Tomorrow we will look at some strong reasons to obey and serve God with joy.

Why bother with good works?

If good works won't make a person more pleasing to God, why should a person be involved in good works?

Study the verses below.

> Therefore do not let sin reign in your mortal body that you should obey its lusts, and do not go on presenting the members of your body to sin as instruments of unrighteousness; but present yourselves to God as those alive from the dead, and your members as instruments of righteousness to God.
>
> –Romans 6:12-13

> Flee immorality. Every other sin that a man commits is outside the body, but the immoral man sins against his own body. Or do you not know that your body is a temple of the Holy Spirit who is in you, whom you have from God, and that you are not your own? For you have been bought with a price: therefore glorify God in your body.
>
> –1 Corinthians 6:18-20

> Whatever you do, do your work heartily, as for the Lord rather than for men; knowing that from the Lord you will receive the reward of the inheritance. It is the Lord Christ whom you serve.
>
> –Colossians 3:23-24

> For the grace of God has appeared, bringing salvation to all men, instructing us to deny ungodliness and worldly desires and to live sensibly, righteously and godly in the present age, looking for the blessed hope and the appearing of the glory of our great God and Savior, Christ Jesus; who gave Himself for us, that He might redeem us from every lawless deed and purify for Himself a people for His own possession, zealous for good deeds.
>
> –Titus 2:11-14

✎ **Now that you have read these verses, mark the statements below as *T* (true) or *F* (false) according to these Scriptures.**

_____ People are to offer themselves to God for service.
_____ People are to honor God with their bodies.
_____ People are to work at whatever they do with all their hearts.
_____ People are to work at everything as if they are working for the Lord.
_____ People are to live self-controlled lives and do good works.
_____ People are to deny ungodliness and worldly desires.

Here's how to honor God

> ### HOW TO HONOR GOD
>
> You should be involved in good works because they represent an opportunity to bring honor to Christ. Your good works do not represent a means to earn righteousness but a way to bring Him delight and glory.

All the statements in the above exercise are true. As you are more and more aware of what God has done for you, your natural response will be to honor Him in your daily life.

Right Things for Right Reasons?

Are you doing the right things for the right reasons? The next question we can answer is what determines whether a deed will honor God.

For no man can lay a foundation other than the one which is laid, which is Jesus Christ. Now if any man builds upon the foundation with gold, silver, precious stones, wood, hay, straw, each man's work will become evident; for the day will show it, because it is to be revealed with fire; and the fire itself will test the quality of each man's work.
–1 Corinthians 3:11-13

Whether, then, you eat or drink or whatever you do, do all to the glory of God.
–1 Corinthians 10:31

But he who doubts is condemned if he eats, because his eating is not from faith; and whatever is not from faith is sin.
–Romans 14:23

✎ **Read 1 Corinthians 3:11-15; 10:31 and Romans 14:23, all at left. Check the following statements that affirm what the Scriptures say about whether a deed will honor God.**

❏ Deeds can come from a person's faith.
❏ Deeds can be done to help people.
❏ Deeds can be done for the glory of God.
❏ Deeds can to be done that will impress people.
❏ Deeds can be shown for what they are.

The issue is more than just doing the right things. Are you doing the right things for the right reasons? Jesus had the most trouble with religious people who were doing religious works for the wrong reasons. If you are honest, you probably realize that you perform many of your good deeds to make yourself more acceptable to others, to God, and perhaps to yourself.

But none of these good works will exist forever. Are you motivated to do the right things in response to what Christ has done for you? In motivating others, we need to point people to God and to His grace and let Him motivate them.

➥ **You likely are continuing to work on memorizing the affirmation "My Identity in Christ." Last week you memorized the first two lines of the**

affirmation. This week you can add the next five lines (emphasized earlier in this session on page 53). By the end of this week's study, you likely will have memorized the first seven lines. Look at page 224 if you need help with the first seven lines.

✎ **Write a prayer to God, asking Him to help you do your deeds for His honor and not for self-serving reasons.**

_____

_____

_____

SUMMARY STATEMENTS

- You can do nothing to add to or to take away from what Christ did for you on the cross. As a result of your justification, you are completely forgiven and fully pleasing to God.
- Some people have difficulty thinking of themselves as being pleasing to God because they link pleasing so strongly with performance.
- In motivating others, we need to point people to God and to His grace and let Him motivate them.

DAY 3

Motivations for Obedience

Six Reasons to Obey God

The love of God and His acceptance of us are based on grace. They are not based on our ability to impress God through our good deeds. But if He accepts us on the basis of His grace and not because of our deeds, why should we obey God?

Here are six good reasons to obey Him. We will study the first 3 today and the last 3 in day 4.

GOOD REASONS TO OBEY GOD

1. Christ's love	4. His commands are good
2. Sin is destructive	5. Eternal rewards
3. The Father's discipline	6. Christ is worthy

If you will ask me anything in My name, I will do it. He who has my commandments and keeps them, he it is who loves Me, and he who loves Me shall be loved by My Father, and I will love him, and will disclose Myself to him.

–John 14:15, 21

✎ **Read John 14:15,21 at left. Mark the statements as _T_ (true) or _F_ (false).**

_____ The love of Christ makes people want to obey.
_____ People express love to God by obeying.
_____ People must make themselves obedient.

Christic Love

Expressing love in return

Understanding God's grace makes us want to act because love motivates us to please the One who has so freely loved us. When we experience love, we usually respond by seeking to express our love in return. Obeying God is a way we show our love for Him, which comes from an understanding of what Christ has accomplished for us on the cross (2 Corinthians 5:14-15). We love because He first loved us and clearly demonstrated His love for us at the cross (1 John 4:16-19). Understanding this will highly motivate us to serve Him.

This great motivating factor is missing in many of our lives because we really don't believe that God loves us unconditionally. We expect His love to be conditional, based on our ability to earn it. Our experience of God's love is based on our perception. If we believe that He is demanding or faraway and disinterested, we will not be able to receive His love and tenderness. Instead, we either will be afraid of Him or angry with Him. Faulty perceptions of God often prompt us to rebel against Him.

When I was angry at God . . .

✎ **Think of occasions when you have withdrawn from God or have been angry with Him and rebellious against Him. Write what your thoughts were about Him then.**

_____

_____

_____

Read the following Scriptures.

For God so loved the world, that He gave His only begotten Son, that whoever believes in Him should not perish, but have eternal life. For God did not send the Son into the world to judge the world, but that the world should be saved through Him.

–John 3:16-18

I in them, and Thou in Me, that they may be perfected in unity, that the world may know that Thou didst send Me, and didst love them, even as Thou didst love Me. Father, I desire that they also, whom Thou hast given Me; be with Me where I am, in order that they may behold My glory, which Thou hast given Me; for Thou didst love Me before the foundation of the world.

–John 17:23-24

For while we were still helpless, at the right time Christ died for the ungodly. For one will hardly die for a righteous man; though perhaps for the good man someone would dare even to die. But God demonstrates His own love toward us, in that while we were yet sinners, Christ died for us.

–Romans 5:6-8

But God, being rich in mercy, because of His great love with which He loved us, even when we were dead in our transgressions, made us alive together with Christ (by grace you have been saved), and raised us up with Him, and seated us with Him in the heavenly places, in Christ Jesus.

In order that in the ages to come He might show the surpassing riches of His grace in kindness toward us in Christ Jesus. For by grace you have been saved through faith; and that not of yourselves, it is the gift of God; not as a result of works, that no one should boast.

–Ephesians 2:4-9

✎ **Now that you have read these verses, answer the following questions yes or no, based on what you read.**

_____ Did Christ die for the ungodly?
_____ Did Christ die for us while we were still sinners?
_____ Did God send His Son because He loved the world?
_____ Did God make us alive with Christ because of His great love for us?
_____ Does the love of Christ cause you to want to obey Him?

Our image of God is the foundation for all of our motivations. As we grow in our understanding of His unconditional love and acceptance, we will be better able to grasp that His discipline is prompted by care, not cruelty. We also will be able more and more to perceive the contrast between the joys of living for Christ and the destructive nature of sin.

Sin Is Destructive

✎ **The Bible character Jonah is known for his disobedience. Follow the directions in the box at left. Then read the first chapter of Jonah. Check the statements below that give the results of Jonah's choice of disobedience to God.**

❑ Jonah's sin endangered the lives of those around him.
❑ Jonah was able to continue doing as he pleased.
❑ Jonah lost property.
❑ Jonah involved others in his sin.
❑ Jonah was isolated from God and others.

> **Even before you read the Bible story, you may know something about Jonah's disobedience. Write here what you know .**
>
> _____
>
> _____
>
> _____
>
> _____
>
> _____

Jonah's sin endangered the lives of those around him, resulted in a loss of property, caused Jonah to be unsympathetic to others, caused a loss of personal testimony, involved others in his sin, and ultimately isolated him from God and others.

Satan has blinded us to the painful, damaging consequences of sin. The effects of sin are all around us, yet many people continue to indulge in sins such as rampant self-centeredness, status and pleasure seeking, and sexual wrongdoing, which cause much anguish and pain.

Sooner or later, sin will result in some form of destruction.

Satan contradicted God in the garden when he said, "You surely shall not die!" (Genesis 3:4). Sin may seem pleasant but does so only for a season. Sooner or later, sin will cause some form of destruction.

✎ **Name a specific way that sin affects your self-concept.**

_____

_____

Many times, we're unable to see the full impact of sin on both ourselves and others. Ask the Holy Spirit to help you become more sensitive to the fact that sin always has a serious negative result. As you become more aware of how harmful sin is, you will choose to obey Him more often.

Sin is destructive in many ways. Emotionally, sin causes us to experience the pain of guilt and shame and the fear of failure and punishment. Mentally, sin causes us to experience the anguish of flashbacks–continuing to relive our sin. We also may spend enormous amounts of time and energy thinking about our sins and trying to explain away our guilt.

Physically, sin may cause us to suffer from psychosomatic illnesses or to experience pain through physical abuse. Sin also may result in the loss of property or even the loss of life. Relationally, sin can alienate us from others.

Spiritually, sin causes us to make the Holy Spirit sad, to lose our testimony, and to break our fellowship with God. The painful and destructive effects of sin are so profound that it is a mystery why we don't have an intense dislike for it.

Some effects of sin:
• **Pain of guilt and shame**
• **Fear of failure**
• **Psychosomatic illness**
• **Physical abuse**
• **Loss of property**
• **Loss of life**
• **Loss of fellowship with God**
• **Alienation from others**

✎ **Read Hebrews 12:5-11 at left. Mark the following statements as *T* (true) or *F* (false), based on these verses.**

_____ God disciplines us because He truly loves us.
_____ Discipline is proof that we have become the sons of God.
_____ God disciplines us in love and never punishes us in anger.

The Father's Discipline

Our loving Father has given us the Holy Spirit to convict us of sin. Conviction is a form of God's discipline and serves as proof that we have become sons of God (Hebrews 12:5-11). It warns us that we are making choices without regard either to God's truth or sin's consequences. If we choose to not respond to the Holy Spirit, our Heavenly Father will discipline us in love.

✎ **Before studying further, explain in your own words how you view the difference between discipline and punishment.**

_____

_____

_____

_____

and you have forgotten the exhortation which is addressed to you as sons, "My son, do not regard lightly the discipline of the Lord, nor faint when you are reproved by Him; for those whom the Lord loves He disciplines, and He scourges every son whom He receives." It is for discipline that you endure; God deals with you as with sons; for what son is there whom his father does not discipline? But if you are without discipline, of which all have become partakers, then you are illegitimate children and no sons. Furthermore, we had earthly fathers to discipline us, and we respected them; shall we not much rather be subject to the Father of spirits, and live? For they disciplined us for a short time as seemed best to them, but He disciplines us for our good, that we may share His holiness. All discipline for the moment seems not to be joyful, but sorrowful; yet to those who have been trained by it, afterwards it yields the peaceful fruit of righteousness.
–Hebrews 12:5-11

But when we are judged ourselves rightly, we should not be judged. But when we are judged, we are disciplined by the Lord in order that we may not be condemned along with the world.
–1 Corinthians 11:32

Read 1 Corinthians 11:32 at left. Paul wrote to explain that when discipline does come, it is sent for correction, not condemnation.

Most of us equate discipline with punishment. This misunderstanding of God's intentions causes us to fear God rather than to respond to His love.

The chart on the next page shows the profound contrasts between punishment and discipline.

PUNISHMENT VS. DISCIPLINE		
	PUNISHMENT	**DISCIPLINE**
Source:	God's Wrath	God's Love
Purpose:	To Avenge a Wrong	To Correct a Wrong
Relational result:	Alienation	Reconciliation
Personal result:	Guilt	A Righteous Life-style
Directed toward:	Non-Believers	His Children

Correcting in love

Jesus bore on the cross all the punishment we deserved; therefore, we no longer need to fear punishment from God for our sins. We can seek to do what is right so that our Father will not have to correct us through discipline. When He disciplines us, we can remember that God is correcting us in love. This discipline leads us to righteous performance, which reflects Christ's righteousness in us.

 Read the following statements and check the ones that illustrate God's motivation for discipline.

God disciplines us because—
❏ 1. it is an additional expression of His love for us;
❏ 2. He loves us so much that He doesn't want us to miss His best by continuing in sin;
❏ 3. His motive for discipline always is love, never anger or revenge;
❏ 4. when we realize that His discipline is always for our good, it makes us more open to the lessons He wants to teach us.

 In the blanks below write about a time in the past when you understood that God was correcting you in love.

_____

_____

➡ **It's time to review again your memory work on the first of God's truths. Review the first truth (turn to the inside back cover if you need to read over it quickly) until you can repeat it from memory. By the end of this week you likely will have memorized this truth.**

SUMMARY STATEMENTS

• Our obedience to God can be an expression of our love for Him, which comes from an understanding of what Christ has accomplished for us on the cross.
• As we grow in our understanding of God's unconditional love and acceptance, we will be better able to grasp that His discipline is prompted by care, not cruelty.

More Reasons for Obedience

In day 3 we learned the first three good reasons for obeying God: Christ's love, sin's destructive consequences, and the Father's discipline. Today we will study three more: His commands for us are good, eternal rewards, and Christ is worthy.

His Commands for Us Are Good

✎ **Read Romans 7:12 and 1 John 5:3 below. Then complete the statement that follows these verses.**

> So then, the Law is holy, and the commandment is holy and righteous and good.
>
> –Romans 7:12
>
> For this is the love of God, that we keep His commandments; and His commandments are not burdensome.
>
> –1 John 5:3

God's commands are described as _____ , _____ ,

_____ , and not _____ .

God gives His commands to us for two good purposes: to protect us from sin's destructiveness and to direct us in a life of joy and fruitfulness. We have a wrong perspective if we view God's commands only as restrictions in our lives. Instead, we must realize that His commands are guidelines, given so that we might enjoy life to the fullest. Obeying God's commands never should be considered as a means to gain His approval.

✎ **Read Deuteronomy 5:29; 6:24 at left. List the results of obeying God.**

_____ , _____ , _____ , _____

In today's society we have lost the concept of doing something because it is the right thing to do. Instead, we do things in exchange for some reward or favor or to avoid punishment. Wouldn't it be novel to do something simply because it is the right thing to do? God's commands are holy, right, and good; and the Holy Spirit gives us the wisdom and strength to keep them.

Therefore, since these commands have value in themselves, we can choose to obey God and follow His commands.

✎ **Have you ever obeyed God's command because doing so simply was the right thing to do? Describe one such experience here.**

_____

_____

_____

_____

Oh that they had such a heart in them, that they would far Me, and keep all My commandments always, that it may be well with them and with their sons forever!

–Deuteronomy 5:29

So the Lord commanded us to observe all these statutes, to fear the Lord our God for our good always and for our survival, as it is today.

–Deuteronomy 6:24

> God's commands are valuable simply because they originate from a loving Father. God's commands are guidelines, given to help us enjoy all He has provided. They are good, and they are for our good; therefore, they are worth obeying.

Not just another thing to do

Most of us have a negative attitude about God's commands. If we believe that our worth is based on our performance, then every command is just one more thing we have to do to earn our acceptance. But if we believe that our worth is secure in Christ, then we will view His commands as helpful guidelines.

Eternal Rewards

For we must all appear before the judgment seat of Christ, that each one may be recompensed for his deeds in the body, according to what he has done, whether good or bad.

–2 Corinthians 5:10

Yet another important reason to live the way God wants us to is the fact that He will reward us in heaven for serving Him. Second Corinthians 5:10, which appears in the left margin, explains how this reward works and who will receive it.

Through Christ's payment for us on the cross, we have escaped eternal judgment; however, our actions will be judged when we appear before Christ at the judgment seat of Christ. There God will evaluate our performance and will reward us for our service. He will reward us for deeds that reflect a desire to honor Christ. However, He will reject deeds performed to earn God's acceptance, to earn others' approval, or to meet our own standards.

Read the passages below.

> Now if any man builds upon the foundation with gold, silver, precious stones, wood, hay, straw, each man's work will become evident; for the day will show it, because it is to be revealed with fire; and the fire itself will test the quality of each man's work. If any man's work which he has built upon it remains, he shall receive a reward. If any man's work if burned up, he shall suffer loss; but he himself shall be saved, yet so as through fire.
>
> *–1 Corinthians 3:11-15*

> For we must all appear before the judgment seat of Christ, that each one may be recompensed for his deeds in the body, according to what he has done, whether good or bad.
>
> *–2 Corinthians 5:10*

> By this, love is perfected with us, that we may have confidence in the day of judgment; because as He is, so also are we in this world.
>
> *–1 John 4:17*

> And I saw a great white throne and Him who sat upon it, from whose presence earth and heaven fled away, and no place was found for them. And I saw the dead, the great and the small standing before the throne, and books were opened; and another book was opened, which is the book of life; and the dead were judged from the things which were written in the books, according to their deeds.
>
> *–Revelation 20:11-15*

Do you not know that those who run in a race all run, but only one receives the prize? Run in such a way that you may win.

–1 Corinthians 9:24

Suffer hardship with me, as a good soldier of Christ Jesus. No soldier in active service entangles himself in the affairs of everyday life, so that he may please the one who enlisted him as a soldier. And also if anyone competes as an athlete, he does not win the prize unless he competes according to the rules.

–2 Timothy 2:3-5

I have fought the good fight, I have finished the course, I have kept the faith; in the future there is laid up for me the crown of righteousness, which the Lord, the righteous Judge, will award to me on that day; and not only to me, but also to all who have loved His appearing.

–2 Timothy 4:7-8

After these things I looked, and behold, a door standing open in heaven, and the first voice which I had heard, like the sound of a trumpet speaking with me, said, "Come up here, and I will show you what must take place after these things." Immediately I was in the Spirit; and behold a throne was standing in heaven, and One sitting on the throne. And He who was sitting was like a jasper stone and a sardius in appearance; and there was a rainbow around the throne, like an emerald in appearance. And around the throne were twenty-four thrones; and upon the thrones I saw twenty-four elders sitting, clothed in white garments, and golden crowns on their heads. And when the living creatures give glory and honor and thanks to Him who sits on the throne to Him who lives forever and ever, the twenty-four elders will fall down before Him who sits on the throne, and will worship Him who lives forever and ever, and will cast their crowns before the throne, saying, "Worthy art Thou, our Lord and our God, to receive glory and honor and power; for Thou didst create all things, and because of Thy will they existed, and were created."

–Revelation 4:1-4, 9-11

✍ **Based on the Scriptures you just read, mark the following statements as T (true) or F (false).**

_____ Only the lost person will appear before Christ to be judged.
_____ All believers will appear before the judgment seat of Christ.
_____ Each believer before the judgment seat will be judged for what he has done.
_____ Judgment will be only for bad things done on earth.
_____ At the great white throne unbelievers will be judged for rejecting Christ.

Many of us believe that according to these passages, unbelievers will be judged and condemned at the great white throne for rejecting Christ. Though believers will be spared from this condemnation, we will stand before the judgment seat of Christ to have our deeds tested. Those deeds done for the Lord will be honored, but those deeds done for ourselves and for our own selfish interests will be rejected. The Greek word to describe this judgment seat is the same used to describe the platform an athlete stands on to receive a wreath of victory for winning an event. The judgment seat of Christ is for the reward of good deeds, not for the punishment of sin.

✍ **Read 1 Corinthians 9:24 and 2 Timothy 2:3-5; 4:7-8 in the left margin. Match the correct answers with the following questions.**

_____ 1. How should we run the race of life? A. Crown of righteousness
_____ 2. How do you get the victor's crown? B. To get the prize
_____ 3. What is in store for a Christian?   C. By competing

Does the thought of an eternal reward make you want to obey more? Explain why you feel this way.

_____

_____

_____

Although we do not become more acceptable to God because of our rewards, our rewards represent our faithful service to Him. Rewards, then, are an honor God gives us because we have honored Him.

Christ Is Worthy

Our most noble motivation for serving Christ simply is that He is worthy of our love and obedience.

✍ **Read Revelation 4:1-4, 9-11 in the left margin. Then below in your own words describe John's vision and his response to God's glory.**

_____

_____

Christ deserves our affection and obedience. No other person, no goal, no fame or status, and no material possession can compare with Him. The more we understand His love and majesty, the more we will praise Him and desire to honor Him at the expense of everything else. Our hearts will echo the words of the psalm in the box below.

> Whom have I in heaven but Thee? And besides Thee, I desire nothing on earth. But as for me, the nearness of God is my good; I have made the Lord God my refuge, that I may tell of all Thy works.
>
> –Psalm 73:25,28

Read the following verses.

> Do you not know that you are a temple of God, and that the Spirit of God dwells in you? If any man destroys the temple of God, God will destroy him, for the temple of God is holy, and that is what you are.
>
> –1 Corinthians 3:16-17

> But you are a chosen race, a royal priesthood, a holy nation, a people for God's own possession, that you may proclaim the excellencies of Him who has called you out of darkness into His marvelous light.
>
> –1 Peter 2:9

✎ **What do these passages state should be the purpose of your life?**

_____

_____

Here's why I'm on this earth

Write a short purpose statement for your life.

_____

_____

You are to reflect His image through the way you live and to proclaim the great things about Him to those around you.

✎ **Review the lesson for day 4 so far and then complete the following summary.**

> We obey God because. . .
>
> 1. Christ's _____ motivates us to live for Him.
>
> 2. _____ is destructive and should be avoided.
>
> 3. We will receive eternal _____ for obedience.

What really motivates you?

 How much does each of these six reasons to obey God motivate you? Reflect on these motivations and rate each on the following scale of 0 to 10.

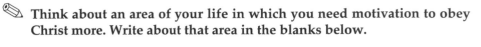

| 0 (no motivation to you at all) | → | 10 (a persistent, conscious, compelling motivation) |

_____ Christ's love motivates us to live for Him.
_____ Sin is destructive and should be avoided.
_____ His commands for us are good.
_____ We will receive eternal rewards for obedience.
_____ Our Father lovingly disciplines us for wrongdoing.
_____ He is worthy of our obedience.

Usually, each person ranks one or two of these motivations higher than he or she does the others. All of these are good and proper motivations. In particular situations any of them could be the most important. However, it seems that the motivations to honor God and to express our love for Him are higher because they focus on Christ and represent a response to His love and majesty. Simple and pure devotion to Christ is our highest and best motivation for serving Him.

Where do you need work?

 Think about an area of your life in which you need motivation to obey Christ more. Write about that area in the blanks below.

_____

_____

_____

➡ It's time to review again your memory work on the affirmation "My Identity in Christ." Review the first seven lines (the two you memorized last week and the next five lines from this week) until you can repeat them from memory. Remember that by the end of this week you likely will have memorized the five seven lines. (Turn to page 224 if you need to refer to the entire affirmation.)

Ask God to help you see what steps of obedience to Him you need to take today.

➡ Stop and pray, asking God's guidance in the area you mentioned that needs concentration. Ask God to reveal Scripture that would be good for you to study and memorize. Ask your prayer partner to pray with you about this area of need. Ask God to help you see what steps of obedience to Him you need to take.

SUMMARY STATEMENTS

- God's commands are given for two good purposes: to protect us from the destructiveness of sin and to direct us in a life of joy and fruitfulness.
- The more we understand God's love and majesty, the more we will praise Him and desire to honor Him at the expense of everything else.
- Simple and pure devotion to Christ is our highest and best motivation for serving Him.

Poor Reasons for Obedience

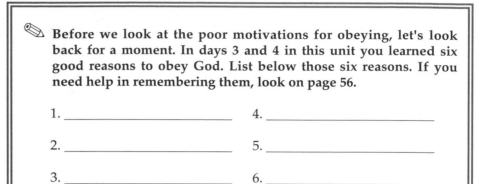

Before we look at the poor motivations for obeying, let's look back for a moment. In days 3 and 4 in this unit you learned six good reasons to obey God. List below those six reasons. If you need help in remembering them, look on page 56.

1. _____   4. _____

2. _____   5. _____

3. _____   6. _____

Pharisees–n. a Jewish religious party which flourished during the last two centuries before Christ and during the first Christian century. Jesus criticized them for their lack of compassion, for their failure to practice what they preached, and for their contempt for people who could not obey the Law as carefully as the Pharisees did. (Mercer)

Poor Motivations for Obeying God and Their Possible Results

Now we'll turn to some reasons for obeying God that aren't the best. Jesus said over and over that He cared about not only *what* we do but also *why* we do it. The **Pharisees** (the left margin tells more about who they were) obeyed many rules and regulations, but their hearts were far from the Lord. Motives are important! The following are some poor motivations for obeying God. In this session you'll learn more about possible results of those poor motivations.

POOR MOTIVATIONS

1. Someone may find out.
2. God will be angry with me.
3. I couldn't approve of myself if I didn't obey.
4. I'll obey to be blessed.

---

1. Someone May Find Out

Many people obey God because they are afraid of what others will think of them if they don't obey. Allen visited prospects for his church because he feared what his Sunday School class would think if he didn't go. Barbara was married but wanted to date a man at work. She didn't because of what others would think.

We've all done it sometime

Think about a time when you did the right thing for the wrong reason—for fear of what others would think. Write about it here.

_____

_____

_____

You will have many problems if you let what others think determine how you behave. To begin with, sometimes no one *is* watching. Maybe you're on a

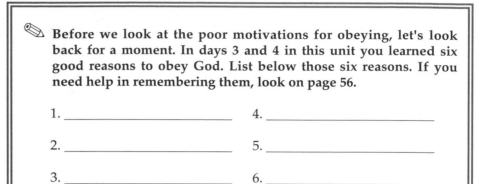

business trip, and you don't know anyone in the city. The motive to stay away from sin is missing, so you indulge in it. Also, sometimes you may decide you want to disobey more than you want to please or more than you want to avoid offending others. Finally, once someone has found out you've sinned, you no longer have a reason to obey. Sherry didn't sleep with her boyfriend for fear of what her mother would say if she found out. One day Sherry slept with her boyfriend, and as she feared, her mother found out. Sherry lost her motivation to obey, so she began sleeping with him regularly. Obeying God because of others' opinions might work for a while, but it won't honor God. Eventually, it won't work at all.

Obeying God because we fear what others will think is another aspect of the fear of rejection. The Lord wants you to obey Him, not to obey the whims of others. Who are the persons for whom you do things in order to please? Can you list them in the box in the left margin? Think about the specific sin you try to avoid in order to please them. For example, you may not show anger because your father scolded you severely when you lost your temper. But in reflecting on the proper motivations for obedience, you can choose to replace that motivation with an understanding that losing your temper dishonors God. Self-control and a proper expression of displeasure bring honor to Him.

2. God Will Be Angry with Me

Some people obey God because they think God will get angry with them if they don't obey. We've already discussed the difference between God's discipline and punishment. We know that God disciplines us in love, not in anger. His response to our sin is grief, not condemnation (see the verse at left).

And do not grieve the Holy Spirit of God, by whom you were sealed for the day of redemption.
–Ephesians 4:30

Hank was afraid that God would "zap" him if he did anything wrong, so he performed for God. He lived each day in fear of God's anger. Predictably, his relationship with the Lord was cold and mechanical.

God doesn't want us to live in fear of His anger but in response to His love. This produces joyful obedience instead of fear. If you believe that God's response to your sin is anger, you feel alienated and bitter toward Him. However, He genuinely is concerned for your welfare. He is sad when sin hurts you. Realizing that He loves you and wants the best for you can prompt you to obey in response to His love. It will motivate you to honor the One who loves you.

There is therefore now no condemnation for those who are in Christ Jesus.
–Romans 8:1

> **Read Romans 8:1 at left and write in your own words what this Scripture says about God's love for you.**
>
> _____

3. I Couldn't Approve of Myself If I Didn't Obey

Some people obey God in an effort to live up to certain standards they've set for themselves. They feel they simply couldn't stand themselves if they didn't obey. Sadly, the idea of yielding their lives to a loving Lord often is far from their minds. They only are trying to live up to their own standards. If they don't meet those standards, they feel ashamed.

These people primarily are concerned with do's and don'ts. Instead of having an intimate relationship with God, they see the Christian life as a ritual, with the key emphasis on rules. Of course, if these people succeed in keeping the rules, they often become prideful. They also may tend to compare themselves with others, hoping to be accepted on the basis of being a little better than someone else.

Do we obey God because we feel that our obedience makes us better than someone else?

Why Phillip didn't curse

Phillip was reared in a strict church family. He was taught that cursing is a terrible sin. All of Phillip's friends cursed, but he never did. He secretly thought that he was better than his friends. Phillip never acted based on what God wanted or because of God's love for him. Instead, he acted because he was determined to live up to his standards. Phillip needed to base his behavior on God and His Word, not on his own standards.

God gave us His commands out of love for us. As we obey Him, we are protected and freed to enjoy life more fully.

✎ Take a moment to think about Christian standards you have set for your life. List some of those standards below. Be ready to share these in your group time.

1. _____

2. _____

3. _____

4. _____

5. _____

He saved us, not on the basis of deeds which we have done in righteousness, but according to His mercy.

–Titus 3:5

Read what the Scripture at left says about how God sees our good deeds.

When we realize that we cannot earn righteousness, no matter how strict we are, we humbly can accept the forgiveness and righteousness that Christ gives. One result is that we will become "zealous for good deeds" (Titus 2:14), not to be accepted but to express our desire to honor Christ.

4. I'll Obey to Be Blessed

If our sole motive to obey is to receive God's blessing or special favor, we simply are attempting to manipulate God. The underlying assumption is: *I've been good enough. . .bless me.* It's true that we will reap what we sow. It's true that obedience keeps us within God's plan for our lives. But our decision to obey never should be based solely on God's rewarding us.

Brian went to church because he thought doing so would cause God to bless his business, not because he wanted to worship God. Cheryl chose not to gossip about Diane. Cheryl had told God she wouldn't spread bad news about Diane if He would get her the raise she wanted.

Do we make deals with God?

✎ Have you ever found yourself trying to make a deal with God or trying to manipulate God for your own good? List below one example of your trying to manipulate or make a deal with God.

_____

_____

_____

Sometimes we think we're as important as God is, and that's why we try to manipulate Him.

One reason you might try to make a deal with God is that you have a view of yourself that is too high. Perhaps you see yourself as an equal with God and as someone who deserves the best from Him. But we are not His equals. He is the awesome, almighty Creator; we are sinful people, deserving eternal condemnation. By His grace He forgives and accepts us.

The appropriate response to His gift of grace is not arrogance but humility and a desire to honor Him. Yes, He is good to you and promises to provide for your needs, but He provides them as your gracious Lord and loving Father.

✎ After learning about these four motivations, think about your own life. Do any of these apply to you? Check below the statement that indicates your reason for obeying God.

❑ God will be angry with me if I don't.
❑ I'll obey to be blessed.
❑ Someone may find out.
❑ I couldn't approve of myself if I didn't obey.
❑ Christ's love motivates me to live for Him.
❑ Other: _____

Changing the Way I Do Things

List here the names of three persons who model the loving characteristics of God to you.

_____

_____

_____

_____

If you want to change your self-serving motivations to motivations that will honor God, several ways exist to get you started. You can start by spending time with other believers who model the loving characteristics of God. In the box at left list the names of some persons you want to strive to be like in this regard.

You also can read the Bible and perhaps look for characteristics of God as you read. You can thank God for His discipline, realizing that it protects us from the destructive nature of sin. You can ask the Holy Spirit to help you appreciate God's commands, knowing that He gives them for our welfare and our spiritual growth. You also can focus not just on the here and now, but you also can keep your sights on eternity, asking God to help you wait for His rewards.

Will you commit to change?

✎ Think about the ways just named that you can change your self-serving motivations. Check the ones you will commit to doing.

❑ I will spend time with believers who model God's loving characteristics.
❑ I will read the Bible to find characteristics of God.

❏ I will ask the Holy Spirit to help me appreciate God's commands, knowing He gives them for my welfare and spiritual growth.

❏ I will thank God for His loving discipline, realizing it protects me from the destructive nature of sin.

❏ I will not just focus on the here and now but also will keep my sights on eternity, asking God to help me wait for His rewards.

God in love will enable us to understand our wrong motives for service, both in our relationship with Him and with others.

Through prayer, relationships with others, and the study of God's Word, He will enable us to experience God's love and compassion. God in love will help us understand our wrong motives for service, both in our relationship with Him and with others.

✎ **Review this week's lessons. Pray and ask God to identify one positive statement that had an impact on your understanding of who you are.**

Write that statement in your own words.

_____

_____

_____

Rewrite your thoughts as a prayer of thankfulness to God.

_____

_____

_____

You probably gained many insights as you worked through this week's lessons. Which insight stands out to you? Write it here.

_____

_____

_____

APPROVAL ADDICT

Case in Point

MOTIVATED TO SERVE?

Randy felt like a vending machine. Anyone wanting something could pull an invisible lever and get it. On the job Randy always was doing other people's work for them. At home his friends continually called on him to help them with odd jobs. His wife insisted that he hold down outside employment so that they could live an affluent life-style. Even people in Randy's church took advantage of him. They knew they could count on "good old Randy" to direct a number of the programs they planned. He said yes until he was exhausted. What was the problem? Was Randy a self-sacrificing saint, did his inability to say no stem from his fear of rejection? (Read about Randy's situation on page 72.) What does Randy need in his life?

What you'll learn this week

This week you'll—

- learn how we react to individuals from whom we seek approval by choosing one individual and examining specific situations based on your experience with that individual;
- study how the fear of rejection affects us and how it can keep us from being all God intended;
- take a test to determine how strongly we fear rejection;
- learn how to rely more on the Holy Spirit to show us continually how to apply the truth that we are fully pleasing to God;
- study the four basic levels of acceptance and rejection and what each level communicates to us.

What you'll study each day

Driven to Please People	What Rejection Feels Like	How Fearing Rejection Zaps Us	The Hazards Go On	How We Treat Others
DAY 1	DAY 2	DAY 3	DAY 4	DAY 5

Memory verse

A key verse to memorize this week

For am I now seeking the favor of men, or of God? Or am I striving to please men? If I were still trying to please men, I would not be a bondservant of Christ.

–Galatians 1:10

Driven to Please People

Though God does not intend it to be this way, our self-concept largely is determined by what others think about us. As a result the need for others' approval can drive us to do whatever we feel we must do to receive it.

Randy felt like a vending machine. Anyone wanting something could pull an invisible lever and get it. On the job Randy always was doing other people's work for them. At home his friends continually called on him to help them with odd jobs. His wife insisted that he hold down outside employment so that they could live an affluent life-style. Even people in Randy's church took advantage of him. They knew they could count on "good old Randy" to direct a number of the programs they planned. He said yes until he was exhausted.

Why can't Randy say no?

What was the problem? Was Randy simply a self-sacrificing saint, or did his ability to say no stem from his fear of rejection? Randy deeply resented those people who, by demanding so much from him, left him little time for himself. Yet he just couldn't refuse them. He longed for others' approval, and he feared their rejection. He believed that by agreeing to their every wish, he would win their approval and would make sure they did not shut him out.

Sometimes we give of ourselves because we feel that doing so will make people appreciate us and not reject us.

Randy typifies many of us. We spend much of our time building relationships and striving to win others' respect. We give of ourselves to the point of exhaustion because we feel that doing so will make people appreciate us and will keep them from rejecting us.

✎ **Describe below a time when you've acted like Randy, saying yes to too many requests and driving yourself to exhaustion because you wanted someone's approval and feared that person's rejection.**

_____

_____

_____

A second false belief associated with such behavior is: I must have approval of certain others to feel good about myself.

In this unit we'll study how this lie causes us to react in ways like Randy did and in other ways as well. We'll also study why we feel we need to believe it, the pitfalls of it, and how we can change our thinking about it.

Looking at what you've learned

✎ **To recap, write below the first two false beliefs and the emotions that arise from them.**

1. I must meet certain _____

_____ , and when I don't meet those

_____

_____

2. I must have _____

_____ , and when I don't have their _____

_____

How Others' Expectations Affect Me

First, let's personalize this lesson a bit by looking at some persons whose approval you need and whose rejection you fear. Only when we study how this situation works in our own lives can we begin to understand why it happens and what we can do about it.

Whose approval do I need?

✎ **List below names of persons whose approval you need and whose rejection you fear. These individuals might include your parents, boyfriend/girlfriend, spouse, peer group, or boss. Even God might be on your list.**

_____

_____

_____

In the following exercise we will see how one of the individuals you listed in the blank above affects you. Choose one of the names you listed and then answer the next four sets of questions about that person. Examine: (a)what you feel would make that person more pleased with you, (b)what you do now that makes the person proud, (c)what that person does to attempt to get you to change, and (d)what you do to win that person's approval. Later in the session we'll examine the causes for some of these reactions.

The example below demonstrates what someone might write if she had chosen her father as the person who she feels rejects or disapproves of her.

Example:
1. My *father* would be more pleased with me if I called him more often, wore my hair the way he wants me to, and got a better job.
2. My *father* is proud of me when I get a promotion, when I remember important family dates, when I win in sports.
3. My *father* criticizes me, is sarcastic with me, and sometimes ignores me in an effort to get me to change.
4. To gain my *father's* approval, I tell him only what he likes to hear, exaggerate the truth a little, and work really hard to be a success.

Now you fill in the blanks, based on your experience.

1. _____ would be more pleased with me if I would—

   a. _____

   b _____

   c. _____

2. _____ is proud of me when I—

    a. _____

    b. _____

    c. _____

3. _____ attempts to get me to change by doing the following.

Looking at my approval needs

    a. _____

    b. _____

    c. _____

4. Things I do or say to get _____ to approve of me include—

    a. _____

    b. _____

    c. _____

An Approval Addict's Confession

Hoping to win others' favor

I easily can identify with people who find themselves hungry for others' approval. My own desire for this often has been so great that I sometimes joke about having been born an approval addict. As I grew up, I always felt that I didn't fit in, that I was different from others, and that something was inherently wrong with me. I desperately hoped that winning others' favor would make up for the negative feelings I had about myself.

Ironically, others' conditional approval never was enough to satisfy me. Instead, being praised only reminded me of the disapproval I might encounter if I failed to maintain what I had achieved. I thus was driven to work even harder at being successful. I occasionally find myself falling into this pattern of behavior even now, despite my improved knowledge, experience, and relationship with God. However, here's what I've learned:

> The only way we can overcome the fear of rejection is to focus on the reality of God's acceptance of us based on our position in Christ rather than on the approval of others based on our performance.

Depending on others for value brings slavery, while abiding in Christ's love and acceptance brings freedom and joy.

Our fear of rejection will control us to the degree to which we base our worth on the opinions of others rather than on our relationship with God. Depending on others for value brings slavery, while abiding in Christ's love and acceptance brings freedom and joy. From this study you will learn why we think we need approval, what ways we experience disapproval, and how the fear of rejection affects us.

DAY 2

What Rejection Feels Like

What is this situation of rejection we fear so greatly? How does rejection show up in our lives? What does it communicate to us? You probably can list more than one occasion in which you've experienced rejection. This rejection may have occurred in a subtle, indirect, or even nonverbal manner. For example, you may have felt it in a friend's disgusted look, a individual's snub after you say hello, a coworker who rudely keeps his eye on his computer screen for minutes after you've entered his office, or a general icy coolness that you detect when you enter a room.

 Think of situations in which someone has communicated rejection to you nonverbally. List these situations here.

A time I was snubbed

1. _____

2. _____

3. _____

You may have felt rejection in a professor's sarcastic remark about your paper or in an impatient answer.

Other times you've felt rejected may have been more direct. For example, you may have felt it in a professor's sarcastic remark about your paper, a potential employer's don't-call-us-we'll-call-you letter, a group's excluding you from a function, an athletic team's choosing you last, or an impatient answer.

List situations in which you have felt someone's rejection of you has been more direct, such as through a critical remark, a put-down, or outright exclusion.

_____

_____

_____

✎ Choose one of the situations you listed on the previous page that represented a time you felt rejection—either through a verbal or nonverbal message. Below list the emotions that accompanied the situation you described.

How did it make you feel?

_____

_____

Did this cause you lowered self-worth? ❏ Yes ❏ No

Why or why not? _____

_____

_____

If we believe the lie, I am what others say I am, *the fear of rejection will plague us.*

Our emotional responses in these situations may vary from slight annoyance to deep hurt, anger, and bitterness. We fear rejection in proportion to the degree to which we base our self-worth on the opinions of others. If we believe the lie, *I am what others say I am,* the fear of rejection will plague us.

How greatly does the false belief, *I must be approved by certain others to feel good about myself* affect you? Take the following test to determine how strongly you fear rejection.

✎ Read each of the statements below. Then, from the top of the test, choose the term that best describes your response. Put in the blank beside each statement the number above the term you chose.

1	2	3	4	5	6	7
Always	Very Often	Often	Sometimes	Seldom	Very Seldom	Never

_____ 1. When I sense that someone might reject me, I become anxious.

_____ 2. I spend lots of time analyzing why someone was critical or sarcastic to me or ignored me.

_____ 3. I am uncomfortable around those who are different from me.

_____ 4. It bothers me when someone is unfriendly to me.

_____ 5. I am basically shy and unsocial.

_____ 6. I am critical of others.

_____ 7. I find myself trying to impress others.

_____ 8. I become depressed when someone criticizes me..

_____ 9. I always try to determine what people think of me.

_____ 10. I don't understand people and what motivates them.

_____ Total (Add the numbers you have placed in the blanks.)

What your score says about you

Interpreting Your Score
If your score is...

57-70
God apparently has given you a very strong appreciation for His love and unconditional acceptance. You seem to be free from the fear of rejection that plagues most people. (One exception: Some people who score this high either are greatly deceived or have become callous to their emotions as a way to suppress pain. Examine your heart to see if this exception applies to you.)

47-56

The fear of rejection controls your responses rarely or only in certain situations. Again, the only major exceptions are those who are not honest with themselves.

37-46

Emotional problems you experience may relate to a sense of rejection. Upon reflection you probably will relate many of your previous decisions to this fear. The fear of rejection also will affect many of your future decisions unless you take direct action to overcome that fear.

27-36

The fear of rejection forms a general backdrop to your life. Probably few days go by in which this fear does not affect you in some way. Unfortunately, this robs you of the joy and peace your salvation is meant to bring.

0-26

Experiences of rejection dominate your memory and probably cause you to have a great deal of depression. These problems will persist until you take definitive action. In other words, this condition will not simply disappear; time alone cannot heal your pain. You need to experience deep healing in your self-concept, in your relationship with God, and in your relationships with others.

How deeply do you need healing?

• •

Here's a thought to remember:

> Turning to others for what only God can provide shows how overwhelmingly we accept Satan's lie that others must accept us before we feel good about ourselves.

Only God, speaking to us through His Word, His Spirit, and His timing, can provide the security we so desperately seek.

➥ **By now you likely will be well into your memory work on the four false beliefs. Today look at the inside back cover and begin memorizing the second false belief. By the end of this week's study, you likely will have memorized this belief, as well as the first false belief you memorized in unit 1.**

SUMMARY STATEMENTS

- We fear rejection in proportion to the degree to which we base our self-worth on the opinions of others.
- If we believe the lie, *I am what others say I am,* the fear of rejection will plague us.
- Turning to others for what only God can provide shows how overwhelmingly we accept Satan's lie that others must accept us before we feel good about ourselves.

How Fearing Rejection Zaps Us

Virtually all of us fear rejection. We can fall prey to it even when we've learned to harden our defenses as we anticipate someone's disapproval. Neither being defensive nor trying to please another person at all costs is the answer to this problem. These approaches to our fear of rejection actually prevent us from dealing with that fear's root cause.

How does the fear of rejection zap us and keep us from being all God intended?

We fear rejection even when we've learned to harden our defenses to it.

 As you read the following list, circle the ways fear or rejection affects you most.

- **Inability to give and receive love**
- **Avoiding people**
- **Susceptibility to peer pressure**
- **Susceptibility to experiment with drugs or sex**
- **Susceptibility to influence on our moral standards**
- **Susceptibility to manipulation**
- **Need to be in control of all situations**
- **Anger, resentment, hostility**
- **Depression**
- **Defensiveness**
- **Passivity**
- **Unwillingness to share our faith**

We will study half of these in this session and half in the next. The explanations of the following results are not exhaustive but are designed to demonstrate how the fear of rejection can affect many areas of our lives.

Inability to Give and Receive Love

One result of our fear of rejection is that we become unable to give and receive love. We find it difficult to open up and reveal our inner thoughts and needs because we believe others will reject us if they know what we're *really* like.

Michael, for example, was reared in a broken home. Since he was quite young, Michael had lived with his father. Michael's father had not wanted custody of the boy, but Michael's mother was too busy with her whirl of social activities to care for him.

Afraid to get too close

After the divorce Michael's father married another woman who had three children. This new wife began to resent Michael.

When Michael grew up and married a wonderful woman who truly loved him, he, not surprisingly, was cautious about sharing his love with her because he had experienced the pain of rejection all his life.

Because of that rejection he withheld his love from someone he truly cared for because he was afraid of becoming too close to his wife. His parents had rejected him, and if she rejected him as they had done, the pain would be too much for him to bear.

Friends at arms' length

✎ Describe a time in which you feared revealing your inner self because you feared rejection.

_____

_____

_____

Avoiding People

These people's friends never really get to know them because they hide behind a wall of words, smiles, and activities.

Some people react to their fear of rejection by avoiding others, thereby avoiding the risk that they'll be rejected. Some people avoid others overtly and spend most of their time alone, while others deal with this fear by having numerous relationships but keeping them on the surface. They actually may be around people much of the time and may be considered socially skilled. They may know how to make friends easily and seem gregarious, but their friendships never are deep ones. Their friends never *really* get to know them because these people hide behind a wall of words, smiles, and activities. These people usually are quite lonely in the midst of all their "friends."

✎ Describe a time in which you avoided people to avoid the risk that they would reject you.

_____

_____

_____

Susceptibility to Peer Pressure

I want to be liked!

Fear of rejection causes us to bow to peer pressure in an effort to gain approval. We may join clubs and organizations, hoping we'll be accepted. We may identify ourselves with social groups, believing that being with these groups will ensure our acceptance and their approval.

Susceptibility to Experiment with Drugs or Sex

Many people admit that they bow to peer pressure for fear that they won't be accepted if they don't. However, drugs and sexual promiscuity promise something they can't fulfill. Experimenting only leaves these people with pain. It also leaves them with a deeper need for self-worth and acceptance.

Susceptibility to Influence on Our Moral Standards

And do not be conformed to this world, but be transformed by the renewing of your mind, that you may prove what the will of God is, that which is good and acceptable and perfect.
–Romans 12:2

Some of us have established our moral standards based on the approval or disapproval of others. Rather than letting God speak to us through His Word as our authority on matters of life, we have referred to people, doing what they approve of or encourage us to do. This may have led some of us to compromise our sexual purity, moral and ethical integrity, and our walk with God. God has revealed His good, acceptable, and perfect will for our lives in His Word, as the Scripture in the left margin shows. We must learn to embrace and apply His truths and refuse to believe the lie, *I am what others think of me.*

When did the fear of rejection cause you to bow to peer pressure and make a regrettable decision? Write about it here.

_____

_____

_____

God is the only One who loves us and appreciates us unconditionally. He has provided a solution to the fear of rejection.

Write in the margin box about a time in which the fear of rejection caused peer pressure to rule in your life.

 Based on the results we've studied so far, check below the ways you can see that the fear of rejection shows up in your life.

- ❏ I'm unable to give and receive love.
- ❏ I avoid people.
- ❏ I'm susceptible to peer pressure.
- ❏ I'm susceptible to experimenting with drugs or sex.
- ❏ I'm susceptible to having my moral standards influenced.

The reason we experience the fear of rejection and its accompanying problems is because we believe Satan's lie that our self-worth = performance + others' opinions. We crave love, fellowship, and intimacy, and we turn to others to meet those needs. However, the problem with basing our worth on the approval of others is that God is the only One who loves and appreciates us unconditionally. He has provided a solution to the fear of rejection.

SUMMARY STATEMENTS

- When we fear rejection, we find it difficult to open up and reveal our inner thoughts and needs because we believe others will reject us if they know what we're *really* like.
- The reason we experience the fear of rejection and its accompanying problems is because we believe Satan's lie that our self-worth = performance + others' opinions.
- God is the only One who loves us and appreciates us unconditionally. He has provided a solution to the fear of rejection.

DAY 4

The Hazards Go On

As if those hazards weren't enough, the list showing what the fear of rejection does to people continues in this session. Besides the results we just studied, the fear of rejection also causes people to experience the following situations, which we'll discuss fully in day 4.

- **Susceptibility to manipulation**
- **Need to be in control of all situations**
- **Anger, resentment, hostility**
- **Depression**
- **Defensiveness**
- **Passivity**
- **Unwillingness to share our faith**

Susceptibility to Manipulation

Just about anything to please

Those who believe that their self-worth is based on others' approval likely will do just about anything to please people. They truly believe that they will be well liked if they comply with the requests of others. Many of them inevitably end up despising those who manipulate and resent what they feel they have to do for others' approval. Although some praise is given to help us, build us up, and encourage us through appreciation, some praise can be a form of manipulation.

Some people use praise to get us to accomplish their goals, to contribute to their program, or to help them look good in front of others. In that sense, praise is a subtle but powerful form of rejection. Unfortunately, many of us fall prey to this harmful, manipulative praise because we so desperately want to be appreciated.

✎ **Think about a time someone praised you in a manipulative way. Describe here what that person said to you. Write how you felt about it then and how you feel about it now.**

_____

_____

_____

✎ **Check below the response you feel when people praise you only to manipulate you.**

Does this make you feel used?

❑ I feel used, like an object.
❑ I resent being used.
❑ I get angry with the person.

If you perceive that someone is praising you only to manipulate you, then you very well may feel used, like an object instead of a person. You may feel very angry at the person.

> People who manipulate us with praise are using us as tools to accomplish their goals and are rejecting us as people. It creates a kind of sickness of spirit in us. Do we really need others' approval so much that we'll tolerate this treatment?

Need to Be in Control of All Situations

In their fear of rejection and in their efforts to avoid being hurt, many people constantly try to maintain control of others and dominate most situations. Greg needed to control so much that he refused to attend parties unless he was the host. If coworkers needed five minutes of his time to discuss a project, he was too busy. Yet Greg showed up frequently in coworkers' offices unannounced and demanded their uninterrupted time, even if it were inconvenient for them. Such people are skilled in controlling by giving out approval or disapproval. They are unwilling to let others be themselves and to make their own decisions without their consent. People who fear rejection are so insecure that the thought of not controlling every situation horrifies them.

People who fear rejection are so insecure that the thought of not controlling every situation horrifies them.

Think for a moment about the following question.

If I run from rejection, who really is in control of my life? Am I really the master controller that I see myself to be? Write your answer here.

_____

Can you really be so very much in control if you're running from rejection all the time?

If you run from rejection, whoever you avoid actually is determining your actions and therefore is your controller. As you begin to experience freedom from the control of others' opinions, your life increasingly will be focused on the Lord, and He will control it. This will result in your growth and in His glory.

Anger, Resentment, Hostility

Anger usually is our most common response to rejection or to the fear of rejection. Some of us are honest about our anger. We may deny it exists; we may suppress it; and we may assume that it will go away. We may vent our anger in a destructive explosion. Or we may use sarcasm or neglect to express anger in a more indirect way. If we don't resolve our anger through honesty and forgiveness, we become deeply hostile and resentful. One motive for retaining anger is the desire for revenge.

Depression

Depression is the result of a deep sense of loss or repressed, pent-up anger. This anger can stem from past rejections that make the present fear of rejection even more intense. Or it can stem from feeling used by others' manipulation in our great desire for approval. When people do not handle anger properly, their bodies and minds respond to its intense pressure. The person's emotions and sense of purpose become dulled.

Defensiveness

Our fear of rejection makes us run from any type of open discussion of issues. Fred always bristled and found an excuse to avoid meeting when members of the church committee he chaired approached him with a concern. Instead of making possible an honest, helpful talk, Fred went on the defensive immediately. He feared rejection so much he ran from any situation in which he thought he might feel pain.

What makes Fred bristle?

Passivity

We may become passive because of our fear of rejection. We may withdraw by avoiding decisions and activities in which we might be criticized. We also avoid activities in which we can't be sure we'll be successful. Our goal in these instances usually is to avoid the pain of rejection by not doing anything that might be objectionable. This also prevents us from enjoying the pleasures of healthy relationships and achievements.

Unwillingness to Share Our Faith

Perhaps the most critical result of the fear of rejection is that it keeps many of us from sharing our faith. Nonbelievers are well aware of the pain of rejection,

Nonbelievers use the pain of rejection to threaten us so they won't have to deal with the gospel.

and they use it to threaten us so they won't have to deal with the gospel. Their rejection quickly sends the message, "I don't care about you or what you have to say." So, since we fear rejection anyway, we quickly back off. Some things they say are:

- "You don't believe all that Christianity junk, do you?"
- "How could anyone with any brains be a Christian?"
- "Christianity is a crutch."
- "I believe religion is a personal issue; don't talk to me about it."
- "Only losers are Christians."

In the left margin write about a time when someone used a put-down remark to try to prevent you from sharing the gospel.

What are nonbelievers doing? They are rejecting us (inflicting emotional pain) to silence us. Identifying this fear and working through it may enable us to more readily initiate conversation with others about the gospel.

✎ **Based on the results we've studied in this session, check below the ways you can see that the fear of rejection shows up in your life.**

❑ I'm susceptible to others' manipulating me.
❑ I feel that I always must be in control.
❑ I have a great deal of anger, resentment, and hostility.
❑ I'm always on the defensive.
❑ I have a great deal of depression.
❑ I'm unwilling to share my faith.

• •

In looking back over the list, every one of the results mentioned stems from our desire for approval, and the Bible has quite a bit to say about this. In Galatians 1:10 Paul clearly drew the line concerning our search for approval. Read in the left margin what he said. According to this passage, we ultimately seek either people's approval or God's approval as the basis of our self-worth. We cannot seek both. God wants to be the Lord of our lives. He is unwilling to share that rightful lordship with anyone else.

➡ **It's time to review again your memory work on the second false belief. Review the first two beliefs (the one you memorized in unit 1 and the next one from this week) until you can repeat them from memory. By the end of this week, you likely will have memorized both lines. (Turn to the inside back cover if you need to review the four false beliefs.)**

Write about a time when someone used a put-down remark to keep you from sharing the gospel.

_____

_____

_____

For am I now seeking the favor of men, or of God? Or am I striving to please men? If I were still trying to please men, I would not be a bondservant of Christ.
–Galatians 1:10

SUMMARY STATEMENTS

- People who manipulate us with praise are using us as tools to accomplish their goals and are rejecting us as people.
- People who fear rejection are so insecure that the thought of not controlling every situation horrifies them.
- Perhaps the most critical result of the fear of rejection is that it keeps many of us from sharing our faith. Nonbelievers use it to threaten us so they won't have to deal with the gospel.

How We Treat Others

Can I Be Completely Free?

Probably not. It may be impossible for us totally to shed our need for others' approval and our fear of rejection. Many may be surprised to learn this. Perhaps they assume that reading this book and completing its exercises will keep them forever from basing their self-worth on what others think of them.

I don't believe that any of us will gain complete freedom from this tendency until we're with the Lord someday. Our God-given instinct to survive compels us to avoid pain. Knowing that rejection and disapproval bring pain, we will continue our attempts to win the esteem of others whenever possible.

> The good news is that we are fully pleasing to God. We need not be devastated when others respond to us in a negative way.

We may not totally free ourselves from the need for approval, but the Holy Spirit will keep teaching us areas in which we need work.

As we grow in our relationship with God, the Holy Spirit will continue showing us how to apply this liberating truth to different aspects of our lives at an increasingly deeper level. In fact, one way we see Him working in us is the ability to see new areas of our lives in which we are allowing the opinions of others to determine our sense of worth. With spiritual maturity we will be able to identify these areas more often and will choose to find our significance in God's unconditional love for us and complete acceptance of us. With spiritual maturity we will recognize the false beliefs about ourselves for what they are, and we will overcome them as God speaks to us through the truths from His Word.

✎ **From memory write below the first two false beliefs.**

1. I must meet certain _____

_____

2. I must have _____

_____

Watching what we say

We Do Our Share of Rejecting, Too

Before we can be sure we're on the right track toward overcoming our fear of rejection, we must look at how we treat other people. We communicate rejection to others, as well. Have you ever been guilty of using disapproval, silence, sarcasm, or criticism to get others to do what you want them to do? If you don't think that you use rejection to motivate others, see if any of these statements sound familiar:

- *"If you loved me, you'd..."*
- *"Come on, Joe, everyone else is going."*

Write a put-down remark
that you've used to
communicate rejection to
others.

_____

_____

_____

- "You didn't know that?"
- "Have you heard what Susie did?"
- "If you can't do better, I'll get someone else who's more competent."
- "That's stupid!"
- "Your hair looks so much better that way."
- "You mean you weren't invited to the party?"
- "Nice shirt. Did that color cost extra?"

In the left margin write a remark that you have used to communicate rejection to others.

Four Basic Levels of Acceptance and Rejection

In studying the nature of your relationships with other people concerning how you are treated and how you treat others, we can study the four basic levels of acceptance and rejection.

> 1. Total rejection
> 2. Highly conditional acceptance
> 3. Mildly conditional acceptance
> 4. Unconditional acceptance

What does one have to do?

These levels center on the question, What does a person have to do to be accepted? Here are examples of what each level communicates.

1. **Total rejection**: "No matter what you do, it's not good enough."

2. **Highly conditional acceptance**: "You must do these things in order for me to be happy with you."

3. **Mildly conditional acceptance**: "I will be happier with you if you do these things."

4. **Unconditional acceptance**: "I love you and accept you no matter what you do. There is nothing you can do that can make me stop loving you."

You may find yourself wondering, How, then, do I relate to persons whose approval I've felt I needed?

After studying the previous sessions, you may find yourself wondering, *How, then, do I relate to persons who manipulate me? How do I relate to persons who I fear will reject me? How do I relate to persons whose approval I feel I so desperately needed?* The answer is this: We relate to them in the way God relates to us. He accepts us unconditionally. We can do nothing to make Him stop loving us or to love us more. He accepts us as we are.

Unconditional acceptance truly is the way to relate to others. This does not mean that we can do as we please or that we are to ignore unacceptable behavior in others. Unconditional acceptance may include loving confrontation; correction; and, in some cases, discipline.

However, the focus in these relationships is on the individual rather than on his or her behavior. We accept this person even if she snubs us, gives us icy glances in the hallways, fails to invite us to parties, and refuses to select us for the athletic team. Perhaps we also can begin to look in another direction for the major source of our friendship and support.

God's approval is enough

But we also can turn this person loose in terms of the power he or she holds over us. We do not need this person's approval for our self-worth. We have God's approval, and that's all that matters.

This list also guides us in relating to other people. What do we communicate about our acceptance of them?

A Note for Parents

Parents can take special note of how they communicate rejection to their children. By verbal attacks on the child's character and abilities, by comparisons to other siblings, by silence, by prolonged absences from home, and by physical abuse, parents can communicate rejection that carries with it lifetime scars. That is why many children rebel when they reach adolescence and why many leave home.

 List one technique you've observed that parents use to communicate rejection to children. Then list one technique you've observed that parents use to communicate acceptance to children.

_____

_____

We must communicate love for the child and dislike for the misdeed.

Again, unconditional acceptance is the answer for parents. This doesn't mean we approve of our children's wrongdoing. Sometimes confrontation and discipline are needed. But we are communicating in a godly way, "I love you; I just don't like your misdeed."

Are some changes needed?

 Think about a major relationship in your life: a family member, a friend, a coworker, someone at school, a fellow church member, or a neighbor. Then answer these questions.

How does this person tend to treat you?

How do you tend to treat this person?

Which pattern of acceptance/rejection do you use in relating to this person?

Do you need to put fewer demands and conditions on your acceptance of this person? How will you do that?

What Will You Do?

Will you commit to remembering that you need not fear rejection because God loves you?

What will you commit to do to end your approval addiction? Will you commit to understanding your self-worth based on God's Word as God speaks to us through it about our importance to Him? Will you commit to remembering that your self-worth is not based on others' approval and that you need not fear rejection because God loves you?

✎ **Here is what I commit to do to make profound changes in the way I view my self-worth, based on others' acceptance:**

1 _____

2. _____

3. _____

✎ **Review this week's lessons. Pray and ask God to identify one positive statement that had an impact on your understanding of who you are.**

Write that statement to your own words.

_____

_____

_____

Rewrite your thoughts as a prayer of thankfulness to God.

_____

_____

_____

You probably gained many insights as you worked through this week's lessons. Which insight stands out to you? Write it here.

_____

_____

_____

RECONCILIATION

FEELING UNPARDONABLE

Edith was an unmarried woman who gave birth to a child. Although she was a Christian before this event occurred, Edith later stopped attending church because she no longer felt close to God. Although she believed God forgives some sins, she felt that her action was on God's unpardonable list. She spent much of her adult life feeling unworthy of God's love. (Read more about Edith's situation on page 96.) What does Edith need in her life?

What you'll learn this week

This week you'll–

- study the biblical basis and application of reconciliation;
- learn that because of reconciliation we have gone from being an enemy to a friend of God;
- learn the importance of having other Christians in our lives—for strength, encouragement, comfort, and love;
- learn that God is loving, protective, gracious, and compassionate even if our parents were poor role models of these characteristics;
- learn to distinguish between healthy and unhealthy relationships.

What you'll study each day

Becoming Friends	Acceptable and Accepted	Nothing Makes Us Unacceptable	A New Way to React to Hurt	The Role of Relationships
DAY 1	DAY 2	DAY 3	DAY 4	DAY 5

Memory verse

A key verse to memorize this week

And although you were formerly alienated and hostile in mind, engaged in evil deeds, yet He has now reconciled you in His fleshly body through death, in order to present you before Him holy and blameless and beyond reproach.

–Colossians 1:21-22

WordWatch

Words to help you understand this week's lessons

reconciliation–n. to restore to friendship or harmony; to settle or resolve something. (*Example: You are acceptable to God because of reconciliation.*)

mercy–n. the outward sign of pity; God's attitude toward people in distress; compassion for the ills of others. (*Example: God saved us according to His mercy.*)

DAY 1

Becoming Friends

Feeling Unacceptable

Three years after Pam married, she committed adultery with a coworker. Although she confessed her sin to God and to her husband and had been forgiven, guilt continued to plague her. Four years after the affair she still could not forgive herself for her actions, and she felt unacceptable to God.

As Pam sat in my office, we explored why she could not accept God's forgiveness. "It sounds as though you believe that God can't forgive the sin you committed," I said. "That's right," she replied. "I don't think He ever will."

I told her that God doesn't base His love and acceptance of us on our performance.

"If any sin is so filthy and vile that it makes us less acceptable to Him, then the cross is not enough," I continued. "If the cross isn't enough to take care of all sin, then the Bible is in error when it says that God forgave all your sins [see the verse at left]. God took our sins and canceled them by nailing them to Christ's cross. In this way God also took away Satan's power to condemn us for sin. So you see, nothing you ever will do will wipe out that **reconciliation** and make you unacceptable to God."

> And when you were dead in your transgressions and the uncircumcision of your flesh, He made you alive together with Him, having forgiven us all our transgressions, having canceled out the certificate of debt consisting of decrees against us; and He has taken it out of the way, having nailed it to the cross.
> –Colossians 2:13-14

Pam is like many of us. We look back on our lives and think about something we've done that seems so horrible, so inexcusable, so terribly wrong that we don't think we'll ever feel acceptable again. We think, *I deserve to be rejected because of this big mess.*

When we've messed up badly

 Think for a moment about a time you messed up badly in the past and you still have a tinge of guilt about it. In fact, you still may be wondering how you can be acceptable in God's eyes because of it.

God's solution to that dilemma is **reconciliation**. Because of reconciliation God has wiped out of his memory some action that the world might see as a big mess.

> *Because of reconciliation, God has wiped out of His memory some action that the world might see as a big mess.*

At left is the dictionary's definition of *reconciliation*. Write the definition here in your own words.

_____

_____

> **reconciliation**–n. to restore to friendship or harmony; to settle or resolve something (Webster's)

God's solution to the fear of rejection is based on Christ's sacrificial payment for our sins. Through this payment we find forgiveness, reconciliation, and total acceptance through Christ.

> Reconciliation means that those who were enemies have become friends.

And although you were formerly alienated and hostile in mind, engaged in evil deeds, yet He has now reconciled you in His fleshly body through death, in order to present you before Him holy and blameless and beyond reproach.
–Colossians 1:21-22

In the verse at left Paul described how we went from a relationship of being enemies to being friends with God. Below is a summary of that verse.

Because of your sin you were an enemy of God and were hostile in mind. Your sin made you subject to God's wrath; but if you have trusted Christ, you now are declared holy in His sight, without blemish and free from accusation.

✎ **Complete this chart, basing your answers on the above summary of Colossians 1:21-22.**

Before Christ	After Christ
Subject to God's _____	_____ in His sight
An _____ of God	Without _____
_____ in mind	Free from _____

Not Simply a Ticket to Heaven

The fact that Christ accepts us unconditionally is a profound, life-changing truth. Salvation is not simply a ticket to heaven. It is the beginning of a dynamic new relationship with God.

Justification, which we studied in unit 3, is the doctrine that explains the judicial facts of our forgiveness and righteousness in Christ. Reconciliation explains our salvation's relational aspect. The moment we receive Christ by faith, we enter a personal relationship with Him.

An instant relationship

> We are united with God in an eternal and inseparable bond. The Holy Spirit has sealed us in that relationship, and we are absolutely secure in Christ.

Ephesians 1:13-14 states, "Having also believed, you were sealed in Him with the Holy Spirit of promise, who is given as a pledge of our inheritance, with a view to the redemption of God's own possession, to the praise of His glory."

✎ **Read Romans 5:8-11 at left and choose the correct answers below.**

Who initiated restoring your relationship with God?
- ❏ You initiated the restoring.
- ❏ God, who deeply loves you, restored your relationship with Him.

How did God reconcile you to Himself?
- ❏ God reconciled you to Himself through the death of His precious Son, Jesus Christ.
- ❏ God reconciled you to Himself through punishment for your sins.

But God demonstrates His own love toward us, in that while we were yet sinners, Christ died for us. Much more then, having now been justified by His blood, we shall be saved from the wrath of God through Him. For if while we were enemies, we were reconciled to God through the death of His Son, much more, having been reconciled, we shall be saved by His life. And not only this, but we also exult in God through our Lord Jesus Christ, through whom we have now received the reconciliation.
–Romans 5:8-11

What is your response to God's reconciliation?

❑ You can greatly delight in God, knowing that He loves you and has reconciled you to Himself.

❑ God can't forgive the sin you have committed.

Recently, in a group prayer meeting someone prayed, "Thank You, God, for accepting me when I am so unacceptable." This person understood that we cannot earn God's acceptance by our own merit. However, this person seemed to have forgotten that we are accepted unconditionally in Christ. We no longer are unacceptable—the cross made us acceptable! Through Christ's death and resurrection we have become acceptable to God. This did not occur because God decided He could overlook our sin but because Christ forgave all our sins so that He could present us to the Father holy and blameless.

We no longer are unacceptable—the cross made us acceptable!

 What is wrong with the statement you just read: "Thank you, God, for accepting me when I am so unacceptable"? Write your response below.

_____

_____

_____

You are acceptable to God! He does not just tolerate you.

 Mark the following statements as *T* (true) or *F* (false).

_____ I am acceptable to God right now.
_____ I am not at this moment acceptable to God.
_____ I am 99.99 percept acceptable to God.
_____ I am 100 percent acceptable to God.
_____ I am acceptable because I do good deeds.
_____ I am acceptable because Christ has paid the price.

100 percent acceptable!

You are 100 percent acceptable to the highest Judge: the perfect, holy, and righteous God Almighty. You are acceptable to God for one reason: Christ has abolished the barrier and made peace with God through His blood on the cross. You have the righteousness of Christ (2 Corinthians 5:21). You can never be any more acceptable to God than you are now (Romans 5:8-10; Ephesians 2:14-18; Colossians 1:21-22).

You fear rejection when you believe the lie, *I am what others think of me* instead of believing God's truth, *I am totally acceptable and accepted because of Christ*. You never will begin to experience freedom from the fear of rejection until you realize that God has completely accepted you. If you refuse to believe God's statement, the only other option is to turn to others to meet your need for acceptance and significance. As you studied in unit 4, turning to others will leave you painfully disillusioned. The primary issue is this: Whose acceptance do you value more, God's or people's?

You never will begin to experience freedom from the fear of rejection until you realize that God has completely accepted you.

The Biblical Theme of Reconciliation

 No greater theme exists in Scripture than the reconciliation of people to God. At the end of each day's work for this week you will see several

As far as the east is from the west, So far has He removed our transgressions from us.

–Psalm 103:12

for this is My blood of the covenant, which is poured out for many for forgiveness of sins.

–Matthew 26:28

For God so loved the world, that He gave His only begotten Son, that whoever believes in Him should not perish, but have eternal life.

–John 3:16

Scriptures that deal with reconciliation. Study the passages in the left margin and answer the question after each one.

Psalm 103:12. What happens to our transgressions (sins)?_____

_____

Matthew 26:28. Why was Christ's blood shed? _____

_____

John 3:16. What is God's promise? _____

_____

 By now you likely will be well into your memory work on God's four truths. Today look on the inside back cover and begin memorizing the second truth. By the end of this week's study you likely will have memorized this truth, as well as the first of God's truths you memorized in unit 3.

SUMMARY STATEMENTS

- Because of reconciliation God has wiped out of His memory some action that the world might see as a big mess.
- Through Christ's death and resurrection we have become acceptable to God.
- You never will begin to experience freedom from the fear of rejection until you realize that God has completely accepted you.

DAY 2

And I, brethren, could not speak to you as to spiritual men, but as to men of flesh, as to babes in Christ. I gave you milk to drink, not solid food, for you were not yet able to receive it. Indeed, even now you are not yet able, for you are still fleshly. For since there is jealousy and strife among you, are you not fleshly, and are you not walking like mere men? For when one says, "I am of Paul," and another, "I am of Apollos," are you not mere men?

–1 Corinthians 3:1-4

Acceptable and Accepted

Because of reconciliation we are completely acceptable to God and are completely accepted by God. We enjoy a full and complete relationship with Him. In this relationship He does not determine our value based on our performance. However, we may question what this relationship means as we attempt to apply it in our day-to-day experience. Let's analyze this issue.

Hard to Change Our Outlook

When we are born again as spiritual beings in right standing with God, we are still tilted toward the world's way of thinking. Because the world's outlook and values have conditioned us, we find it hard to look at things any other way.

Indeed, when Paul wrote to the Christians at Corinth, he called them *men of flesh*. Though they were Christians, these individuals had not yet developed into the complete, mature believers God intended them to be. He even called them *babes in Christ*. (This verse appears in the margin.)

Many of us are like the Christians at Corinth. We still try to get our significance the world's way—through success and approval. Often, we look only to other people for that worth rather than to Christ Himself. Sometimes we do this even through our church activities. We learn to use the right Christian words, claim that the Lord is guiding us, and organize programs. Yet so often, it's as though we have on a spiritual front that lacks depth and substance. Our spiritual activities become human efforts lacking the real touch of the Master. In effect, we live a lie.

Do I see myself in Janet?

For five years in a row Janet had organized the churchwide picnic. She was well known for her lavish decorations and her efficiency at putting committees to work. Then one year the youth in the church asked if they could be in charge of the picnic so they could learn leadership skills. Janet became so angry that she refused to cooperate when the youth asked her for assistance. Janet and her family eventually began attending another church because Janet felt her entire self-worth was based on her history as the church-picnic organizer.

✎ **Think for a moment whether you've ever acted like Janet and felt your self-worth was lessened when you lost a role you held in a church or another organization. Describe what you did about it.**

_____

_____

The desire for success and approval constitutes the basis of an addictive, worldly self-worth. Certainly, we may feel some pain as we withdraw from this dependency and as we begin to base our self-worth on something different. Yet we will begin to discover true freedom and maturity in Christ only when we understand that our lives mean much more than what success or the approval of others can bring.

✎ **Write below the second false belief and the truth from God's Word to refute Satan's lie.**

False belief:_____

Truth:_____

The Free Gift

If we base our self-worth on others' approval, we are saying that their approval is more highly valued than is Christ's payment on the cross.

We can do nothing to contribute to Christ's free gift of salvation; furthermore, if we base our self-worth on others' approval, we actually are saying that their approval is more highly valued than is Christ's payment on the cross. We are the sinners, the depraved, the wretched, and the helpless. He is the loving Father, the seeking, searching, patient Savior who has paid for our sins on the cross and has extended to us His grace and sonship. We add nothing to our salvation.

It is God who seeks us out, convicts us of sin, and reveals Himself to us. It is God who gives us the very faith with which to accept Him. Our faith is simply our response to what He has done for us. Let's look further at what God has done for us.

As far as the east is from the west, So far has He removed our transgressions from us.

−Psalm 103:12

For I am convinced that neither death, nor life, nor angels, nor principalities, nor things present, nor things to come, nor powers, nor height, nor depth, nor any other created thing, shall be able to separate us from the love of God, which is in Christ Jesus our Lord.

−Romans 8:38-39

 Psalm 103:12 tells us that God has placed our transgression "as far as the east is from the west." Romans 8:38-39 tells us that nothing separates us from God's love. Both of these verses are at left.

In the blanks below write how it makes you feel to realize what these verses tell you about what God has done for you.

_____

_____

_____

_____

Do We Need Other People?

So then, our worth lies in the fact that Christ's blood has paid for our sins; therefore, we are reconciled to God. We are accepted on that basis alone, but does this great truth indicate that we don't need other people in our lives? On the contrary, God very often uses other believers to demonstrate His love and acceptance to us. The strength, comfort, encouragement, and love of Christians toward one another represent a visible expression of God's love. In the margin box list some persons whose friendship to you demonstrates God's love. We need people like them in our lives!

Name some persons whose friendship to you demonstrates God's love.

_____

_____

_____

However, our acceptance and worth do not depend on others' acceptance of us, even if those persons are fellow believers! Sometimes we seem to take it especially hard if fellow Christians do not give us the acceptance and approval we feel we need.

Although it's easy to be disappointed when this happens, it truly doesn't matter whether others—Christians or not—accept us. We still are deeply loved, completely forgiven, fully pleasing, totally accepted, and absolutely complete in Christ. He alone is the final authority on our worth and acceptance.

The Biblical Theme of Reconciliation

Truly, truly, I say to you, he who heard My word, and believes Him who sent Me, has eternal life, and does not come into judgment, but has passed out of death into life.

−John 5:24

My sheep hear my voice, and I know them, and they follow Me; and I give eternal life to them, and they shall never perish; and no one shall snatch them out of My hand.

−John 10:27-28

 Continue your study on the theme of reconciliation by looking at the Scriptures at left and by answering these questions.

John 5:24. What is the promise to the person who knows and believes?

_____

_____

John 10:27-28. What do His sheep have? Will they perish? _____

_____

Of Him all the prophets bear witness that through His name everyone who believes in Him receives forgiveness of sins.
–Acts 10:43

Acts 10:43. Of what did the prophets bear witness? _____

_____

➥ You likely are continuing to work on memorizing the affirmation "My Identity in Christ." By the end of unit 3 you likely will have memorized the first seven lines. This week you need to add the next three lines. By the end of this week's study, you likely will have memorized the first 10 lines. Look on page 224 if you need help with the lines.

SUMMARY STATEMENTS

- If we base our self-worth on others' approval, we actually are saying that our ability to please others is worth more than is Christ's payment on the cross.
- We may feel some pain as we withdraw from the world's view of self-worth. Yet we will discover true maturity in Christ when we learn that our self-worth is based on more than others' approval.
- Even if other Christians don't accept us, we still are deeply loved, completely forgiven, fully pleasing, totally accepted, and complete in Christ. He alone is the final authority on our worth and acceptance.

DAY 3

And although you were formerly alienated and hostile in mind, engaged in evil deeds, yet He has now reconciled you in His fleshly body through death, in order to present you before Him holy and blameless and beyond reproach.
–Colossians 1:21-22

Nothing Makes Us Unacceptable

When God chose to redeem us, He did not make us partially righteous, nor has He allowed our poor performance to mar that righteousness. Christ's death on the cross is enough to pay for all sin. Because of this we are holy and righteous before God, even in the midst of sin.

This does not make sin less damaging to our lives. Instead, it makes even greater the indescribable sacrifice of Christ.

Read once again what the Bible says about this in Colossians. The Scripture is in the margin.

Read those last words again. At this very moment God sees us as holy and blameless and beyond reproach (which means beyond disapproval). This does not merely refer to our future standing; it describes our present status as well. It tells us something very significant: We are totally accepted by God.

 List below the ways the verse at left says that Jesus presents you to the Heavenly Father.

1. _____

2. _____

3. _____

> Blessed be the God and Father of our Lord Jesus Christ, who according to His great mercy has caused us to be born again to a living hope through the resurrection of Jesus Christ from the dead, to obtain an inheritance which is imperishable and undefiled and will not fade away, reserved in heaven for you.
>
> –1 Peter 1:3-4

Don't waste critical years!

No Sin Too Filthy!

Is there any sin so filthy that it can prevent a Christian from going to heaven? Absolutely not! A believer is eternally secure; heaven is a certainty for this person. (Read this promise to us at left.) But salvation is more than just a ticket to heaven when we die. It is the basis of a relationship. God received us into a loving, intimate, personal relationship the moment we placed our faith in Christ. We are united with God in an eternal and inseparable bond (Romans 8:38-39).

Edith was an unmarried woman who gave birth to a child. Although she was a Christian before this event occurred, Edith later stopped attending church because she no longer felt close to God. Although she believed God forgives some sins, she felt that her action was on God's unpardonable list. She spent much of her adult life feeling unworthy of God's love.

Only in her senior-adult years did she become convinced of God's unconditional acceptance of her. She later learned that even the sin of sexual intercourse outside marriage was not too filthy in God's eyes to be forgiven. She later regretted wasting so many critical years of her life that she could have used in God's service.

➡ **Do you have any sin in your past or present for which you cannot forgive yourself of which you are not certain God has forgiven you? Do you have a sin that you feel is too filthy to forgive? Name that sin.**

> Is any sin so filthy that it can prevent a Christian from going to heaven? Absolutely not!

✎ **Mark the following statements as *T* (true) or *F* (false).**

_____ I am deeply loved by God.
_____ I am completely forgiven by God.
_____ I am fully pleasing to God.
_____ I am totally accepted by God.
_____ I am absolutely complete in Jesus Christ.

Can a Christian can do anything to become more acceptable to God? No! If such a thing were possible, then the cross would not be enough. If we can do anything to be more acceptable to God, then Christ either lied or was mistaken when He cried out on the cross, " 'It is finished!' " (John 19:30).

If that is the case, what He should have said was, "It is almost finished, and if you live a perfect life, you and I together might make you acceptable."

The Biblical Theme of Reconciliation

> and through Him everyone who believes is freed from all things, from which you could not be freed through the Law of Moses.
>
> –Acts 13:39

✎ **Based on what you have learned about reconciliation, read the verse at left and those on the next page and complete the following exercise.**

Acts 13:39. What does belief do? _____

for all have sinned and fall short of the glory of God, being justified as a gift by His grace through the redemption which is in Christ Jesus.

–Romans 3:23-24

Blessed are those whose lawless deeds have been forgiven, and whose sins have been covered.

–Romans 4:7

For if while we were enemies, we were reconciled to God through the death of His Son, much more, having been reconciled, we shall be saved by His life.

–Romans 5:10

For you have not received a spirit of slavery leading to fear again, but you have received a spirit of adoption as sons by which we cry out, "Abba! Father!"

–Romans 8:15-17

Romans 3:23-24. By what are we justified? _____

_____

Romans 4:7. Who is blessed? _____

_____

Romans 5:10. Through what are we reconciled? _____

_____

Romans 8:15-17. Describe the nature of our relationship with God.

_____

 It's time to review again your memory work on the second of God's truths. Review the first two truths (the one you memorized in unit 3 and the one you memorized earlier this week) until you can repeat them from memory. By the end of this week you likely will have memorized both of these truths. (Turn to the inside back cover if you need to review the list of God's truths.)

SUMMARY STATEMENTS

- Salvation is more than just a ticket to heaven when we die. It is the basis of a relationship. God received us into a loving, intimate, personal relationship the moment we placed our faith in Christ.
- Christ's death on the cross is enough to pay for all sin. Because of this we are holy and righteous before God, even in the midst of sin.
- God has reconciled us in His fleshly body through death in order to present us before Him holy and blameless and beyond reproach. This status refers not only to the future but also to the present.
- We have all sinned. We have all been forgiven unconditionally.

DAY 4

mercy–n. the outward sign of pity; God's attitude toward people in distress; compassion for the ills of others (Vine's)

A New Way to React to Hurt

Since our relationship with God was bought entirely by the blood of Christ, it is the height of pride to think that our own good works can make us acceptable to God.

But the Bible says something totally different: "He saved us, not on the basis of deeds which we have done in righteousness, but according to His **mercy**" (Titus 3:5). (Look in the left margin for a definition of mercy.)

Christ has reconciled us to God, and He allows us to experience the incredible truth, *We are totally accepted by and acceptable to God.*

> Based on the Bible's teachings about our acceptability, what, then, should we do when someone disapproves of us or when we experience rejection? Here's a practical way to summarize this biblical truth:
>
> "It would be nice if _____ (my boss liked me, I had made the team, he had asked me instead of my best friend for a date, that person hadn't snubbed me, and so forth), but *I'm still deeply loved, completely forgiven, fully pleasing, totally accepted, and absolutely complete in Christ.*"

This statement doesn't mean that we won't feel pain or anger when things don't go our way. We probably never will stop smarting when someone ignores us, makes fun of us, declines to hire us, manipulates us, or criticizes us. We need to be honest about our feelings. Covering them up doesn't help.

Learning a new response

However, a statement like the one above simply is a way to gain quickly God's perspective on whatever we are experiencing. It is not magic, but it enables us to reflect on the implications of biblical truth. It enables us to look at the situation the way God would. We can apply this truth in every difficult situation, whether that situation involves someone's disapproval, our own failure to accomplish something, or the failure of another person.

➡ **Memorize the truth that appears in italics in the above statement in the box. Begin to apply it in your situations and relationships.**

Now practice it!

✎ **Think of a situation in your recent past when you felt that someone whose acceptance and approval was important to you rejected you. This person might be a spouse, a family member, a close friend, your boss, or a church-staff member. Answer the questions below as they relate to this specific event.**

Briefly describe the situation. _____

_____

_____

How did that person's rejection make you feel?_____

_____

_____

What emotions do you remember experiencing when the rejection occurred? (Example: anger, shame, guilt, insecurity)

_____

_____

Now, place that person's name in the blank below and reject the false belief that you must have his or her acceptance to feel good about yourself; then replace the false belief with the truths of God's Word.

I do not have to have _____'s acceptance or approval to feel good about my self because I am deeply loved, completely forgiven, fully pleasing, totally accepted, and complete in Jesus Christ.

Your example might have looked something like this:

Situation: Frank laughed at my idea in the committee meeting. (Others laughed too.)

Feelings: I felt deeply hurt and didn't say another word. I left as soon as the meeting was over.

Emotions: Hurt, anger, rejection, and fear.

New response: I do not have to have Frank's (or the other committee members') acceptance to feel good about myself, because I am deeply loved, completely forgiven, fully pleasing, totally accepted, and absolutely complete in Jesus Christ.

Make it a habit in your life

You can use this same format with any situation in your life when you have experienced rejection and that rejection has caused you pain or hurt. After you have used it several times, it will start to become a habit. Satan's lie says that we must have the acceptance and approval of others to feel good about ourselves; but God's Word says we still are loved by Him, completely forgiven, fully pleasing, totally accepted, and absolutely complete in Christ.

On which of these two statements will you base your self worth?

The Biblical Theme of Reconciliation

✎ **Continue your study on the theme of reconciliation by reading the following Scriptures (they appear at left) and answering these questions:**

Who will bring a charge against God's elect? God is the one who justifies.
–Romans 8:33

Romans 8:33. Who will accuse us? _____

_____

For I am convinced that neither death, nor life, nor angels, nor principalities, nor things present, nor things to come, nor powers, nor height, nor depth, nor any other created thing, shall be able to separate us from the love of God, which is in Christ Jesus our Lord.
–Romans 8:38-39

Romans 8:38-39. Of what was Paul convinced? _____

_____

Therefore if any man is in Christ, he is a new creature; the old things passed away; behold, new things have come.
–2 Corinthians 5:17

2 Corinthians 5:17. Describe what we are in Christ. _____

_____

_____

It's time to review again your memory work on the affirmation "My Identity in Christ." Review the first 10 lines (the first seven from unit 3 and the next three lines from this week) until you can repeat them from memory. By the end of this week you likely will have memorized the first 10 lines.

SUMMARY STATEMENTS

- We probably never will stop smarting when someone ignores us, makes fun of us, declines to hire us, manipulates us, or criticizes us, but we need to gain God's perspective quickly on what we experience.
- Satan's lie says that we must have the acceptance and approval of others to feel good about ourselves; but God's Word says we still are loved by Him, completely forgiven, fully pleasing, totally accepted, and absolutely complete in Christ.

The Role of Relationships

DAY 5

It's tough to understand that God is loving, compassionate, protective, and gracious when our parents weren't that way.

For many of us the unconditional love, forgiveness, and acceptance of Christ is hard for us to understand. We may understand how these character traits work, but it's hard for them to make them part of our experience. Often, we can trace this difficulty to our parental relationships.

Parents and Models

God intends for parents to model His character to their children. Scripture says parents are to give their children affection, compassion, protection, provision, and loving discipline. When parents provide this kind of environment in their home, children usually can understand that God has these characteristics. They can understand that He is loving, compassionate, protective, gracious, and loving in His discipline.

Many of us, however, have not received this parental model of God's character. Although some of us had relatively healthy relationships with our parents, others have experienced various forms of neglect, condemnation, and manipulation. Still others have suffered the deeper wounds of sexual abuse, physical abuse, or abandonment. The greater the degree of dysfunction (or poor modeling) in a family, the greater the potential for emotional, spiritual, and relational wounds.

Put another way, the poorer the parental model we have of God's love, forgiveness, and power, the harder time we have experiencing and applying these characteristics in our lives.

Why we don't feel lovable

If we have been deeply wounded, we may recoil from the truth of God's love instead of being refreshed by it. We may believe that we are unlovable.

We may fear reaching out and being hurt again. We withdraw from the very idea of being loved and accepted.

✎ **Think about your understanding of who God is, based on your parents' role modeling. Check the box beside the descriptions that apply.**

❑ Your father was aloof and distant; therefore, you think of God as someone far away and unreachable.

❑ Your mother never was around when you needed her; therefore, it's hard for you to think about God as someone who will be there for you.

❑ Your mother never let you forget it when you did something wrong; therefore, it's hard for you to think about God as kind and forgiving.

❑ Your father was undependable; therefore, you think of God as someone on whom you can't rely.

❑ Your father believed in you and thought you could accomplish anything; therefore, you think of God as someone who has great plans in store for you.

❑ Your mother was warm and kind; therefore, it's easy for you to think of God as having these same characteristics.

❑ Other: _____

New Models

Persons who have received poor parental modeling need new models—loving Christian friends—to help them experience the love and grace of God. Through His body of believers God often provides us with models of His love, so that our perception of His character slowly can be reshaped into one that is more accurate. This results in a healthier relationship with Him. Then our deep emotional, spiritual, and relational wounds can begin to heal, and we more fully can experience God's unconditional love.

Some of us already are involved in strong relationships with people who are understanding and patient with us; some of us haven't yet been able to cultivate relationships like these. We're still looking for these kinds of situations. If the latter is your circumstance, you may need to find a pastor or counselor to help you get started. This person may direct you to one or more believers who can minister to you. A small fellowship group or Bible study is an excellent resource for intimate sharing, comfort, and encouragement. If you have tried to cultivate healthy relationships but haven't found any yet, don't give up! The Lord wants all of us to be in an environment in which we can experience more of His love through relationships with other believers.

The Lord wants all of us to be in an environment in which we can experience more of His love through relationships with other believers.

If you ask God for guidance and if you are willing to continue putting forth the effort, He will lead you in His perfect time to some persons who can provide this kind of an environment for you.

A little help from a friend

✎ **If you need good role models who can model God's love, acceptance, and approval for you, stop right now and ask for God's guidance. Make a list of persons who might help you. Take this list to your pastor, or a group leader, and ask for his guidance. Your discovery group can become a place to find God's love and acceptance. Make your list now and begin to cultivate these relationships.**

_____   _____

_____   _____

Healthy vs. Unhealthy Relationships

 As you read the following paragraphs, underline characteristics of healthy relationships. Circle characteristics of unhealthy relationships.

Because many of us are so vulnerable when we begin allowing ourselves to experience the pain that usually accompanies growth, it is wise to have a basic understanding of healthy and unhealthy relationships.

We first must understand that while God often shows His love and affirmation for us through believers and non believers alike, He wants our relationships with others to help us know Him more fully. His work through others, in part, is to serve as a channel by which we can better understand His divine love and acceptance of us. Sadly, we all are likely to miss His message and to mistake His messenger(s) as the source of our fulfillment. When this misperception is carried to an extreme, we can fall into emotional dependency. We become emotionally dependent when we believe that someone else's presence and/or nurturing is necessary for our personal well-being.

Healthy relationships are turned outward rather than inward. Healthy relationships encourage individuality rather than conformity and are concerned with independence rather than emotional dependence. Healthy relationships point one's focus toward the Lord and to pleasing Him rather than toward the friendship and pleasing one another.

Based on what you just read, fill in this chart. I've completed the first line for you.

Characteristics of a healthy relationship:	Characteristics of an unhealthy relationship:
1. *Turned outward*	1. *Turned inward*
2. _____	2. _____
3. _____	3. _____
4. _____	4. _____

A Checklist for Relationships

Have we crossed the line?

How do we know when we've crossed the line from a healthy relationship to one that is emotionally dependent? When either party in a relationship—

- experiences frequent jealousy, possessiveness, and a desire for exclusivism, viewing other persons as a threat to the relationship;
- prefers to spend time alone with this friend and becomes frustrated when this does not happen;
- becomes irrationally angry or depressed when this friend withdraws slightly;
- loses interest in a friendship other than this one;

- has romantic or sexual feelings leading to fantasy about this person;
- becomes preoccupied by the person's appearance, personality, problems, and interests;
- is unwilling to make plans that do not include the other person;
- is unable to see the other's faults realistically;
- becomes defensive about this relationship when someone asks about it;
- displays physical affection beyond what is appropriate for a friendship;
- refers frequently to the other in conversation; feels free to "speak for" the other.

Our relationships matter to God

Our relationships with one another are so important to God that He has placed unity among the brethren as a priority in our relationship with Him (see Matthew 5:23-24 in the left margin). This is because God has reconciled us to Himself as a body in Christ (Ephesians 2:16). He therefore intends for us to interact as members of one another (Ephesians 4:25).

➡ **Pray that God will guide you to relationships that will encourage you to be honest, practice the truth of His Word, affirm you and thereby help you develop an appropriate love for yourself, and make you want to focus on Him as the gracious provider of your needs.**

In the margin write the names of three persons who you help you be honest about yourself. Eventually, your gratitude to God will motivate you to practice pleasing Him rather than pleasing other people.

✎ **Review this week's lessons. Pray and ask God to identify one positive statement that had an impact on your understanding of who you are.**

Write that statement in your own words.

_____

_____

_____

Rewrite your thoughts as a prayer of thankfulness to God.

_____

_____

You probably gained many insights as you worked through this week's lessons. Which insight stands out to you? Write it here.

_____

_____

_____

> **Name three persons who help you be honest about yourself.**
>
> _____
>
> _____
>
> _____

THE BLAME GAME

NO RIGHT TO FEEL GOOD

When he was a teenager, Matt and several friends from school stepped inside a downtown department store and tried to slip out without paying for some cassette tapes. A security guard caught them and escorted all of them to the manager's office. Matt never heard the end of the incident. Every time he made a mistake at home, his father reminded him of what he had done. "You're a liar and a thief, and you'll never amount to anything!" his father told him. Matt never forgot his humiliation. As a young adult, Matt believed he had no right to feel good about himself. "After all, no one as worthless as I am has a right to feel happy," Matt said. (Read more about Matt's situation on page 105.) What does Matt need in his life?

What you'll learn this week

This week you'll–

- learn about the destructive nature of condemnation, whether it is pointed at another or at ourselves;
- learn how to change our response to others from condemnation to Christlike compassion;
- take a test to determine the influence of the false belief—*Those who fail are unworthy of love and deserve to be punished*;
- learn four problems caused by the fear of punishment and how these problems have a strong impact on our lives as we deal with others;
- learn how blame works in our lives and in our treatment of others.

What you'll study each day

The Compulsion to Condemn	Responding to Those Who Fail	Blame's Paralyzing Fear	What Happens to Us	How Blame Works
DAY 1	DAY 2	DAY 3	DAY 4	DAY 5

Memory verse

A key verse to memorize this week

Beloved, if God so loved us, we also ought to love one another.

–1 John 4:11

WordWatch

A word to help you understand this week's lessons

retribution–n.the dispensing of punishment (*Example: Society has conditioned us to use **retribution**.*)

The Compulsion to Condemn

Our perception of success and failure often is the main way we evaluate ourselves and others. If we believe that performance reflects one's value and if we believe that failure makes one unacceptable and unworthy of love, then we usually feel completely justified in condemning those who fail, including ourselves.

Any form of condemnation is a powerfully destructive force.

Self-condemnation may include name-calling (*I'm so stupid! I can't do anything right!*), making jokes or statements at our own expense, or simply never allowing any room for error in our performance. With others we may be harsh (physically or verbally abusive) or relatively subtle (sarcastic or silent). But any form of condemnation is a powerfully destructive force that communicates, *I'll make you sorry for what you did.*

 List below the third false belief and the emotions that arise within us when we hold that belief.

Those who fail _____

_____

No Right to Feel Good

Matt made a serious mistake early in his life and never was able to overcome it. At age 14 he and several friends from school stepped inside a downtown department store and tried to slip out with some cassette tapes without paying for them. They made it to the glass doors past the cashier's stand before a security guard caught them and escorted all of them to the manager's office.

Matt's unforgettable mistake

Matt never heard the end of the incident. Every time he made a mistake at home, his father reminded him of what he had done. "You're a colossal failure!" his father screamed. "You've got no values whatsoever! You're a liar and a thief, and you'll never amount to anything!"

Matt never was able to forget his humiliation. At age 20, he sat in my office and very seriously told me that on some days he discovered that he actually was happy until he realized that he was feeling good. Believing he had no right to feel good about himself, he then began to feel depressed again. "After all," he reflected, "no one as worthless as I am has a right to feel happy."

 Describe a time you have sustained some type of humiliation that made you feel unworthy of love.

_____

_____

_____

Brainwashed and broken

Many times we have been like Matt—brainwashed and broken by the false belief, *Those who fail are unworthy of love and deserve to be punished.*

The Search for a Culprit

Pointing an accusing finger

Whether consciously or unconsciously, we all tend to point an accusing finger, assigning blame for virtually every failure. Whenever we fail to receive approval for our performance, we likely search for a reason, a culprit, a scapegoat. More often than not, we can find no one but ourselves to blame, so the accusing finger points right back at us. Self-condemnation is a severe form of punishment.

retribution–n. the dispensing of punishment (Webster's)

If possible, we often will try to blame others (and fulfill the law of **retribution**-that people should get what they deserve.). For most of our lives, we have been conditioned to make someone pay for failures or shortcomings. When someone misses a deadline at work, we let everyone know it's not our fault. "I know the report was due yesterday, but Frank didn't get me the statistics until this morning," we say. If someone leaves a household chore undone, we quickly look to our other family members to determine who is responsible. For every flaw we see around us, we usually search for someone to blame. We hope to clear ourselves from blame by making sure that others properly identify and punish the one who failed.

✎ **Think about a time when something went wrong in your world and you were determined to make sure someone other than you got blamed. Write about it here.**

_____

_____

Another reason we blame others is that our success often depends on their contribution. Their failure is a threat to us. When another's failure blocks our goal of success, we usually respond by defending ourselves and blaming them. We often use condemnation to manipulate them to improve their performance. Blaming others also helps put a safe distance between their failure and our fragile self-worth.

✎ **Check the reasons you may have used to assign blame for past failures.**

❑ I condemn myself for past failures to punish myself so I won't do it again.
❑ I blame others for past failures to relieve my conscience.
❑ I defend myself for past failures by blaming these failure on others' shortcomings.
❑ Blaming others makes me feel better about myself.

Determined to blame ourselves

Whether we focus our accusations on ourselves or on others, we all tend to believe that someone must take the blame. When Ellen discovered that her 15-year-old daughter was pregnant, Ellen didn't sleep for a week. She tossed and turned, trying to determine who was at fault. Was her daughter to blame for bringing this embarrassment on the family, or had Ellen failed as a mother? All Ellen knew was that someone had to take responsibility for the crisis.

Blame makes us feel better

Rather than being objective and looking for a solid, biblical solution to our problems, we often either accuse someone else or berate ourselves. Sometimes we blame others to make ourselves feel better. By blaming someone else who failed, we feel superior. In fact, the higher the position of the one who failed (parent, boss, and so on), the farther they fall and often, the better we feel. This desire to be "one up" on someone is at the root of gossip.

In other situations, however, just the opposite is true. When a parent fails, a child usually accepts the blame for that failure. Even as adults, we readily may take the blame in our relationships with those in authority. We feel it's important for us to support those we depend on. Many of us don't like to think of our parents, pastors, or supervisors as weak, so we take great steps to cover for them, even if that means accepting blame for them when they're clearly at fault.

We don't like to think of our parents, pastors, or supervisors as weak, so we take great steps to cover for them.

This is one reason why denial is so strong in abusive families. For example, one woman said, "I never told anybody that Daddy was molesting me when I was a child because I thought that somebody would take him away from our family."

 Stop and pray, asking God to help you have an open mind during this week's study about blame. Ask Him to help you understand why you often are determined to blame yourself or others.

SUMMARY STATEMENTS

- If we believe that performance reflects one's value and that failure makes one unacceptable and unworthy of love, then we usually feel completely justified in condemning those who fail, including ourselves.
- For most of our lives, we have been conditioned to make someone pay for failures or shortcomings.
- Many of us don't like to think of our parents, pastors, or supervisors as weak, so we take great steps to cover for them, even if that means accepting blame for them.

DAY 2

Beloved, if God so loved us, we also ought to love one another.
–1 John 4:11

Responding to Those Who Fail

How should we respond when someone else fails? If the person who failed is a Christian, we need to affirm God's truth about him or her: He (or she) is deeply loved, completely forgiven, fully pleasing, and totally accepted by God and absolutely complete in Christ.

This perspective eventually can change our condemning attitude to one of love and a desire to help. By believing these truths, we gradually will be able to love this person just as God loves us (read at left what the Bible says about this), to forgive him or her just as God has forgiven us (Ephesians 4:32), and to accept him or her just as God has accepted us (Romans 15:7).

This does not mean that we will become blind to others' faults or failures. We will continue to see these faults, but over time we will change our response to them considerably. We will change our response from condemnation to compassion. As we depend less on other people for our self-worth, their sins and mistakes will become less of a threat to us, and we will desire to help them instead of feeling that we must punish them.

✎ **Match the false belief with the truth of God's Word that we can use.**

___ I must be meet certain standards to feel good about myself.

A. I am complete in Jesus Christ.

___ I must have the approval of certain others to feel good about myself.

B. I am fully pleasing to God.

___ Those who fail are unworthy of love and deserved to be punished.

C. I am totally accepted by God.

___ I am what I am. I cannot change.

D. I am deeply loved by God.

And He said to him, "You shall love the Lord your God with all your heart, and with all your soul, and with all your mind" This is the great and foremost commandment. The second is like it, "You shall love your neighbor as yourself."

-Matthew 22:37-39

But I say to you who hear, love your enemies, do good to those who hate you, bless those who curse you, pray for those who mistreat you.

–Luke 6:27-28

"Love Your Neighbor" Means Unbelievers, Too

But how should we respond to unbelievers? Although unbelievers haven't yet trusted in the cross of Christ so that their condemnation is removed before God, Jesus was clear about how we are to treat them. In Matthew 22:37-39 Jesus told His disciples about how they to love their neighbors, both believers and unbelievers. (See first verse at left.) Later in the Bible He was even more specific about this. Read the second verse at left to see what He said in Luke.

Christ didn't come to love and die only for the lovely, righteous people of the world. If He had, we all would be in trouble! He came to love and die for all the unrighteous, the inconsiderate, and the selfish. As we understand more and more about His love for us and as we continue to understand that He rescued us from the righteous condemnation we deserve because of our sins, we gradually will become more patient and kind to others when they fail. We can remember that no one can do anything to me that can compare with my sin of rebellion that Christ has forgiven completely.

✎ **Check below the reasons you deserve to feel good about yourself.**

❏ I am a child of God.
❏ God accepts me.
❏ God loves me.
❏ God has made me complete in Jesus Christ.

God's precious son or daughter

You deserve to feel good about yourself because you are God's precious son or daughter. He accepts you, loves you, and has made you complete. Because of this no one should feel better about himself than you do! You may think that anyone who failed as badly as you have at something important has no right to feel good about himself. When you think about it, no one really deserves to feel good about himself. We all deserve God's condemnation, but you can feel great about yourself because Christ loves, forgives, and accepts you.

✎ **Describe an incident in which you feared being blamed or punished. As you describe this incident, include the reasons you were afraid.**

When I feared blame . . .

_____

_____

Perhaps you feared being blamed or punished because you didn't measure up to someone's standards. Maybe someone threatened to punish you (either emotionally or physically) if you didn't please him or her. You have this fear because the world operates under the false belief that failure must be punished. Therefore, if you've failed, you probably will conclude that you'll be punished in some way.

Two Major Errors in Punishing Others

1. Blaming people for mistakes

We tend to make two major errors when we punish others for their failures. The first is that we condemn people not only for genuine sin but also for their mistakes. When people who have tried their best fail, they do not need our biting blame. They need our love and encouragement. Again, we often tend to blame others because their actions (whether they reflect overt disobedience or honest mistakes) make us look like failures and our own failure is unacceptable to us. Write in the box at left about times you've done this.

> List below four statements you have used to condemn others for their past failures.
>
> _____
>
> _____
>
> _____
>
> _____

Husband-wife, parent-child, and employer-employee relationships are especially vulnerable to one's being threatened by the failure of another. A wife gets angry with her husband for his not-so-funny joke at an important dinner party; a parent criticizes a child for accidentally spilling milk; a manager scowls at an employee because an error in the employee's calculations has made the manager look foolish to his supervisor. People generally experience difficulty in dealing with their *sins;* let's not compound their problems by condemning them for their *mistakes.*

➡ **Stop and pray for others you have condemned for their mistakes. Ask God to forgive you for times you have been heartless when someone has made an error. Ask those you have hurt to forgive you, too.**

2. Blaming to right a wrong

A second major error we often make by condemning others is believing that we are godly agents of condemnation. Unable to tolerate injustice, we seem to possess a great need to balance the scales of right and wrong.

We are correct in recognizing that sin is worthy of criticism and deserves condemnation; yet God has not licensed us to punish others for their sins. Judgment is God's responsibility, not ours.

Jesus dealt specifically with this issue when several men decided to stone a woman caught in adultery. He told them that the person without sin should throw the first stone. Beginning with the older ones, all of the accusers walked away as they remembered their own sins. (Read about this in John 8:3-9.) In light of their own sinfulness, they no longer saw fit to condemn the sins of another. As this incident clearly illustrates, we can leave righteous condemnation and punishment in the hands of the One worthy of the responsibility. Our response can be love; affirmation; and possibly, compassionate correction.

✎ **You may find you have made one or both of these errors made in punishing others for their mistakes. Below describe a time you have done this, and explain why.**

_____

_____

When Someone Hurts Our Feelings

Is it best to explode or stifle our emotions when we're angry or insulted?

When others offend or insult us, should we tell them that they have made us angry or hurt our feelings? This question can be difficult to answer. Some psychologists tell us that we should vent all of our emotions because stifling our emotions, or repression, is unhealthy. Others tell us that our emotions always will be positive and controlled if we truly walk with the Lord.

We should avoid both of these extremes. Venting our anger uncontrollably is not a healthy solution, but neither is continued repression and denial.

We need a safe environment to express our emotions. A good friend or counselor can help us get in touch with our true feelings, which we may have kept buried for years. We also can learn to express ourselves fully to the Lord and tell Him our true feelings, fears, hopes, and dreams. (If you want to read some Bible verses about this, the Psalms are filled with honest expressions of anger, pain, confusion, hope, and faith.)

To deal with our emotions:
1. Find a friend
2. Tell it to the Lord
3. Read some Scriptures
4. Learn how to communicate

In this safe environment we slowly can learn how to communicate appropriately with those who hurt us. This requires wisdom, because each situation and each person may require a different form of communication.

➡ **Stop now and pray, asking God to help you turn to the person you selected in unit 2 to encourage and affirm you in this course. Ask God to help you have the courage to tell this individual your true feelings, even if you have kept them buried for years. Thank God for providing an encourager for you in this circumstance. Ask God to help your encourager help you to learn how to communicate with persons who have injured you.**

As we learn to relate appropriately with those who have hurt or injured us in some way, we will begin to develop a healthy sense of assertiveness—an important component in shaping other persons' behavior toward us.

For example, if others are rude but never realize it because we passively accept their behavior so that we won't upset them, at least two things usually happen: We resent them, and they never have to come to terms with their negative impact on others. They then miss an important opportunity to change, and we in effect prolong their hurtful behavior.

Both appropriate and inappropriate ways exist to communicate our sense of anger or resentment to others, but we need to speak up about these feelings—for others' benefit and for ours.

Learning to express our feelings appropriately is a process. Be patient with yourself!

Learning to express our feelings appropriately is a *process*. It takes time to learn how to respond firmly and clearly and to express years of repressed pain. Be patient with yourself!

✎ **Write about a time when you passively accepted someone's rude behavior and did not confront the person because you feared upsetting this person.**

_____

_____

➥ By now you may have at least half of the four false beliefs memorized. Today look at the inside back cover and begin memorizing the third false belief. By the end of this week, you likely will have memorized this belief and the first two beliefs you memorized earlier.

SUMMARY STATEMENTS

- As we depend on others less for our self-worth, their sins and mistakes will become less of a threat to us, and we will desire to help them instead of feeling that we must punish them
- When people who have tried their best fail, they do not need our biting blame. They need our love and encouragement.

**DAY
3**

Blame's Paralyzing Fear

Not a Permanent Blot

We have a choice in our response to failure: We can condemn ourselves or others who fail, or we can learn from times when we mess up. We all fail, but this doesn't mean that we're failures. Failing can be a step toward maturity, not a permanent blot on our self-esteem. Like children learning to walk, we stumble and fall. And, like children, we can pick ourselves up and begin again. We don't have to allow failure to keep us from being used by God.

Blessed be the God and Father of our Lord Jesus Christ, the Father of mercies and God of all comfort.

–2 Corinthians 1:3

During many times of my life, I have felt that God would punish me by causing me to lose all that I had. I thought this would happen either because of something I had done or had failed to do. This wrong perception of God has driven me away from Him on many occasions when I've needed Him most. It also goes completely against what we know about God. Read how Paul in the Scripture at left describes God.

If we have trusted Christ for our salvation, God has forgiven us and wants us to experience His forgiveness daily. Moses was a murderer, but God forgave him and used him to deliver Israel from Egypt. David was an adulterer and a murderer, but God forgave him and made him a great king. Peter denied the Lord; but God forgave him, and Peter became a leader in the church. Paul persecuted other Christians, but God turned his life around and made him a bold witness.

The book of the genealogy of Jesus Christ, the son of David, the son of Abraham. To Abraham was born Isaac; and to Isaac, Jacob; and to Jacob, Judah and his brothers; and to Judah were born Perez and Zerah by Tamar; and to Perez was born Hezron; and to Hezron, Ram; and to Ram was born Amminadab; and to Amminadab, Nahshon; and to Nahshon, Salmon; and to Salmon was born Boaz by Rahab; and to Boaz was born Obed by Ruth; and to Obed, Jesse; and to Jesse was born David the king. And to David was born Solomon who by her who had been the wife of Uriah;

–Matthew 1:1-6

God rejoices when His children learn to accept His forgiveness, pick themselves up, and walk after they have stumbled. But we also must learn to forgive ourselves. God wants us to view our failure as a way we move forward in our relationships with Him. He does not want us to view our failures as threats to our self-esteem.

✎ **Read Matthew 1:1-6 at left. In this passage you find among Jesus' ancestors the name of David, who sinned against God. You also will find the name of Rahab, a prostitute, and of Tamar, a person who was involved in an extremely immoral incident. God used both of them to help bring His Son into the world. As you read the Scripture at left, circle the names of these individuals God used and did not give up on.**

The Scripture below reassures us that Jesus understands about weakness and helps us in our need.

> Therefore, since we have a great high priest who has gone through the heavens, Jesus the Son of God, let us hold firmly to the faith we profess. For we do not have a high priest who is unable to sympathize with our weaknesses, but we have one who has been tempted in every way, just as we are–yet was without sin. Let us then approach the throne of grace with confidence, so that we may receive mercy and find grace to help us in our time of need.
>
> Hebrews 4:14-16, NIV

Some of us tend to look at Jesus and God as having different characteristics in their relationship with us. We sometimes think of Jesus as our friend and of God as a harsh disciplinarian. Yet the author of Hebrews described Jesus as the "radiance of [God's] glory and the exact representation of His nature" (Hebrews 1:3).

Studying passages like these and spending time with compassionate, forgiving Christians have enabled the Holy Spirit over the years to reshape my thinking about God. I continue to feel remorse when I fail. But rather than hide from God and fear His punishment, I try to appreciate Him for what His love has done for me.

Blame's Negative Consequences

Both assuming and assigning blame for failure can have many negative consequences. Many psychologists today believe that blame is the core of most emotional disturbances. They believe the answer is for each of us to stop blaming ourselves and others and to accept ourselves in spite of our imperfections.

We daily can claim His complete forgiveness and acceptance.

How right they are! Christ's death is the complete payment for sin. We daily can claim His complete forgiveness and acceptance.

Many emotional problems stem from the false belief that we must meet certain standards to be acceptable. We feel that the only way to deal with our weaknesses and shortcomings is to punish ourselves and others for them. It's impossible for us to shoulder such a heavy burden.

Our guilt will overpower us. The weight of our failures will break us.

The false belief, *Those who fail (including myself) are unworthy of love and deserve to be punished,* is at the root of our fear of punishment and our tendency to punish others. How deeply does this lie affect you? How does believing it cause you to act? Take the test on the next page to determine how much influence this lie has in your life.

What does this lie do to you?

Fear of Punishment/Punishing Others Test

✎ Read each of the following statements; then, from the top of the test, choose the term that best describes your response. Put in the blank beside each statement the number above that term.

1	2	3	4	5	6	7
Always	Very Often	Often	Sometimes	Seldom	Very Seldom	Never

_____ 1. I fear what God might do to me.

_____ 2. After I fail, I worry about God's response.

_____ 3. When I see someone in a difficult situation, I wonder what he or she did to deserve that situation.

_____ 4. When something goes wrong, I tend to think that God must be punishing me.

_____ 5. I am very hard on myself when I fail.

_____ 6. I find myself wanting to blame people when they fail.

_____ 7. I get angry with God when someone who is immoral or dishonest prospers.

_____ 8. I am determined to make sure others know about it when I see them doing wrong.

_____ 9. I tend to focus on others' faults and failures.

_____ 10. God seems harsh to me.

_____ Total (Add the numbers you have placed in the blanks.)

What your score says about you

Interpreting Your Score
If your score is...

57-70
God apparently has given you a very strong appreciation for His unconditional love and acceptance. You seem to be freed from the fear of punishment that plagues most people. (One exception, however: Some people who score this high either are greatly deceived or have become callous to their emotions as a way to suppress pain.)

47-56
The fear of punishment and the determination to punish others control your responses rarely or only in certain situations. Again, the only exceptions to this are people who are not honest with themselves about how strongly these matters affect them.

37-46
When you experience emotional problems, they may have to do with a fear of punishment or with an inner urge to punish others. Upon reflection you probably can relate many of your previous responses to this fear. The fear of punishment and/or the determination to punish others also will affect many of your future responses unless you take direct action to overcome these tendencies.

27-36
The fear of punishment forms a general backdrop to your life. Probably few days go by that the fear of punishment and the tendency to blame others do not affect you. Unfortunately, this robs you of the joy and peace your salvation is meant to bring.

0-26

Experiences of punishment dominate your memory. You probably have suffered a great deal of depression as a result of them. This condition will not simply disappear; time alone cannot heal your pain. You need to experience deep healing in your self-concept, in your relationship with God, and in your relationships with others.

Making sure someone pays

If you are preoccupied by your weaknesses and failures, you probably often are discouraged because you believe that when something goes wrong, someone is to blame. You blame yourself and others to be sure that someone pays for the failure.

If you perform well, you feel worthy of love, so you reward yourself. If you fail, you feel unworthy of love, so you blame yourself. You probably treat others the same way.

● ●

We usually give ourselves demeaning labels because we fail over and over. These labels are different for each individual. Some of these terms might be:

lazy, ugly, klutz, stupid, dumb, incompetent

What labels do you use?

These may be used in comparison to someone else. For example, you might say, "I'm not as pretty as _____. My grades are lower than _____'s. My ideas are not as bright as _____'s; I'm a stupid fool."

✎ **What are the four most negative terms you use to describe yourself?**

1. _____ 3. _____

2. _____ 4. _____

Condemning yourself does not make you a better person. Using a guilt/blame motivation to make your performance perfect (and thus to feel good about yourself) is not what the Bible says to do. It hurts you.

For a short time blame may motivate you to perform better, but your self-concept will suffer from your condemnation. Ultimately, your self-concept is far more important than is your short-term performance.

SUMMARY STATEMENTS

- God wants us to view our failure as a way we move forward in our relationships with Him rather than viewing our failures as threats to our self-esteem.
- The false belief, *Those who fail (including myself) are unworthy of love and deserve to be punished,* is at the root of our fear of punishment
- Condemning yourself does not make you a better person. Using a guilt/blame motivation is not what the Bible says to do. It hurts you.

What Happens to Us

The logical result of Satan's deception, Self-worth = Performance + Others' Opinions, is fear—the fear of failure, rejection, and punishment. When we base our security and value on how well we perform and how we want others to perceive us, failure poses a tremendous threat to us.

When we are threatened, we often withdraw from the source of our fear and/or become very controlling of ourselves and others. For example, to try to avoid failure, we may stick to a fairly rigid schedule in which we're fairly certain of success, and we may avoid activities we feel less sure about. Also, sometimes others' failure threatens us because we fear that that same failure might happen to us. So we likely will try to control others' behavior as well. If we also believe that those who fail deserve to be punished, we make ourselves or others victims for virtually any wrongdoing.

How we react to the fear of failure:
We avoid new activities.
We try to control others.
We make ourselves victims.
We are blind to our faults.
We don't see we need God.
We believe it's God's fault.
We punish ourselves.
We make excuses for others.

✎ **Think of a time when you reacted to the fear of failure in one of the ways the above paragraph describes. Write here about that time.**

_____

_____

_____

Because we are insecure, some of us are so self-protective that we rarely are able to see ourselves as being in the wrong. We may be quick to pinpoint—and condemn—others' weaknesses, but we may be blind to our faults and weaknesses. This attitude may prompt us to think that others (who we see as "more needy") should turn to God, but it may prevent us from seeking Him because we can't see we need Him. Also sometimes when we fail, we may believe that it's all His fault. Some of us may fall on the other end of the spectrum. We may be so absorbed in our performance and so demanding of ourselves that when failure enters our circumstances, we believe that we are solely responsible. Rather than laying blame on someone else, we inflict punishment on ourselves.

We explain away others' shortcomings to protect those who hurt us. In the box are some of the excuses we make for others in order to protect them.

> - *She didn't mean what she said.*
> - *I'm sure that he loves me; he just has a hard time showing it.*
> - *If you just knew what he is going through, you'd understand why he responded so rudely.*
> - *It's all because she travels so much. When she's home, she's too tired to think about other people.*

If we tend to punish ourselves for failures, we may believe that we must feel remorse for a certain length of time before we can experience peace and joy again. In a twisted form of self-motivation, we may think that if we condemn ourselves enough, then perhaps we won't fail again.

 Describe below a time when you felt you had to punish yourself by feeling remorse because of a failure.

_____

_____

_____

**Some other ways we react:
We judge others' failure.
We try to play God.
We live it up and enjoy sin.**

Still others of us are so hard on ourselves that we pass our self-condemning attitude on to others. Passing judgment on to others may be a response to our great need for consistency and justice. If we are going to punish failure in ourselves, we reason, then we must be consistent and punish failure in others. Insisting on justice, we also may take it upon ourselves to be God's instrument of correction. We normally don't like to see others getting away with something for which they should be punished (or perhaps for something that we wish we could do ourselves).

Finally, some of us decide that because punishment is bound to happen, we may as well "live it up" and enjoy our sin before the judgment comes.

Check below the ways that your fear of failure and punishment affects you.

❏ I feel that I might as well "live it up" because punishment is inevitable.
❏ I explain away others' mistakes because we feel threatened by their failures.
❏ I need to punish others when they fail God. I am God's instrument of correction.
❏ I concentrate on others' weaknesses and rarely see myself as wrong.

What the Fear of Punishment Causes

The fear of punishment and the tendency to punish others can affect our lives in many ways. The following provides a brief description of common problems that often result from this deception.

We think that if we're hard enough on ourselves, God won't have to punish us.

• **Self-induced Punishment**—Many of us operate on the theory that if we are hard enough on ourselves, then God won't have to punish us. We fail to realize that God disciplines us in love and never punishes us in anger. Because God loves us unconditionally and does not punish us, we don't need to punish ourselves.

• **Passivity**—The fear of punishment is at the root of one of the most common problems in our society: passivity. Passivity is the neglect of our minds, time, gifts, or talents through inaction. God intends for us to cooperate with Him actively, but fear can have a paralyzing effect on our will. Passivity results in a dull life as we avoid risks and miss opportunities.

• **Bitterness**—If we believe that God and others always are punishing us, we soon become very angry at ourselves and others. Holding anger in and continually questioning God's motives result in deep bitterness and pessimism.

• **Punishing Others**—Our specific response to others' failure depends on several factors: our personalities, the nature of their failure, and how their failure reflects on us (for example, we may think thoughts like, *Her mistake makes me look like I'm dumb,* or *a bad parent,* or ...*a poor leader,* or ...*a rotten employee*).

 Describe a time in which your fear of punishment or your tendency to punish others has affected your life in one of the ways mentioned above.

_____

_____

_____

We make people "pay for what they did."

Some ways we condemn those who fail are by using verbal or physical abuse, nagging criticism, withholding appreciation and affection, or ignoring them. These responses usually are designed to "make them pay for what they did."

 Think of a close friend or family member with whom you had a conflict. Check below what you said or did to inflict emotional pain on that person because of the conflict.

❑ Withdrew love, affection, and encouragement
❑ Made sarcastic remarks or laughed at the person
❑ Spoke to him or her abruptly
❑ Abused him or her verbally or physically
❑ Gave the person the silent treatment for several days
❑ Got even through a harmful deed to the person

You probably reacted this way because you believe that those who fail are unworthy of love and failure must be punished. You even may have appointed yourself to carry out the sentence of punishment.

Christ did all this for us!

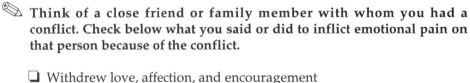

We can overcome the fear of punishment and the desire to punish others by realizing that Christ took on the punishment we deserve.

Christ's motives toward us are loving and kind. His discipline is designed to correct us and to protect us from the destruction of sin, not to punish us.

➥ **It's time to review your memory work on the third false belief. Review the first three beliefs (the two you memorized earlier and the one from this week) until you can repeat them from memory. By the end of this week, you likely will have memorized all three. (Turn to the inside back cover if you need to review the four false beliefs.)**

DAY

5

How Blame Works

The fact that we use blame so much shows how effective it is. We often believe that we deserve to be blamed for any significant shortcoming. We think self-inflicted punishment will clear us of guilt and will enable us to feel good about ourselves again.

Both self-inflicted punishment and the feeling we must punish others result from the false belief, *Those who fail are unworthy of love and deserve to be punished.*

✎ **Write here the first three false beliefs:**

1. I must meet certain _____

_____

2. I must have _____

_____

3. Those who _____

_____

Believing You Must Pay

Paul's stepfather was a corporate executive who was driven to succeed. Nothing Paul did was good enough for him. He often laughed at Paul and called him an idiot and a wimp. Why do we use such terms to describe ourselves and others? (In the left margin list some of these terms.)

We use these because we believe that condemnation motivates us and provides favorable change. However, the only way this really will work is if the target will accept the message that she is unworthy of love.

After he betrayed Christ for 30 pieces of silver, Judas experienced such unbearable guilt that he flung the money across the temple floor and cried, " 'I

Write some put-down terms you have used to punish yourself.
_____
_____
_____

have sinned by betraying innocent blood' " (Matthew 27:4). He then went out and hanged himself! All people, even nonbelievers, believe that they must pay for their sins.

Without even realizing it, you probably have inside you a concept that sounds like this, *When I fail, I am unworthy of love (and when others fail, they are unworthy of love) and deserve to be punished.* We have been conditioned to accept personal blame or condemnation every time our performance is unsatisfactory. After reading this, some people immediately recognize that they automatically respond this way. They say to themselves, *Yes, that describes me perfectly.* Others are blind to it. You may think that this false belief does not affect you at all—but it probably does.

One of our automatic responses is, I'm personally to blame every time my performance is unsatisfactory.

✎ **Think about the two statements below and check the statement that you find to be true in your own life.**

❑ When something fails, I generally have an urge to blame someone else.
❑ When I fail, I look for excuses.

If one or both of these is true about you, then you need to recognize that this false belief has a controlling effect on your life.

Rather than working out our problems and objectively evaluating our performance, most of us tend to defend ourselves. Counterattack triggers counterattack. The more we criticize other people, the more defensive they usually get and the less likely they are to admit their errors (especially to us). Criticism can lead to a counterattack from both sides. Pretty soon it's like a volleyball game, with each person intensifying the pace while returning blame to the other person's side.

An emotional volleyball game

However, it sometimes is even more destructive for people to accept blame automatically without defending themselves. Tom was becoming an emotional zombie under his wife's constant condemnation, but instead of fighting back, he kept thinking, *Yes, Suzanne's right. I am an incompetent fool.* He attacked himself over and over so that he became like the worn-out punching bag of a heavyweight fighter.

Feeling badly about ourselves is a way of trying to pay for our sins by our own deeds or feelings. If we believe that those who fail are unworthy of love and deserve to be blamed and condemned, then we probably will use feelings of guilt as a form of self-condemnation. We think that if we feel badly enough for long enough (the severity and length depending, of course, on how large the sin is), the sin will be forgiven and we can go on with life.

John lied to the IRS. Sam committed adultery. Christy got drunk at a party. Sherman was insensitive to his wife. Rick stole from his employer. Which of these persons should feel badly about himself or herself the longest? That question, of course, is a ridiculous one; but it shows the attitude of some people who feel that a certain type of sin should carry with it a longer period of regret and blame. When they repent of the sin, their repentance represents only a promise to themselves to avoid being embarrassed again.

Please note: No one should feel good about sin. Dishonoring the Lord and harming ourselves and others produce a sorrow that is right and proper. But God intends for this sorrow to be a response to the destructiveness of sin and

For the sorrow that is according to the will of God produces a repentance without regret, leading to salvation; but the sorrow of the world produces death.
–2 Corinthians 7:10

the righteousness of Christ, not an effort to pay for sin through blame. Read the Scripture at left to see how Paul describes godly sorrow. The regret of which he speaks is regret without self-punishing bad feelings. The death of which he speaks is spiritual deadness.

✎ **Write about a time that you feel you truly failed your Heavenly Father and tried to avoid God.**

_____

_____

✎ **Stop and pray, asking God to help you have regret about your sin without having self-punishing bad feelings that harm yourself and others.**

Do you feel that God is waiting to "lower the boom" on you?

If you believe that God is waiting to "lower the boom" on you, then you probably won't want to pray. No one likes to be punished, so if you believe that God's attitude toward you is anger and condemnation, you will try to avoid Him. Most people have the wrong idea about God's character. As a result, they live in fear of what God will do to them because of their sin. But God has demonstrated His love for us on the cross when Christ paid our sins in full. Therefore, God doesn't punish us for our sins. Christ bore that punishment on the cross.

✎ **Review this week's lessons. Pray and ask God to identify one positive statement that had an impact on your understanding of who you are.**

Write that statement in your own words.

_____

_____

_____

Rewrite your thoughts as a prayer of thankfulness to God.

_____

_____

_____

You probably gained many insights as you worked through this week's lessons. Which insight stands out to you? Write it here.

_____

_____

_____

PROPITIATION

ALWAYS ON HER MIND

Mary thought she had forgiven her brother for his cruelty to her when they were children, but during arguments between the two, she kept bringing up past incidents. When Mary and her brother were together, it seemed that she always was stewing about these past misdeeds. Shirley had been cold for two weeks to Greg, who had offended her. She would forgive him, all right—as soon as she was through punishing him. (Read Mary's and Shirley's stories on page 131.) What do Mary and Shirley need in their lives?

What you'll learn this week

This week you'll–

- study the meaning of and the effects of propitiation;
- learn that God's response to our sin and rebellion is not anger but love, which caused Him to send Jesus to die for our sin;
- learn about some problems in our lives that can result from a lack of forgiveness;
- learn to look at others' offenses in a different light when we compare the offenses to our sin that Christ has forgiven completely;
- study how to look at our children the way our Heavenly Father see us, then learn to approach their misdeeds with sadness rather than anger;

What you'll study each day

Christ, Our Substitute	Freedom from Punishment	Forgiving Others	Forgiveness Is Not Erasure	Avoiding Unholy Anger
DAY 1	DAY 2	DAY 3	DAY 4	DAY 5

Memory verse

A key verse to memorize this week

And be kind to one another, tender-hearted, forgiving each other, just as God in Christ has forgiven you.

–Ephesians 4:32

WordWatch

A word to help you understand this week's lessons

propitiation–n. describes what happened when Christ, through His death, became the means by which God's wrath was satisfied and God's mercy was granted to the sinner who believes on Christ. (*Example: **Propitiation** is the greatest demonstration of God's love to people.*)

Christ, Our Substitute

When Christ died on the cross, He was our substitute. He took upon Himself the righteous wrath of God that we deserved. The extreme nature of what God did for us reveals His deep love for us: The holy Son of God became a human being and died a horrible death in our place.

Two Bible passages state this very well. Isaiah, who anticipated that Christ would come to earth, wrote the first one:

He was crushed for our sins

> Surely our griefs He Himself bore, and our sorrows He carried; yet we ourselves esteemed Him stricken, smitten of God, and afflicted. But He was pierced through for our transgressions, He was crushed for our iniquities; the chastening for our well-being fell upon Him, and by His scourging we are healed. All of us like sheep have gone astray, each one of us has turned to his own way; but the Lord has caused the iniquity of us all to fall on Him.
>
> –Isaiah 53:4-6

The second is from the New Testament:

He came so we could live

> By this the love of God was manifested in us, that God has sent His only begotten Son into the world so that we might live through Him. In this is love, not that we loved God, but that He loved us and sent His Son to be the propitiation for our sins. Beloved, if God so loved us, we also ought to love one another.
>
> –1 John 4:9-11

The Greatest Act of Love

propitiation–n. describes what happened when Christ, through His death, became the means by which God's wrath was satisfied and God's mercy was granted to the sinner who believes on Christ (Vine's)

Propitiation (see definition at left) describes this substitution that occurred when Christ died on the cross. *Propitiation* means that the anger of someone who has been wronged unjustly has been satisfied. It is an act that soothes hostility and satisfies the need for getting even.

Providing His only begotten Son as the propitiation for our sin was the greatest possible demonstration of God's love for people. Jesus' death, which was the substitute for our sin, satisfied the anger of God.

 Write below about an act that a friend or someone else has done for you that you feel demonstrates that person's love for you. _____

_____

Most of us have experienced acts of kindness done for us. Even if we've had difficult lives and felt like we've had few friends, most of us usually can look back on some small act of kindness that made us feel loved.

God did this extremely loving act for people who have hurt Him mightily since creation!

What God did for us, however, in sending His Son to die on the cross was an even more loving act than the one you just listed. And to think He did it for people who have hurt Him mightily since the beginning of creation!

Actually, to understand God's wondrous gift of propitiation, we must go back to Adam and Eve and remember what He has put up with since people first existed. Adam and Eve's sin in the garden of Eden was the first hurtful act against Him, but people's wrongdoing continues even now with the terrible sin we see in our world today. God has seen His children involved in greed, hatred, lust, and pride.

For all of us have become like one who is unclean, And all our righteous deeds are like a filthy garment; And all of us wither like a leaf, And our iniquities, like the wind, take us away.

–Isaiah 64:6

All of these actions show how greatly people rebel against the God of love and peace. If we don't act with a desire to glorify Him, even our "good" deeds are like filthy garments to God, as the verse at left shows.

✎ **Check each of the statements below that helps explain the meaning of** *propitiation.*

> ❑ 1. Christ's death was a substitution for my sins.
> ❑ 2. God's anger is satisfied.
> ❑ 3. I must pay for my own sins.
> ❑ 4. Christ paid for my sin penalty.
> ❑ 5. My sin deserves God's anger, but Christ's death does away with that anger.

Propitiation means *satisfaction. Propitiation* refers to Christ's death on the cross, which satisfied, or took care of, the penalty for our sins. Christ's death propitiates, or does away with, God's anger. God's righteous anger is directed against all sin and, therefore, against all sinful people. Christ's death removed God's anger from those who are sorry and turn away from their sins. You should have checked 1, 2, and 4 in the list of statements above.

God is light, and in Him there is no darkness at all.

–1 John 1:5

Our sin deserves God's righteous anger. He is the Almighty, the rightful judge of the universe. He is absolutely holy and perfect. Read the verse at left for another description of God. Because God is like this, He cannot overlook sin, nor can He compromise by accepting sinful behavior. For God to condone even one sin would mar His holiness. It would be like smearing a white wedding gown with black tar.

More loving than we can imagine!

Because God is holy, He used His righteous anger to show how much He dislikes sin. However, God not only is righteously angry about sin, but He also is more loving than we ever can imagine. In His holiness God condemns sin, but in the most awesome example of love the world ever has seen, He decided that His Son would die to pay for our sins. God sacrificed the sinless, perfect Savior to turn away—to propitiate—His great wrath.

✎ **Based on what you've just read, describe here how you believe it is possible for God to be both righteously angry about our sin and yet loving toward us.**

_____

_____

_____

For while we were still helpless, at the right time Christ died for the ungodly. For one will hardly die for a righteous man; though perhaps for the good man someone would dare even to die. But God demonstrates His own love toward us, in that while we were yet sinners, Christ died for us. Much more then, having now been justified by His blood, we shall be saved from the wrath of God through Him. For if while we were enemies, we were reconciled to God through the death of His Son, much more, having been reconciled, we shall be saved by His life. And not only this, but we also exult in God through our Lord Jesus Christ, through whom we have now received the reconciliation.

–Romans 5:6-11

Describe a time when someone did something nice for you although you mistreated that person.

_____

_____

_____

He made Him who knew no sin to be sin on our behalf, that we might become the righteousness of God in Him.

–2 Corinthians 5:21

For I am convinced that neither death, nor life, nor angels, nor principalities, nor things present, nor things to come, nor powers, nor height, nor depth, nor any other created thing, shall be able to separate us from the love of God, which is in Christ Jesus our Lord.

–Romans 8:38-39

For you have not received a spirit of slavery leading to fear again, but you have received a spirit of adoption as sons by which we cry out, "Abba! Father!"

–Romans 8:15

God cannot overlook sin—not even a "little one." Even what we consider to be the slightest wrongdoing to Him is like the filthy garment the verse we read earlier describes. Every wrong we do makes Him sad, but He sent Jesus to pay the price for it all.

 Stop and pray. Thank God that He sent Jesus to pay the price for your sins, even if you might not fully understand yet all that this involves. Pray that God will help you understand more about this during this week's study.

For Whom Did Christ Die?

And for whom did Christ die? Was it for a world that appreciated His sinless life and worshiped Him? No! Christ died for us while we were rebelling against Him. Read more about this in the Scripture at left.

 As you read Romans 5:6-11, circle the characteristics of persons for whom the Scripture says Christ died.

Write in the margin box about a time when someone did something nice for you, even though you had treated that person badly. That's exactly what happened when Christ died for us.

It's one thing to do something nice for someone who does nice things for you; it's another matter to do a good deed for someone who has hurt you.

God knew full well what was happening to Christ, His Son, on earth. Surely He saw Christ's mistreatment––the scourging, the humiliation, the beatings––at the hands of sinful people. Surely God, who created the world, could have delivered Christ from the entire ordeal.

And yet the God of heaven peered down through time and saw you and me. Though we were His enemies, He loved us and longed to rescue us from our sins. He sent the sinless Christ to become our substitute. Only Christ could turn away God's righteous wrath against sin, so in love the Father kept silent as Jesus hung from the cross.

God poured on Christ all of His anger we ever would deserve, and Christ became sin for us (Read about this in 2 Corinthians 5:21 at left).

God no longer looks upon us through the eyes of judgment. Instead, He now lavishes His love upon us. The Scriptures teach that absolutely nothing can separate us from God's love (Romans 8:38-39). He has adopted us into a tender, intimate, and powerful relationship with Him (Romans 8:15).

Read 2 Corinthians 5:21; Romans 8:15, 38-39, all of which appear at left. Tell in your own words what these passages say to you about what God has done for you.

_____

_____

_____

Our Worth—Based on God's Love

We can't imagine such a gift!

Because we are His children, performance no longer is the basis of our worth. We are unconditionally and deeply loved by God. We were spiritually dead, but the Lord has made us alive and has given us the high status of sonship to the Almighty God. It will take all of eternity to understand the wealth of His love and grace. Paul explained this amazing gift this way:

But God, being rich in mercy, because of His great love with which He loved us, even when we were dead in our transgressions, made us alive together with Christ (by grace you have been saved), and raised us up with Him, and seated us with Him in the heavenly places, in Christ Jesus, in order that in the ages to come He might show the surpassing riches of His grace in kindness toward us in Christ Jesus. For by grace you have been saved through faith; and that not of yourselves, it is the gift of God; not as a result of works, that no one should boast (Ephesians 2:4-9).

God loves us infinitely, eternally, and unconditionally.

Propitiation, then, means that through His payment of sin, Christ has satisfied God's anger. He had only one reason to do this. He loves us infinitely, eternally, and unconditionally. God the Father loves us with the love of a father, reaching to snatch us from harm. Christ loves us with the love of a brother, laying down His life for us. He alone has turned away God's wrath from us. We can do no amount of good deeds that can pay for our sins. Instead, Christ conclusively has paid for them so that we can escape eternal condemnation and can experience His love and purposes now and forever.

● ●

A weapon against low self-worth

Christ not only paid for our sins at one point in time, but He also continues to love us and teach us day after day. We have a weapon to use against Satan as he attacks us with doubts about God's love for us. Our weapon is the fact that Christ took our punishment upon Himself at Calvary. We no longer have to fear punishment for our sins because Christ paid for them all—past, present, and future. This tremendous truth of propitiation clearly demonstrates that we are truly and deeply loved by God.

✎ **Write below the third false belief, the emotion that arises within us, and the truth of God's Word to refute that false belief.**

Those who _____

_____

Emotions you might feel: *Fear of* _____

The truth of God's Word to refute this false belief: _____

_____

_____

➥ **How easily did you remember the third truth from God's Word in the above exercise? Look on the inside back cover and begin memorizing this third truth. By the end of this week's study you likely will have memorized this truth as well as the other two truths you memorized in previous weeks.**

➡ Stop and pray, asking God to help you understand what it means to be unconditionally and deeply loved by God.

SUMMARY STATEMENTS

- Providing His only begotten Son as the propitiation for our sin was the greatest possible demonstration of God's love for people.
- Because we are His children, performance no longer is the basis of our worth. We are unconditionally and deeply loved by God.
- The fact that Christ took our punishment upon Himself at Calvary is a weapon to use against Satan as he causes us to doubt our worth.

DAY 2

Freedom from Punishment

Satan's lie states: *Those who fail are unworthy of love and deserve to be punished.* We will be freed more and more from this lie as we understand and apply the truth of propitiation in the context of loving and supportive relationships. In these relationships we can express ourselves honestly and receive both the warmth of affirmation and the challenge of God's Word.

The Accuser

The Scriptures indicate that Satan accuses believers of being unworthy of God's grace. Satan wants us to hide under the fear of punishment. Consider this passage, Revelation 12:10-11:

And I heard a loud voice in heaven, saying, "Now the salvation, and the power, and the authority of His Christ have come, for the accuser of our brethren has been thrown down, who accuses them before our God day and night. And they overcame him because of the blood of the Lamb and because of the word of their testimony, and they did not love their life even to death."

How are we to overcome Satan, the accuser, and to feel accepted in Christ?

We must stop trying to overcome our feelings of failure by acts that we think make up for our wrongdoing.

According to the Scripture above, only one way exists for doing this: by the sacrificial blood of Christ on the cross. To do this, we first can stop trying to overcome our feelings of failure by trying to make up for our wrongdoing by certain acts. We never can do enough on our own to justify our sins.

✎ List below three actions you have undertaken in the past because you thought they would help you overcome your feelings of failure. (You might list something like "I tried to do extra good things.")

1. _____

2. _____

3. _____

At times in my life I thought that I couldn't possibly feel forgiven until I had done certain acts to pay for my sin. These occasions caused me to be depressed, because I hardly could complete my acts to make up for one sin before I had sinned again. Then I would have to feel badly about that for a period of time, only to sin again . . . and again . . . and again. Eventually, I realized that I could do one of three things: I could continue trying to make up for my sin by mourning over it for as long as it seemed necessary (although that wasn't getting me very far); I could try to deny that I had sinned (even though I knew that I had); or I could trust in Christ's forgiveness. Initially, of course, I did not understand these choices as well as I do now.

What we can do about sin:
- **Try to pay for it**
- **Deny it**
- **Accept Christ's forgiveness**

No matter how much we do to make up for our sin, we will continue to feel guilty and will believe that we need to do more unless we resist Satan, our accuser. This can be accomplished only because Christ's blood has completely paid for our sins and has delivered us from eternal condemnation.

Secondly, we can verbalize what Christ's death on the cross has done for us: *We are deeply loved, completely forgiven, fully pleasing, totally accepted, and absolutely complete in Christ.*

➡ **Repeat aloud the segments of the affirmation "My Identity in Christ" that you have memorized thus far. Stop and pray, thanking God that you are special in His eyes, even though you still are in the process of understanding fully this condition of being special to Him.**

✎ **Read 1 John 4:9-10 and mark these statements as *T* (true) or *F* (false).**

> By this the love of God was manifested in us, that God has sent His only begotten Son into the world so that we might live through Him. In this is love, not that we loved God, but that He loved us and sent His Son to be the propitiation for our sins.
>
> –1 John 4:9-10

_____ God's love for me depends on my performance.

_____ My Father deeply loves me.

_____ God demonstrated His love for me when He poured out His wrath on His Son instead of on me.

_____ God's love for me depends on whether I always succeed.

_____ Based on the truth of God's Word, I am deeply loved by God.

✎ **When you reflect on what this verse says about God's love for you, how does it make you feel? Describe that feeling here.**

_____

_____

Consumed with Love

God loves you, and He enjoys revealing His love to you. He enjoys being loved by you, but He knows you can love Him only if you are experiencing His love for you. *Propitiation* means that His wrath has been removed and that you are deeply loved!

✎ **List some ways God has demonstrated His love for you or some experiences in which you have sensed God's love.**

_____

_____

How great it feels to be loved!

 Try to recall an experience in which someone special loved you. That person adored you and wanted to be with you. You didn't have to perform; just being with you was enough. The thought of that person's selecting you to love was intoxicating. All other facets of life seemed to diminish. He or she loved you, and that love was soothing to you and satisfied many of your inner longings.

If a person's love can make us feel this way, consider how much greater joy the Heavenly Father's love can bring! We truly can't experience the Father's love unless we realize that it goes beyond any experience we ever have known of being loved by another man or woman.

Frederick Faber was consumed with love for the Father. A song he wrote reveals his single-minded devotion:

> *Only to sit and think of God,*
> *Oh what a joy it is!*
> *To think the thought, to breathe the Name;*
> *Earth has no higher bliss.*
> *Father of Jesus, love's reward!*
> *What rapture it will be,*
> *Prostrate before Thy throne to be,*
> *And gaze and gaze on Thee.*[1]

One of Faber's sermons says of Christ:

Wherever we turn in the church of God, there is Jesus. He is the beginning, middle, and end of everything to us .... There is nothing good, nothing holy, nothing beautiful, nothing joyous which He is not to His servants. No one need be poor, because, if he chooses, he can have Jesus for his own property and possession. No one need be downcast, for Jesus is the joy of heaven, and it is His joy to enter into sorrowful hearts. We can exaggerate about many things; but we can never exaggerate our obligation to Jesus, or the compassionate abundance of the love of Jesus to us. All our lives long we might talk of Jesus, and yet we should never come to an end of the sweet things that might be said of Him. Eternity will not be long enough to learn all He is, or to praise Him for all He has done, but then, that matters not; for we shall be always with Him, and we desire nothing more.[2]

 Stop and pray, thanking God for His great love for you. Thank Him now for some past occasion in which He has demonstrated His love for you and for which you forgot to thank Him. Say His name over and over until merely doing this act brings you joy, as the poem above says.

Many of us have a distorted concept of the Heavenly Father. We believe that God is thrilled when we accept Christ and are born into His family. But many of us also believe that He is proud of us only as long as we perform well. We believe that the better our performance, the happier He is with us. We may perceive of God as being like the management in a factory. If we produce, the management loves us; if we don't produce, we're fired. We may believe that if we really foul up, God is going to put us on the shelf somewhere. He will take care of our most basic needs because He has obligated Himself to do that, but only the beautiful, producing Christians will enjoy His love and acceptance.

God won't put us on the shelf

Many, O Lord my God, are the wonders which Thou hast done, And Thy thoughts toward us; There is none to compare with Thee; If I would declare and speak of them, They would be too numerous to count.

–Psalm 40:5

In reality, God loves us, and not a moment goes by that He isn't thinking loving thoughts about us. Read the Scripture at left to see just how often this happens. *Propitiation* means that Jesus Christ by His death has satisfied the Father's righteous condemnation of sin. The Scriptures give only one reason to explain this incredible fact: God loves you!

 You now may be finalizing your work on memorizing the affirmation "My Identity in Christ." By the end of unit 6 you likely have memorized the first 10 lines. This week you can add the last five lines. By the end of this week's study, you likely will have the entire affirmation memorized. Look on page 224 if you need help.

SUMMARY STATEMENTS

- We can stop trying to overcome our feelings of failure by trying to make up for our wrongdoing with certain acts. Defending ourselves or trying to pay for our sins by our actions is impossible.
- No matter how much we do to make up for our sin, we will continue to feel guilty and to believe that we need to do more unless we resist Satan, our accuser.

DAY 3

Don't cut God's power flow!

Forgiving Others

Even though God has forgiven us, as we read, we seem to forget about this fact when we decide how we will treat others. We inflict punishment on those around us by refusing to forgive *them*. We add up all the times someone has wronged us and all the things we don't like about someone. Refusing to forgive represents a sure way of cutting the flow of God's power in our lives. It causes several negative outcomes. Before we examine these, let's look at some of the reasons we may refuse to forgive.

Reasons We Don't Forgive

1. The offense was too great.
2. The person won't accept responsibility.
3. The person isn't truly sorry.
4. The person never asked for forgiveness.
5. The person did it too many times.
6. The person did it again.
7. I simply don't like the person.
8. The person did it deliberately.
9. If I forgive, I'll have to treat the offender well.
10. Someone has to punish the person.
11. Something keeps me from forgiving.
12. I'll be a hypocrite if I forgive.
13. I'll forgive, but I won't ever forget.
14. I've found an excuse for the offense, so I'll forgive.

Reasons We Don't Forgive

We often fail to forgive others (and ourselves) because we don't think it's possible to do so. We forget how God graciously has forgiven all of our sins through Christ's death, and we come up with reasons we can't forgive.

 The following represent many of the countless excuses we make for our unwillingness to forgive ourselves and others. Draw a line to match each of the case studies below with one of the reasons in the left margin.

The person never asked for forgiveness

The offense was too great

The person did it again

The person won't accept responsibility

I simply don't like the person

The person did it too many times

The person isn't truly sorry

1. Grant's wife left him for another man, and Grant was bitter toward his wife. Her infidelity was too great a sin for him to forgive.

2. Janet's mother emotionally abused her as a child. Her mother never will own up to her harsh treatment of Janet. Janet refuses to forgive her mother.

3. John pulled a practical joke on you, which caused you to be late for class, and your professor refused to accept your paper because you didn't turn it in on time. John doesn't see anything wrong with a little joke. Oh, he made some rather insincere statements about being sorry, but he still thinks the incident was hilarious.

4. Darrell knew he made you angry when he deliberately didn't invite you to his Christmas open house. He never got around to asking you for forgiveness. You decide to withhold forgiveness until it's requested.

5. Candy's husband had been out late playing cards every Friday night for three years. Some nights he didn't come home at all. "Me? Forgive that jerk? Look how many times he's wronged me!" Candy exclaimed.

6. David had been a horrible husband to Mandy. However, after much effort, Mandy forgave his greater concern for the guys on his softball team; his lack of affection for the children; and his callous, domineering attitude. Then David began to change. His relationship with Mandy started to improve—until he stayed out late again with the guys. He had done it again!

7. Cindy just plain didn't like Martha, who constantly was trying to make Cindy look bad at work. Every emotion in Cindy called for getting back at her coworker. She certainly wasn't interested in forgiving her.

Which of the above reasons has kept you from forgiving in the past? Below, describe how that reason interfered with your ability to forgive.

_____

_____

_____

_____

Here are some more of the countless excuses we make for our unwillingness to forgive ourselves and others. Again, draw a line to match each of the case studies below with a reason in the left margin.

I've found an excuse for the offense

Someone has to punish the person

The person did it deliberately

Something keeps me from forgiving

If I forgive, I'll have to treat the offender well

I'll be a hypocrite if I forgive

I'll forgive but I won't ever forget

1. George's best friend, Hal, swindled George out of $10,000. George's mind raced through times he had been generous to Hal. Hal had used him. George felt he never could forgive Hal.

2. Ben excused his slander of Steve by pointing out how Steve had offended him. He felt justified in lying to destroying Steve's reputation. Forgiving him might mean Ben would have to be nice to this scoundrel.

3. Shirley had been cold for two weeks to Greg, who had offended her. She would forgive him, all right—as soon as she was through punishing him.

4. Gloria felt John, her pastor, wasted the church's money. Gloria, who led the church women's group, felt she was supposed to be the divining rod for John. Soon the church had taken sides—pro-John or anti-John.

5. Steve knew he should forgive Joe, but something kept him from it. He told others that the devil kept him from having an unforgiving spirit toward Joe, but Steve showed no signs of trying to resist Satan, either.

6. Mary thought she had forgiven her brother for his cruelty to her when they were children, but during arguments between the two, Mary kept bringing up past incidents. When Mary and her brother were together, it seemed that she always was stewing about these past misdeeds.

7. Hank had been irresponsible during the early years of his marriage. His wife, Sally, always had been able to forgive him by placing the blame on his mother, who babied Hank even after he was grown. Sally thought she had forgiven Hank when she really had just excused him.

✎ With which of the above case studies do you most readily identify? Below, describe a situation in which the excuse used in that case study has kept you from forgiving.

_____

_____

_____

When We Don't Forgive

When we fail to forgive others, our lives and our relationships suffer. Let's take a look at some problems in our lives that stem directly from a lack of forgiveness.

• **Stress:** Sarah announced to the group that her husband did not deserve to be forgiven. She vowed that she wasn't going to forgive him even if it meant her life. It turned out that it did. Sarah died of kidney failure, which physicians said related to the extreme stress under which she lived. She wanted to kill her husband, but in reality she caused her own death.

Countless people experience extreme stress because they hold inside such bitterness and anger because they haven't forgiven someone. In the margin write about a time that relates to this type of unforgiveness.

• **Self-inflicted Reinjury:** Robert recalled this incident: "As I drove home, I saw flashing through my mind the face of a guy I played basketball with in college. He was a great enemy of mine. He was one of the few people I ever met whom I truly wanted to punch out. I began to remember the unkind things he did to me. Soon anger started creeping up inside of me. I had not thought about this fellow for years, and I'm sure that he doesn't remember me at all. Yet my reliving this event caused me a lot of pain. I had not properly dealt with it in the beginning."

• **No More Love:** "I don't know if I can ever love someone again" is a frequent complaint from those offended by someone about whom they care deeply. Our deepest hurts occur at the hands of those we love.

One way we deal with the pain of being offended is simply to withdraw, refusing to love anymore. We often make this unconscious decision when we have not adequately dealt with an offense. We desperately may want to love again but feel that we are incapable of it. Both refusing to experience love and feeling unable to love are devastating conditions.

✎ **Which of these three problems stemming from lack of forgiveness do you most readily spot in your life? Describe it here.**

_____

_____

_____

Has failing to forgive someone put an ugly snarl on your face?

• **Bitterness:** Emotions trace their lines on our faces. We think others don't notice what's going on inside us, but even the casual observer usually can detect our anger. Kristin recalled seeing a neighbor go through difficulties in her marriage. Hatred was so much a part of the neighbor's life that her face became permanently snarled. Kristin described the neighbor as still having that ugly look on her face. Unforgiveness produces ugliness of all sorts.

• **Perpetual Conflict:** A husband and wife, both of whom had been married previously, received counseling several years ago. Having been hurt in their first marriage, each anticipated hurt from the present spouse. At the smallest offense each reacted as if the spouse were about to deliver the final blow. This husband and the wife constantly were on the defensive, protecting themselves from the attacks they imagined their mate would deliver.

Having been offended in the past, they anticipated more hurt in the present and the future. They reacted in a way that perpetuated the conflict.

• **Walls That Keep Others Out:** Many of us refuse to experience love from those who love us. We often may become anxious and threatened when personal intimacy becomes possible.

Jane hoped and prayed that her husband Frank would come to know the Lord. She thought that if he were a Christian, he would be more loving toward her and toward their children.

One day Frank accepted Christ. Over time his life began to change. He paid more attention to Jane and started spending time with her and the children. He was sensitive and loving. Was it a dream come true? Instead of rejoicing, Jane deeply resented Frank for not changing sooner! *If Frank is able to love us like this now, then he's always had the ability*, she thought. She also felt confused and guilty about her anger.

Hiding behind a wall of unforgiveness is a lonely experience.

Jane's anger was a defense mechanism to keep distance between Frank and herself. The closer they might get, the more pain she might experience if he reverted to his old ways. She never really had forgiven Frank, so the bricks of unforgiveness were stacked to form a wall that kept him from getting too close. Hiding behind a wall of unforgiveness is a lonely experience.

✎ **Do you see any of these results of unforgiveness in your life? Review these last three results of unforgiveness, and describe a time one or more of these problems has affected you.**

_____

_____

_____

Abusing our bodies and emotions

We have looked at what happens to us when we don't forgive. God loves us and expects us to care about ourselves because we are His creation. When we abuse our bodies and our emotions by not forgiving, we are not living the way God wants us to live. Not forgiving also hinders our relationships with others, our brothers and sisters in Christ about whom God cares deeply, too. We can choose to stop acting in a way that harms ourselves and others.

➥ **Stop and pray, asking God to help you forgive others and to help you remember that forgiving others is a part of his plan.**

➥ **It's time to review again your memory work on the third of God's truths. Review the first three truths (the ones you memorized earlier in the study plus the one you memorized earlier this week) until you can repeat them from memory. By the end of this week you likely will have memorized all three of these truths. (Turn to the inside back cover if you need to review the list of God's truths.)**

SUMMARY STATEMENTS

- Failing to forgive others can cause stress and bitterness, can block love, can shut others out of our lives, can cause constant conflict, and can cause us to injure ourselves again and again.
- When we abuse our bodies and our emotions by not forgiving, we are not living the way God wants us to live.
- Not forgiving hinders our relationships with others, our brothers and sisters in Christ about whom God cares deeply.

Forgiveness Is Not Erasure

Sometimes we think that forgiveness is somewhat like a large eraser that wipes our offenses off the books. However God never has forgiven like this. For each offense He demanded full payment. This is the reason for the cross. Christ has paid for our sins in full.

Christians have a special ability to forgive because they can forgive as God does. God has forgiven us fully and completely. We, of all people, know what it is like to experience unconditional forgiveness. As a result, we in turn can forgive those around us.

Think of it this way: No one can do anything to me (insult me, lie about me, annoy me, and so on) that can compare with what Christ has forgiven me for doing.

And be kind to one another, tender-hearted, forgiving each other, just as God in Christ has forgiven you.

–Ephesians 4:32

We can look at others' offenses in a different light when we compare them to our sin of rebellion that Christ has forgiven completely. Read in the left margin what Paul said in Ephesians about this kind of forgiveness.

✎ **List 10 things for which you are glad God in Christ has forgiven you. This can prompt you to be willing to forgive everyone who has done wrong to you.**

God has forgiven me for . . .

1. _____   6. _____

2. _____   7. _____

3. _____   8. _____

4. _____   9. _____

5. _____   10. _____

Then Peter came and said to Him, "Lord, how often shall my brother sin against me and I forgive him? Up to seven times?" Jesus said to him, "I do not say to you, up to seven times, but up to seventy times seven. For this reason the kingdom of heaven may be compared to a certain king who wished to settle accounts with his slaves. And when he had begun to settle them, there was brought to him one who owed him ten thousand talents. But since he did not have the means to repay, his lord commanded him to be sold, along with his wife and children and all that he had, and repayment to be made. The slave therefore falling down, prostrated himself before him, saying, 'Have patience with me, and I will repay you everything.' And the lord of that slave felt compassion and released him and forgave him the debt."

–Matthew 18:21-27

➡ **Stop and pray, thanking God for forgiving you for the matters you mentioned above.**

The exercise on the next page will help you understand biblical principles of forgiveness and will help you apply them to your relationships with others. Read Matthew 18:21-27 at left.

✎ **In these verses how great was the debt of the king's servant? Do you feel he ever could repay it? Why or why not?**

_____

_____

The debt of the king's servant was about $10 million. To put this in perspective, in his book, *Healing for Damaged Emotions* David Seamands states that the entire annual taxes of Judea, Samaria, Galilee, Perea, and Idumea were $800,000.[3] So the debt of the king's servant was impossible to repay, and the fact of this impossibility is exactly the point in this story!

Your debt to God was more impossible to repay than was the servant's debt to the king. If Christ hadn't died on the cross, you would have carried an impossible debt all your life. You would know that when you died, you would have to pay for that enormous debt.

✎ **What did the servant in the passage beg the master to do?**

_____

What did the servant's master do for the servant?

_____

Did the servant ask for forgiveness of the debt? No. He asked for time to repay it. The king, though, had compassion and forgave him the entire debt.

> But that slave went out and found one of his fellow slaves who owed him a hundred denarii; and he seized him and began to choke him, saying, "Pay back what you owe." So his fellow slave fell down and began to entreat him, saying "Have patience with me and I will repay you." He was unwilling however, but went and threw him in prison until he should pay back what was owed.
> –Matthew 18:28-30

✎ **In verses 28-30 at left we find the king's servant being extremely harsh with his fellow servant over a small debt. Write here why the servant was so angry.**

_____

_____

The king's servant apparently did not believe he had been forgiven and was trying to collect enough money to pay back the debt. He took the king's words to mean, *I'll give you a little more time. Work hard and pay me back.* But the king offered total forgiveness by wiping out the debt. The debt was *gone.* He did not owe one penny of the $10 million. (Note: We don't experience forgiveness until we fully accept it.)

> Our ability to extend grace and forgiveness to others directly relates to the degree to which we personally have experienced grace and forgiveness.

> And be kind to one another, tenderhearted, forgiving each other, just as God in Christ also has forgiven you.
> –Ephesians 4:32

> And so, as those who have been chosen of God, holy and beloved, put on a heart of compassion, kindness, humility, gentleness and patience; bearing with one another, and forgiving each other, whoever has a complaint against anyone; just as the Lord forgave you, so also should you.
> –Colossians 3:12-13

✎ **Read Ephesians 4:32 and Colossians 3:12-13 in the left margin. Based on your reading about God's forgiveness of us, answer the following questions.**

To what extent are we to forgive others?

_____

_____

Describe how you feel God has forgiven you.

_____

_____

We are to forgive others just as God in Christ also has forgiven us (Ephesians 4:32). Our every thought and deed, regardless of its motives or results, has been forgiven. That forgiveness is totally unearned. We have done absolutely nothing to deserve it.

A lack of forgiveness on our part may cause us to be harsh toward others; to be self-critical, demanding, guilt-ridden, and resentful; to find fault; to be motivated by "ought to's" (I ought to do this; I ought not to do that); to hold grudges; and to work hard to make up for shortcomings.

✎ **Examine your life for a moment and think about times you might have been harsh with others, resentful, or self-critical because you did not feel forgiven. Describe one of those times.**

_____

_____

_____

_____

Many of us harbor ill feelings toward one or more persons but have suppressed those feelings. We often are not aware of these feelings until the Holy Spirit reveals them to us so that we can deal with them. Sometimes we have a general feeling of uneasiness about someone, but we don't know why.

Do you know people whom you don't like to be around? or whom you can't look in the eye? or with whom you get angry every time you even think of them?

Do you have a sin for which you haven't experienced God's forgiveness? Do you have a sin for which you can't forgive yourself? God the Father has forgiven you because Christ has paid for your sin. Are you refusing to forgive something God has forgiven? Think this through carefully:

> The extent to which you will be able to love and forgive others depends on how much you accept God's love for you and on how much you accept His forgiveness for your sins.

✎ **Use the following exercise to recognize any lack of forgiveness in your life and to forgive freely as God in Christ has forgiven you.**

Do you recognize a lack of forgiveness in your life?

Offense: List in some detail an event which caused you pain.

_____

_____

_____

_____

Persons to be Forgiven: List all who participated in the offense..

_____

_____

_____

Reasons for Not Forgiving: Go through the list of 14 reasons for unforgiveness listed on page 129. List the ones that apply in this case.

_____

_____

Example:			
Persons to Be Forgiven	**Offense**	**Date**	**Reasons for Not Forgiving**
My brothers, Harry and Frank	Never having anything to do with me	12/1/89 through 12/1/90	1, 2, 4, 5, 9

✎ **Insert the person's name and the offense in the statement below. Use this prayer as a means to correct any lack of forgiveness in your life.**

Dear Lord,
I forgive _____ for _____ (offense) because God freely has forgiven me and has commanded me to forgive others. I have the capacity to do this because of Christ's forgiveness in my life. I do not excuse this person's offense in any way, nor do I use any excuse for not extending forgiveness. Thank You, Lord Jesus, for enabling me to forgive.

I also confess that I have sinned by using the following excuses for not forgiving:

_____   _____

Thank You, Lord Jesus, for forgiving me for this sin.

We can avoid most of the pain if we will learn to deal with offenses rather than relive them.

Sometimes others offend us repeatedly. We go through periods when it seems that almost everybody is letting us down. We want freedom from being offended, but that doesn't always occur. Both the experience and the reliving of it hurt us. However, we can avoid most of the pain if we will learn to deal with offenses rather than relive them countless times.

✎ **It's time to review again your memory work on the affirmation "My Identity in Christ." Review the entire affirmation (the part you memorized in earlier sessions plus the last five lines you're memorizing this week) until you can repeat them from memory. Look on page 224 if you need help.**

DAY 5

Avoiding Unholy Anger

One of the most common problems parents have is dealing with their children's misbehavior. Most parents find it painful to face up to their child's wrongdoing. But a main reason why a child's misbehavior is so painful and so embarrassing is that parents tend to blame themselves for it. We also are unable to forgive ourselves for what we think we have caused to occur in the child's life.

Between spells of crying, Joyce said, "Mary wouldn't act like this if I'd been the mother I should have been." Dave, on the other hand, ignored his son's misbehavior with the excuse that his boy was simply "going through a stage." He rationalized his son's wrongdoing because he couldn't face the guilt of failing as a parent.

 Think about how you respond when your children misbehave. If you're not a parent, think about what you've observed others do. Do you blame yourself as Joyce did in the above example? Or do you tend to ignore misdeeds as Dave did because you don't want to face failure? Describe a typical response to a child's misbehavior.

_____

_____

_____

Is our personal worth wrapped up in our performance as parents?

When their children get into trouble, parents usually alternate between blaming themselves and blaming their children. After all, we have taught ourselves to believe that someone has to be blamed. The problem in either case is not that parents love their child too much or too little but that their personal significance is wrapped up in their performance as parents.

Therefore, when a child does well, the parents feel good about themselves. When a child does poorly, parents often blame each other or the child.

Beneath it all is the internalized and unconscious belief, *Someone must take the blame.* Also beneath it all is our inability to forgive ourselves for times we have made mistakes as parents. Somehow that lack of forgiveness and blame gets translated into how we react to our child's misdeeds.

God deeply loves the parent and the child as persons, and He has completely forgiven the parent and the child for their failures. God totally accepts the parent and the child as persons of infinite worth.

Our worth is totally secure in Christ.

Our worth is totally secure in Christ, so our children's success or failure doesn't affect our value in the least. If they whine, make the dean's list, or throw tantrums in the grocery aisle, it doesn't affect our self-worth.

We need to see our children the way our Heavenly Father sees us: deeply loved, completely forgiven, fully pleasing, and totally accepted. Then, when they disobey, our discipline will be like the Father's discipline of us: in love, not anger.

✎ **Think about what you've just read about God's love for us. Then describe some specific ways a parent can respond to a child's misbehavior if he or she remembers that the heavenly Father disciplines us in love, not anger.**

_____

_____

_____

What a Difference!

If we approach our children with an attitude of sadness about their misdeeds rather than anger when they disobey, it will make a tremendous difference! We will be amazed at what happens if we always go to our children with the attitude and words "It's sad that you disobeyed. It was harmful to you, and I love you so much that I don't want you to harm yourself. I will need to discipline you to help you remember not to do it again. Remember, the reason I am disciplining you is that I love you so much!"

We will be amazed at what happens when we approach our children without an angry attitude.

We can respond this way instead of with words like these: "You've done it again, and I'll make sure you regret it! I wonder if you'll ever amount to anything!"

Karen, a mother of two, recalls her mother's disciplining her for pinching another child in Sunday School when Karen was four. Instead of scolding her harshly, her mother turned to her with tears in her eyes and said, "It makes me sad that you pinched your friend. It hurt him, and it hurts you, too, for you to behave that way." Karen says this means of correction impressed her more than any time her mother spoke to her angrily for a misdeed.

Changing our angry response:
- **No fear of parents**
- **No angry relationship**
- **Loving view of God**

Responding to our children in sadness instead of anger will have a major impact on them and us. Our children won't be afraid of us; our relationship with them won't be marred by rage; and they more likely will be able to view God as a loving Father rather than as a tyrant.

As parents dealing with our children, we will have a more accurate perception of God's love and gracious discipline, and we will be more in control of our emotions. This keeps us from letting our anger build and build until we explode.

Instead, we will be able to express our displeasure more acceptably because we will express it in wholesome sadness instead of unholy anger.

 Check the statements below that indicate how a parent's responding to the child's failures with a sense of sadness instead of anger affects the child.

❑ The child won't be afraid of the parent.
❑ The child will punish himself as he deserves.
❑ The relationship won't be marred by anger.
❑ The child will be more likely to view God as a loving Father.

All of the above statements except the second one are true.

➡ **Stop and pray, asking God to help you respond to your child's failures (or the failures of any child with whom you come in contact) with a sense of sadness instead of anger. Ask Him to forgive you for times you have not done this well.**

God disciplines us because sin is destructive, and He does not want us to self-destruct.

As we studied earlier, God does not punish His children, but He does discipline them. Discipline is rooted in love. God disciplines us because sin is destructive, and He does not want us to self-destruct.

The goal of His discipline is to restore, develop, and perfect. Punishment, on the other hand, is retaliation and is used to impose a penalty. Christ has borne your punishment and blame for sin.

We can understand the difference between discipline and punishment. God's discipline can be severe, but it is prompted by sadness, not anger. His willingness to discipline you indicates His love for you.

 Write below your understanding of punishment and God's discipline.

Punishment: _____

God's discipline: _____

When we make mistakes

Punishment often is done in anger, when our emotions are out of control. Our Father disciplines us in love, not anger. He has forgiven us of our failure, and He accepts us as people of infinite worth. Therefore, when He disciplines us, it is not as a tyrant but as a loving Father.

When we think about this subject, we can remember what we've learned about forgiveness. Yes, sometimes we make mistakes—as parents and as people in general. Yes, sometimes our children make mistakes, and those mistakes make us sad. When this happens, we can remember the statement below:

> Because of what Christ has done for us, no misdeed—either one we do or one our children do—is so horrible that it can't be forgiven.

✎ **Review this week's lessons. Pray and ask God to identify one positive statement that had an impact on your understanding of who you are.**

Write that statement in your own words.

_____

_____

_____

Rewrite your thoughts as a prayer of thankfulness to God.

_____

_____

_____

You probably gained many insights as you worked through this week's lessons. Which insight stands out to you? Write it here.

_____

_____

_____

Notes
[1]Frederick Faber, as cited by A.W. Tozer, *The Pursuit of God* (Camp Hill, PA: Christian Publications, Inc., 1982), 40–41.
[2]Ibid., 41.
[3]David Seamands, *Healing for Damaged Emotions* (Wheaton, IL: Victor Books, 1981), 26.

SHAME

Case in point

NO WAY OUT?

Susan was the product of heartless parents. Although she was an attractive child, Susan never seemed quite as confident or as outgoing as her brothers and sisters did. One reason for this was that Susan's father had sexually abused her by the time she was 8 years old. Overcome by the shame this caused her, Susan withdrew from others and looked for an escape. By age 16 Susan was addicted to alcohol and drugs and frequently stole, in addition to selling her body for merchandise. Although she was ashamed of her life-style and wanted to change, she saw no way out. The only people who didn't seem to reject her were the ones who used her. She not only was ashamed, but she also felt trapped and alone. (Read Susan's story on page 150.) What does Susan need in her life?

What you'll learn this week

This week you'll–

* learn that often we have allowed our past performance to control how we perceive ourselves but that our worth is secure in Christ;
* study the meaning of shame and how it affects our lives;
* study eight problems shame can cause in our lives;
* study the meaning of regeneration—God's answer to shame—and its powerful effect on our lives;
* learn the three steps necessary in the process of experiencing your new self.

What you'll study each day

Poor Self-esteem	What Shame Does to Us	How Shame Leaves Its Mark	God's Answer: Regeneration	We Can Grow and Change
DAY 1	DAY 2	DAY 3	DAY 4	DAY 5

Memory verse

A key verse to memorize this week

Fear not, for you will not be put to shame; Neither feel humiliated, for you will not be disgraced.

-Isaiah 54:4

WordWatch

Words to help you understand this week's lesson

shame–n. A painful emotion caused by awareness of guilt, shortcomings, or improper behavior, a condition of humiliating disgrace. (*Example: Shame can rob a person of the joy and peace of his salvation.*

regeneration–n. the renewing work of the Holy Spirit that literally makes each believer experience a new birth the moment he trusts Christ. (*Example: Regeneration took place at our conversion to Christ.*)

<table>
<tr><td>

DAY
1

</td><td>

Poor Self-esteem

</td></tr>
</table>

When we base our self-worth on past failures, dissatisfaction with personal appearance, or bad habits, we often develop a fourth false belief: *I am what I am. I cannot change. I am hopeless.* This lie binds people to the hopeless pessimism—or the belief that things can't get better—associated with poor self-esteem.

"I just can't help myself," some people say. "That's the way I've always been, and that's the way I'll always be. You can't teach an old dog new tricks." We assume that others should have low expectations of us, too. "You know I can't do any better than that. What do you expect?"

 Do you recognize anything in the list below that you can't keep from doing? These are habits you may have tried to stop, but you find yourself doing them over and over.

What can you not stop doing?

- Adultery
- Alcohol or drug abuse
- Premarital sex
- Eating disorder
- Gambling
- Homosexuality
- Other:

- Smoking
- Blatant lying
- Exaggeration of the truth
- Cheating
- Stealing
- Destructive personal habits

When you try to change but you fail instead, you begin to view yourself as a failure with no hope. You feel guilty and helpless.

 List below things about your appearance or past performance that prevent you from viewing yourself as a totally accepted person.

Appearance: Anything from head to toe: height, weight, bone structure, acne, wrinkles, facial features, hair, chest, legs, feet, or teeth.

_____

_____

_____

Past Performance: Failure of your marriage or friendships; disappointing your parents; not making good grades; sloppiness; an addiction; being uncoordinated, deceitful, obnoxious, lustful, gay, adulterous, unforgiving; failing in business.

_____

_____

_____

Stuck like Glue to the Past

If we excuse our failures with an attitude of hopelessness too often, our personality can become glued to them. Our self-image becomes no more than a reflection of our past.

Why did Janet's poise vanish?

When Leslie approached Janet about serving a term as the president of the Ladies' Auxiliary, Janet's outward poise and confidence vanished. "Are you serious?" she stuttered. "You know I've never been a leader and have never even gotten along well with people. No, no, I'd simply embarrass you. No, I can't do it, don't you see?" Janet suffered from low self-esteem. Her opinions of herself were based on her past failures. Those failures kept her from enjoying new experiences.

A young man named Jeff once questioned me when I told him that he needed to separate his past from the present. I told him that no law required him to remain the same individual he always had been. I told Jeff that he could rise above his past and build a new life for himself. "But how?" Jeff asked. "I'm more of a realist than that. I know myself. I know what I've done and who I am. I've tried to change, but it hasn't worked. I've given up now."

Why did Jeff give up?

I explained to Jeff that he needed a new perspective, not just new efforts based on his old, pessimistic attitude. He needed to develop a new self-concept based on the unconditional love and acceptance of God. Both Jeff's past failures and God's unconditional love were realities. The question, however, was this: Which one would Jeff value more? If he continued to value his failures, he would continue to be caught up in self-pity.

Instead, Jeff needed to be honest. He needed someone with whom he could talk openly so that he could express his feelings without fearing rejection. And he needed someone to encourage him to study and to apply the truths of God's Word. As he continued at this process, his sense of self-worth would begin to change. Besides having a changed self-worth, Jeff eventually would experience changes in every area: his goals, his relationships, and his outlook. Too often, our self-image rests solely on how we look at our past behavior. We end up measuring ourselves only through a memory. Day after day, year after year we tend to build our personalities on the rubble of yesterday's personal disappointments.

We tend to build our personalities upon the rubble of yesterday's disappointments.

✎ **Describe how you feel your past failures have affected your sense of self-worth.**

_____

_____

_____

Do Our Failures Make Us Comfortable?

Perhaps we find a strange kind of comfort in our personal failings. Perhaps we find security in accepting ourselves as much less than we can become. That reduces the risk of failure considerably. Certainly, if we expect little from ourselves, we seldom will be disappointed!

Nothing forces us to remain in the mold of the past. By the grace and power of God, we can change! We can persevere and overcome!

> No one forces us to keep shifting our feet in the muck of old failures. We can dare to accept the challenge of building a new life.

Releasing the Old Trapeze Bar

Sometimes to grab a new bar, we have to release the old one.

Paul Tournier once compared life to the experience of a man hanging from a trapeze. The trapeze bar was the man's security, his pattern of existence, his life-style. Then God swung another trapeze into the man's view, and the man faced a confusing dilemma. Should he give up his past? Should he reach for the new bar? Tournier explained that the moment of truth came when the man realized that to grab the new bar, he must release the old one.

In our past relationships we may have experienced the intense pain of neglect, abuse, and manipulation. If we do not begin the process of healing, however, we will be unable to experience the joy and the challenge of the present. We also will be unable to be realistic about the possibility of failure again.

✎ **Which of these events or situations in your own life have been the most damaging to your self-worth?**

What gives me low self-worth?

❑ What parents have said or done to me
❑ What friends have said or done to me
❑ Comparing myself with others
❑ What a supervisor at work has said or done to me
❑ Others: _____

Describe why this event you checked or listed contributed to your low self-worth.

_____

_____

My Struggles

For most of my life I have struggled with this process of change. I may have felt badly about myself because I was reared in a poor family, or because I often felt very awkward as I grew up, or because my home life was not ideal. For whatever reasons, I grew up with a sense of shame about myself and my circumstances.

I had the impression that I just didn't measure up.

Because I felt inadequate during my childhood, I had the impression that I just didn't measure up. Others might not have thought I felt this way, but my sense of inadequacy often was intense. Because I was exceptionally tall and lanky, I was uncomfortable with the way I looked. I felt out of place among my peers. Because I felt inferior, I did not date for a number of years. I was afraid I would be rejected, so I withdrew from social occasions. I preferred to spend time with the few friends with whom I felt most comfortable.

The truth that I am deeply loved, fully pleasing, completely forgiven, and totally accepted by the God of the universe has taken me a lifetime to comprehend. But gradually, by studying God's Word and by experiencing loving relationships with other believers who truly care for me and appreciate me, I have continued to gain a better understanding of the way God values me. This has improved my sense of self-worth considerably.

God has used each situation to teach me that despite my circumstances, my worth is secure in Him.

Many of my past memories still are painful for me, and I imagine they always will be. But through Christ my present attitude about myself continually changes. Knowing that I have no reason to feel ashamed has motivated me to pursue a number of challenges that I wouldn't even have considered undertaking a few years ago. In the process I have experienced failure and success. God has used each situation to teach me that despite my circumstances, my worth is secure in Him.

 Write here about a failure that you have experienced in the past or are experiencing now that you believe is a horrible scar on your life.

_____

_____

➡ **Stop and ask God to help you remember that despite the experience you just listed, your worth is secure in Him.**

➡ **By now you likely will be completing your memory work of the four false beliefs. Today look on the inside back cover and begin memorizing the fourth false belief. By the end of this week's study, you likely will have memorized this belief as well as the first three beliefs you memorized earlier.**

SUMMARY STATEMENTS

- Too often, our self-worth rests solely on how we look at our past behavior. We end up measuring ourselves only through a memory.
- Nothing forces us to remain in the mold of the past. By the grace and power of God, we can change!
- Whether we experience failure or success, God can use each situation to teach us that our worth is secure in Him.

DAY 2

What Shame Does to Us

We can be honest about the pain, the anger, the disappointment, and the loneliness of our past. We can put ourselves in relationships that will encourage us to experience feelings we may have suppressed for many years. This will enable us to begin (or continue) to experience hope and, eventually, healing. Change is possible, but it is a process.

Does this effort seem strange? Does it seem difficult? We may have trouble giving up what is familiar (though painful) for what is unfamiliar because we fear the unknown more than we fear the pain of a poor self-concept. It seems right to hang on. Proverbs 16:25 says, "There is a way which seems right to a man, but its end is the way of death."

Relating in a new way

Any change in our behavior requires us to release our old self-concept, which often is founded in failure and in others' expectations. We can learn how to relate to ourselves in a new way. To accomplish this, we can begin to base our self-worth on God's opinion of us and to trust in His Spirit to accomplish change in our lives. Then, and only then, can we overcome Satan's deception that holds sway over our self-perception and behavior.

✎ **Draw a line to match each false belief on the left with the corresponding truth from God on the right.**

False Beliefs	God's Truths
I am what I am. I cannot change. I am hopeless.	Because of *reconciliation* I am totally accepted by God. I no longer have to fear rejection.
Those who fail (including myself) are unworthy of love and deserve to be punished.	Because of *propitiation* I am deeply loved by God. I no longer have to fear punishment or punish others.
I must meet certain standards to feel good about myself.	Because of *regeneration* I have been made brand-new, complete in Christ. I no longer need to experience the pain of shame.
I must have the approval of certain others to feel good about myself.	Because of *justification* I am completely forgiven by and fully pleasing to God. I no longer have to fear failure.

Turn to the inside back cover and check your work.

If you are evaluating yourself by your past performance or appearance, you are viewing yourself incorrectly. The amount that you evaluate your worth based on your past successes or failures determines how much your past affects you. Recognize that God has made you into a new creature through

Christ's death on the cross. God says you are deeply loved, fully pleasing, completely forgiven, and totally accepted by Him and absolutely complete in Christ.

shame–n. a painful emotion caused by awareness of guilt, shortcomings, or improper behavior, a condition of humiliating disgrace

Shame (read its definition at left) can have a tremendous impact on us if we believe that we never can be different from what we have been. We may view ourselves as persons made up of all of our past actions, and we may believe that we will never be able to change. Left in this hopeless state, we likely will feel trapped in helplessness about ourselves and our future. Because much of what we do is based on our self-concept, our every action reinforces this negative perception of ourselves. Shame often occurs when we consider a failure in our performance or a "flaw" in our appearance so important that it creates a permanently negative opinion about our self-worth.

✎ **Write below the fourth false belief.**

I am what _____

_____

_____

How much does this lie affect us?

✎ By believing Satan's lie, *I am what I am; I cannot change; I am hopeless*, we expect the worst possible outcome and have a poor self-concept. Take this test to determine how strongly this false belief affects you.

Read each of the following statements; then, from the top of the test, choose the term that best describes your response. Put in the blank beside each statement the number above the term you choose.

1	2	3	4	5	6	7
Always	Very Often	Often	Sometimes	Seldom	Very Seldom	Never

_____ 1. I often think about past failures or experiences of rejection that have occurred in my life.

_____ 2. I cannot recall certain things about my past without experiencing strong, painful emotions (for example: guilt, shame, anger, and so on).

_____ 3. I seem to make the same mistakes over and over again.

_____ 4. I want to change certain aspects of my character, but I don't believe I ever can do so successfully.

_____ 5. I feel inferior.

_____ 6. I cannot accept aspects of my appearance.

_____ 7. I generally am disgusted with myself.

_____ 8. I feel that certain experiences basically have ruined my life.

_____ 9. I perceive of myself as an immoral person.

_____ 10. I feel that I have lost the opportunity to experience a complete and wonderful life.

_____ Total (Add the numbers you have placed in the blanks.)

What your score says about you

Interpreting Your Score
If your score is...

57-70
God apparently has given you a very strong appreciation for His love and

unconditional acceptance. You seem to be free from the shame that plagues most people. (One exception, however: Some people who score this high are either greatly deceived or have become callous to their emotions to suppress pain.)

47-56

Shame controls your responses rarely or only in certain situations. Again, the only major exceptions are those who are not honest with themselves.

37-46

Emotional problems you experience may relate to a sense of shame. When you think about some of your previous decisions, you probably will relate many of them to your feelings of worthlessness. Feelings of low self-esteem may affect many of your future decisions unless you take direct action to overcome those feelings.

27-36

Shame forms a generally negative backdrop to your life. Probably, few days go by when shame does not affect you in some way. Unfortunately, this robs you of the joy and peace your salvation was meant to bring.

0-26

Experiences of shame dominate your memory and probably have caused you to experience a great deal of depression. These problems will remain until you take definitive action. In other words, this condition will not simply disappear one day; time alone cannot heal your pain. You need to experience deep healing in your self-concept, in your relationship with God, and in your relationships with others.

➡ **Stop and pray, asking God to help you understand times in your life when you felt that you never could change and that you were hopeless. Ask Him to remind you that you are a new creature in Christ and no longer need to experience the pain of shame.**

➡ **By now you likely will be completing your memory work on God's four truths. Today look at the inside back cover and begin memorizing the fourth truth. By the end of this week's study, you likely will have memorized this truth as well as the first three of God's truths you memorized earlier.**

SUMMARY STATEMENTS

- By believing Satan's lie, *I am what I am; I cannot change; I am hopeless,* we begin expecting the worst possible outcome about things and have a poor self-concept.
- Shame often occurs when we consider a failure in our performance or a "flaw" in our appearance so important that it creates a permanently negative opinion about our self-worth.
- We must begin to base our self-worth on God's opinion of us and trust in His Spirit to accomplish change in our lives.
- We must learn to give up what is familiar (the past) for what is unfamiliar (the future), even though we fear the unknown more than we fear the pain of a poor self-concept.

DAY 3

How Shame Leaves Its Mark

Susan was the product of heartless parents. Although she was an attractive child, Susan never seemed quite as confident or as outgoing as her brothers and sisters did. She seemed always to hold back in her involvement with others. One reason for this was that Susan's father had approached her for sexual favors by the time she was eight years old. Overcome by the shame this caused her, Susan withdrew from others and looked for an escape.

Susan felt used and trapped

By age 16 Susan was addicted to alcohol and drugs and frequently stole, in addition to selling her body for money. She began to feel that she was nothing more than sexual merchandise. Although she was ashamed of her life-style and wanted to change, she saw no way out. The only people who didn't seem to reject her were the ones who used her. She not only was ashamed, but she also felt trapped and alone.

Unlike Susan, Diana was reared by Christian parents. She had grown up in a conservative Protestant church and was very active in its youth group. Diana always witnessed to her friends at school. She always was an example to others.

Diana felt abandoned

Unfortunately, one night Diana made a mistake that changed her life. Alone for the evening, she and her boyfriend had sexual intercourse. Shocked and ashamed by their actions, they both agreed that they must admit the incident to their parents. Diana, seeking understanding and support, confided in her mother. But Diana's mother lost control and bitterly told her how ashamed and disappointed she was. Diana's father couldn't believe what his daughter had done. He refused even to speak to her.

Her relationship with her parents got worse. Six months later, Diana left home. Heartbroken and overcome by shame, she turned to her boyfriend. Soon they began sleeping together regularly, and both began using drugs. Believing that her parents never would accept her again, Diana sought acceptance in the only way she knew.

Both Susan and Diana suffered from the devastating effects of shame. Shame often overwhelms us when something we do wrong is so overpowering or so disappointing to us that it causes us to have a permanently negative opinion about our self-worth. Others may not know about our failure, but we do. We only may imagine their rejection; but real or imagined, the pain resulting from it cripples our confidence and hope.

 Can you identify with either Susan or Diana? Think about a time when something you did made you feel that others rejected you, even though only you might have known about your sin.

Shame usually causes us to feel guilty and to punish ourselves, but it also can lead us to search for God and for His answers. He created our inner, undeniable need for personal significance to make us search for Him. He alone can fulfill our deep need.

God created our inner, undeniable need for personal significance to make us search for Him.

In God we find peace, acceptance, and love. Through Him we find the courage and power to develop into the men and women He intends us to be. Although

Satan wants to convince us that we always will be prisoners of our failures and past experiences, God's grace can free us from the guilt of our past and can give us a new purpose for our lives.

 Describe here a time that you felt shame caused you to want to punish yourself.

_____

_____

Shame can have powerful effects on our self-esteem, and it can show up in many ways. The following is a brief list of problems shame can cause.

 As you read about the following eight problems, circle the ones that you see existing in your own life.

Inferiority

Not good enough

Shame produces a deep sense of inferiority. Feelings of inferiority develop when patterns of failure occur over and over, or they can stem from only one or two haunting instances. Either way, they can destroy our self-worth. As a result, they can have a bad effect on our emotions and behavior. Doug was smart and good-looking, but shame stemming from his parents' harsh criticisms of him as a child made him refuse to believe he had any good traits. Friends told him how capable he was, but he could not accept others' affirmations because he could not see beyond his own inferiority.

Habitually Destructive Behavior

Life looks bleak

We often behave in a manner that is consistent with how we see ourselves. Therefore, seeing ourselves through the eyes of shame usually results in a pessimistic outlook on life and a life-style of destructive behavior. We can't imagine that things ever will get any better.

Self-pity

Sorry for ourselves

Shame often prompts us to view ourselves as victims. Consequently, whether we blame others or condemn ourselves for our actions, we sink into the depths of feeling sorry for ourselves.

Passivity

Avoiding relationships

Some of us try to make up for gnawing feelings of shame through passivity—sitting idly by and refusing to invest any part of ourselves in relationships and responsibilities. We may be perfectionists in some areas of our lives, but we also may avoid taking risks in relationships or circumstances. We may tend to become absorbed in minor activities (clipping coupons, cleaning the kitchen, filing papers, reading magazines), so that we are "too busy" to experience the reality of relationships and situations.

✎ Have you ever experienced a time in which you took a passive approach to life, as you just read about, rather than take the risk of investing yourself in a relationship? Describe that time here.

_____

_____

_____

Isolation and Withdrawal

No one gets close

Isolation goes along with passivity. As we avoid both the risks of rejection and failure, some of us withdraw from virtually all meaningful interaction. We develop false fronts so that nobody can see our hurt. We may be socially active, but we also may not allow anyone to get close to us. We often fear that if people really knew us, we again would experience hurt and rejection. Our deep sense of shame leads us to withdraw from others, to feel isolated, and to experience the pain of loneliness.

Loss of Creativity

No new ideas

When we are ashamed of ourselves over a period of time, we lose our creativity. We tend to become so preoccupied with our own inferiority that we can't come up with new ideas. Often, believing that whatever we attempt will fail, we may choose to avoid doing anything that isn't a proven success.

Codependent Relationships

Needing to be needed

Trying to overcome their sense of shame, many people become codependent; that is, they depend on being needed by a family member or a friend who has an addictive problem or compulsion. Codependents thus develop a need to "rescue" and to take care of others. This caretaking is the codependent's subconscious way of trying to gain personal significance. Such attempts usually backfire, however, because dependent persons often use shame to manipulate the codependent.

A dependent person's frequent ploy is to tell the codependent that he or she is being selfish for taking care of personal matters rather than those of the dependent person. This locks the codependent into a pattern of rescuing to gain approval and feeling ashamed because of his or her inability to develop a sense of personal value, regardless of how hard he or she tries to do so.

Despising Our Appearance

Ashamed of what we see

Beauty is highly valued in our society. Television commercials and programs, magazine ads and billboards all convey the message that we should prize beauty. But very few of us compare to the beautiful people we see in these ads and programs, and most of us are ashamed of at least one aspect of our appearance. We spend hundreds of dollars and more time and worry than anyone can imagine covering up or altering our skin, eyes, teeth, faces, noses, thighs, and scalps. We refuse to believe that God, in His sovereignty and love, gave us the features He wants us to have.

 What about your physical appearance keeps you from feeling acceptable in God's sight? What do you think it will take for you to overcome this feeling and to experience the joy of your new life in Christ?

_____

_____

_____

Fear not, for you will not be put to shame; Neither feel humiliated, for you will not be disgraced.
                              –Isaiah 54:4a

We don't easily change these views of ourselves; but we can change them through honesty, the affirmation of others, the truths of God's Word, the power and encouragement of the Holy Spirit, and time. Because of Christ's redemption we are worthy, forgiven, loved, accepted, and complete in Him. God, speaking to us through His Word, indicates that He is capable of dealing with our shame (see the Scripture at left). This passage reveals that shame is something that God does not want to be part of our lives.

 It's time to review again your memory work on the fourth false belief. Review the four false beliefs (the three you memorized earlier and the one from this week) until you can repeat them all from memory. By the end of this week, you likely will have memorized all four. (Turn to the inside back cover if you need to review the four false beliefs.)

SUMMARY STATEMENTS

- God created our inner, undeniable need for personal significance to make us search for Him. He alone can fulfill our deep need.
- Although Satan wants to convince us that we always will be prisoners of our failures and past experiences, God's grace can free us from the guilt of our past and can give us a new purpose for our lives.
- Shameful views of ourselves can change through honesty, others' affirmation, the truths of God's Word, the Holy Spirit's power and encouragement, and time.

DAY 4

regeneration–n. the renewing work of the Holy Spirit that literally makes each believer experience a new birth the moment he trusts Christ (Vine's)

God's Answer: Regeneration

Zacchaeus

Perhaps no passage in the Bible better illustrates God's **regeneration** (see at left what that word means) than does the story of Zacchaeus in Luke 19:1-10. Zacchaeus was a tax collector, and the people despised him for overtaxing their meager earnings. People in the Roman world hated tax collectors, who obtained their wealth at others' expense.

One day Zacchaeus learned that Jesus was visiting his town. Zacchaeus climbed a sycamore tree to get a good look at the man who reportedly loved even sinners and outcasts. Jesus saw him in the tree. To everyone's amazement—including Zacchaeus'—Jesus invited Zacchaeus to come down. Jesus then ate dinner at Zacchaeus's house!

During dinner Zacchaeus experienced the unconditional love and acceptance of Christ. As a result, he became a different person. His self-concept was radically changed from that of a cheating, hated tax collector to a person who knew God loved him. His actions reflected this dramatic change. Zacchaeus said he was sorry for his sins and said he would repay those he had swindled by four times the amount he had taken from them. He also promised to give half of his possessions to the poor. Through Christ Zacchaeus developed a new self-concept, new values, new goals, and new behavior.

We are complete because Christ has forgiven us and given us life—the capacity for growth and change.

 Read Luke 19:5 at left. Put the verse in your own words to show Jesus' love and acceptance of Zacchaeus.

And when Jesus came to the place, He looked up and said to him, "Zacchaeus, hurry and come down, for today I must stay at your house."

–Luke 19:5

_____

_____

_____

Not a Self-improvement Program

Regeneration is not a self-improvement program, nor is it a clean-up campaign for our sinful natures. Regeneration is nothing less than the giving of new life. As Paul stated in Ephesians 2:5, "Even when we were dead in our transgressions, [God] made us alive together [with Christ]." Theologian Louis Berkhof explains regeneration by saying that it is a change affecting "the whole man: the intellect the will and the feelings or emotions."[1]

In his letter to the young pastor Titus, Paul also wrote about this incredible transformation process:

For we also once were foolish ourselves, disobedient, deceived, enslaved to various lusts and pleasures, spending our life in malice and envy, hateful, hating one another. But when the kindness of God our Savior and His love for mankind appeared, He saved us, not on the basis of deeds which we have done in righteousness, but according to His mercy, by the washing of regeneration and renewing by the Holy Spirit, whom He poured out upon us richly through Jesus Christ our Savior, that being justified by His grace we might be made heirs according to the hope of eternal life (Titus 3:3-7).

Jesus answered and said to him, "Truly, truly, I say to you, unless one is born again, he cannot see the kingdom of God." Nicodemus said to Him, "How can a man be born when he is old? He cannot enter a second time into his mother's womb and be born, can he?" Jesus answered, "Truly, truly, I say to you, unless one is born of water and the Spirit, he cannot enter into the kingdom of God."

–John 3:3-6

In that wondrous, miraculous moment when we trust Christ, we experience more than swapping one set of standards for another. We experience what Jesus called a new birth (see the passage at left to show how Jesus described this to Nicodemus), a renewal of the human spirit, a reviving and transforming that takes place so that the Spirit lives in us (Romans 8:10).

 Read Romans 8:10-14 below and underline the words or phrases in the verse that help you understand about this new birth Jesus described.

And if Christ is in you, though the body is dead because of sin, yet the spirit is alive because of righteousness. But if the Spirit of Him who raised

Jesus from the dead dwells in you, He who raised Christ Jesus from the dead will also give life to your mortal bodies through His Spirit who indwells you. So then, brethren, we are under obligation, not to the flesh, to live according to the flesh-for if you are living according to the flesh, you must die; but if by the Spirit you are putting to death the deeds of the body, you will live. For all who are being led by the Spirit of God, these are sons of God.

–Romans 8:10-14

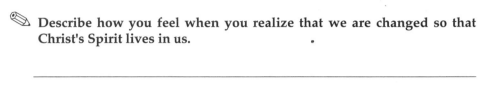 **Describe how you feel when you realize that we are changed so that Christ's Spirit lives in us.**

_____

_____

Complete in Christ

Alive and forgiven in Him

Through the gift of God's grace, we are spiritually alive, forgiven, and complete in Him. Paul wrote the Colossian Christians the following verse, "For in Him [Christ] all the fullness of Deity dwells in bodily form, and in Him you have been made complete, and He is the head over all rule and authority" (Colossians 2:9-10).

In the church at Colossae, false teachers taught that completeness comes through a combination of philosophy, good works, other religions, and Christ. Paul's clear message was that we are made complete through Christ alone.

To attempt to find completeness through any other source, including success, others' opinions, prestige, or appearance, is to be deceived completely (Colossians 2:8).

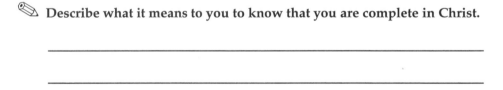 **Describe what it means to you to know that you are complete in Christ.**

_____

_____

We are complete because Christ has forgiven us and given us life–the capacity for growth and change.

Nothing can add to the death of Christ to pay for our sins, and nothing can add to the resurrection of Christ to give us new life. We are complete because Christ has forgiven us and given us life—the capacity for growth and change.

We Stumble and Fall

When we trust Christ and experience new life, forgiveness, and love, our lives will begin to change. Still, regeneration does not mean we change our performance instantly. We will continue to stumble and fall at times, but the Scriptures clearly instruct us to choose to act in ways that reflect our new lives and values in Christ.

As Paul wrote the Ephesians:

that, in reference to your former manner of life, you lay aside the old self, which is being corrupted in accordance with the lusts of deceit, and that you

Laying aside the old self

be renewed in the spirit of your mind, and put on the new self, which in the likeness of God has been created in righteousness and holiness of the truth (Ephesians 4:22-24).

We are to put on this new self that shows Christian character in our attitudes and behavior. We are marvelously unique, created to reflect the character of Christ through our individual personalities and behavior.

✎ **Match the following Scripture references (read the passages in the margin at left) to the correct statements at right to determine how your regeneration was accomplished.**

_____ John 1:12-13   A. By the renewing of the Holy Spirit
_____ John 3:16   B. Through Jesus' death and resurrection
_____ 1 Peter 1:3   C. By the will of God
_____ Titus 3:5   D. Through believing faith in Jesus' death for you

God has made you into a new person. At the instant you trusted Christ, you were born again as a new spiritual being. God creates by "fiat"; that is, He makes something from nothing. Your new birth brought about more than a change of direction. It gave you a completely new nature with new abilities to reflect God's image in your daily life.

➥ **Stop and pray, thanking God that we're not forever bound to our old sinful natures. Thank Him for making you into a new person and giving you a change of direction. Ask Him to help your behavior and your thoughts reflect the new person He has made you.**

➥ **It's time to review the four truths (the ones you memorized earlier in the study plus the one you memorized earlier this week) until you can repeat them from memory. By the end of this week you likely will have memorized all four of these truths. (Review on the inside back cover.)**

SUMMARY STATEMENTS

- Regeneration is the renewing work of the Holy Spirit that literally makes each believer experience a new birth at the moment he trusts Christ as Savior.
- Regeneration is not a self-improvement program, nor is it a clean-up campaign for our sinful natures. Regeneration is nothing less than the giving of new life.

Sidebar (margin, left):

But as many as received Him, to them He gave the right to become children of God, even to those who believe in His name, who were born not of blood, nor of the will of the flesh, nor of the will of man, but of God.

–John 1:12-13

For God so loved the world, that He gave His only begotten Son, that whoever believes in Him should not perish, but have eternal life.

–John 3:16

Blessed be the God and Father of our Lord Jesus Christ, who according to His great mercy has caused us to be born again to a living hope through the resurrection of Jesus Christ from the dead.

–1 Peter 1:3

He saved us, not on the basis of deeds which we have done in righteousness, but according to His mercy, by the washing of regeneration and renewing by the Holy Spirit.

–Titus 3:5

DAY 5

We Can Grow and Change

The truth of regeneration can drive away the haunting memories of the past. God has forgiven our sins. We now can grow and change because we are new people with the Spirit of God living in us. When we sin, we will experience sin's destructive effects and the Father's discipline; but our sin never will change the truth of who we are in Christ.

Confess and Get On with Life

When we sin, we can follow King David's example. When Nathan confronted David about David's sin of adultery with Bathsheba, David confessed his sin to the Lord (2 Samuel 12:1-13). David did not run from his sin or its consequences. He did not deny it, nor did he hide from it. He married Bathsheba, and God was merciful: He enabled Bathsheba to give birth to Solomon, who became the wise king of Israel.

Certainly, God could have brought Solomon into the world another way; but perhaps as a message to us, He chose Bathsheba as the means for this. What a message! Confess your sins, worship God, and get on with your life. You can experience the mercy of God no matter what you've been through.

If we confess our sins, He is faithful and righteous to forgive us our sins and to cleanse us from all unrighteousness.
–1 John 1:9

✎ **Read 1 John 1:9 in the left margin and mark the following statements as *T* (true) or *F* (false).**

_____ God's faithfulness means He will forgive me some of the time.
_____ If I confess (agree with God about) my sins, He will forgive me and cleanse me.
_____ Some types of unrighteousness exist for which God won't forgive me.
_____ The justice of God means He has the legal right to forgive me of my sins.

Thank you for writing that the second statement is true; the rest are false.

A New Creation

At the moment of our conversion to Christ, we were given more than a change of direction; we received new life.

Regeneration is the renewing work of the Holy Spirit by which a person literally becomes a new creation. Our regeneration took place at the instant of our conversion to Christ. At that moment we received more than a change of direction; we received new life.

The part of us that the Holy Spirit regenerated is our spirit. The Holy Spirit has energized our inner spirit with new life. In John 3:3,5-6 Jesus called it a new birth. He said, 'That which is born of the flesh is flesh, and that which is born of the Spirit is spirit' (John 3:6). Regeneration is the Spirit-formed renewal of our human spirit, a transforming resuscitation so that the spirit is alive within us (Romans 8:10). The Holy Spirit has been joined to our human spirit, forming a new spiritual entity. A new birth has produced a new being. "Therefore if any man is in Christ, he is a new creature; the old things passed away; behold, new things have come" (2 Corinthians 5:17).

But the fruit of the Spirit is love, joy, peace, patience, kindness, goodness, faithfulness, gentleness, self-control; against such things there is no law. Now those who belong to Christ Jesus have crucified the flesh with its passions and desires.
–Galatians 5:22-24

✎ **Read the Scriptures that appear in the margin at left and list the characteristics of your new self.**

Galatians 5:22-24: _____

_____

and put on the new self, which in the likeness of God has been created in righteousness and holiness of the truth. Therefore, laying aside falsehood, speak truth, each one of you, with his neighbor, for we are members of one another.
–Ephesians 4:24-25

Ephesians 4:24-25: _____

_____

Remind them to be subject to rulers, to authorities, to be obedient, to be ready for every good deed, to malign no one, to be uncontentious, gentle, showing every consideration for all men.

–Titus 3:1-2

because it is written, 'YOU SHALL BE HOLY, FOR I AM HOLY.'

–1 Peter 1:16

The Spirit Himself bears witness with our spirit that we are children of God, and if children, heirs also, heirs of God and fellow heirs with Christ, if indeed we suffer with Him in order that we may also be glorified with Him.

–Romans 8:16-17

And so, as those who have been chosen of God, holy and beloved, put on a heart of compassion, kindness, humility, gentleness and patience; bearing with one another, and forgiving each other, whoever has a complaint against anyone; just as the Lord forgave you, so also should you. And beyond all these things put on love, which is the perfect bond of unity. And let the peace of Christ rule in your hearts, to which indeed you were called in one body; and be thankful.

–Colossians 3:12-15

Titus 3:1-2: _____

_____

Study the words of these Scriptures carefully. Ephesians 4:24 says that our new self has (already) been created in righteousness and holiness of the truth, but we must yet put on this new self in order to produce godly thoughts and actions progressively—as the acorn produces an oak tree!

✎ **Now read these Scriptures that appear in the margin at left and list more characteristics of your new self:**

1 Peter 1:16: _____

_____

Romans 8:16-17: _____

_____

Colossians 3:12-15: _____

_____

✏ **Describe what difference will occur in your life when you lay aside the old self and put on the new self.**

_____

_____

_____

The process of experiencing your new self involves three steps:

- **Laying aside the old self**—rejecting the old self's hold on you, which dictates how you think, feel, and act, and choosing to stop living in worldliness.

- **Renewing your mind with God's truth**––understanding what Christ has accomplished for you and how that gives you a new capacity to live for Him.

- **Putting on the new self**—in your thoughts, words, actions, values, and relationships.

It is difficult to lay aside the old self because much of your self-worth probably has been based on your performance and on others' opinions. False beliefs have become the primary basis you use to evaluate yourself and the situations you face. The drawing on the next page shows how this happens.

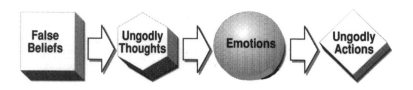

Your beliefs usually influence your thoughts, emotions, and actions. False beliefs are Satan's lies, and they generate ungodly thoughts, painful emotions, and sinful actions. An ungodly performance serves to reinforce these false beliefs, which support the conviction, *I am what I am.*

You may feel trapped and hopeless to be anything different from who you are right now. Take heart! You have hope! Keep in mind the statement below.

> God has made you a new creature! Regeneration provides you with a new system by which you can evaluate yourself and your life.

Or do you not know that the unrighteous shall not inherit the kingdom of God? Do not be deceived; neither fornicators, nor idolaters, nor adulterers, nor effeminate, nor homosexuals, nor thieves, nor the covetous, nor drunkards, nor revilers, nor swindlers, shall inherit the kingdom of God. And such were some of you; but you were washed, but you were sanctified, but you were justified in the name of the Lord Jesus Christ, and in the Spirit of our God.

–1 Corinthians 6:9-11

As you read 1 Corinthians 6:9-11, which appears at left, you will see that regeneration gives you a new beginning. No matter what you have done in the past, God has washed away His remembrance of these sins and set you apart for His own use in the present.

You no longer have to think, feel, and act in the way false beliefs dictate. You now are free to present yourself to God as an instrument of righteousness.

➡ **Picture yourself acting, thinking, and even speaking as a new person would. Picture what your life can be like now that you no longer feel trapped and hopeless. Imagine how free you can feel because you no longer have the guilt that has burdened you. Stop and pray, thanking God that He can bring about this condition in your life.**

Old habits are hard to shake, but it can be done! The drawing below shows how this occurs:

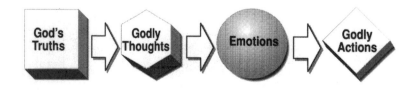

Your life will change

As the Spirit of God renews your mind and as you allow God to speak through His Word to help you apply that Word in relationships with the people of God you encounter, your life progressively will change.

➡ It's time to review again your memory work on the affirmation "My Identity in Christ." Review the entire affirmation (you completed your memory work on it in unit 7) and repeat it now from memory.

✎ Fill in the blanks below as you read the fourth false belief and the truth from God's Word you can use to refute it.

False belief: I am what I am. I cannot _____.

I am _____.

God's truth: Because of _____, I have

been made _____, complete in _____.

I no longer need to experience the pain of _____.

✎ Review this week's lessons. Pray and ask God to identify one positive statement that had an impact on your understanding of who you are.

Write that statement in your own words.

_____

_____

_____

Rewrite your thoughts as a prayer of thankfulness to God.

_____

_____

You probably gained many insights as you worked through this week's lessons. Which insight stands out to you? Write it here.

_____

_____

_____

Notes
[1]Louis Berkhof, *Systematic Theology* (Grand Rapids: William B. Eerdmans Publishing Co., 1941), 468.

OVERCOMING OBSTACLES

Case in point

> ## FEELING SHAMEFUL AND UNFORGIVEN
>
> Jason grew up in a troubled home with parents who abused him verbally and physically. Because he feared his parents' put-downs, Jason never felt he could truly be honest when he felt hurt, angry, or even hopeful or joyful. As an adult, he always felt full of shame and had a difficult time accepting Christ's forgiveness. Highly involved in his church, he wanted to grow as a Christian but never felt totally worthy of being loved. (Read more about Jason's story on page 165.) What does Jason need in his life?

What you'll learn this week

This week you'll–

- look at some of the reasons we fail to grow in our faith;
- learn more about how Christ's forgiveness can give us freedom from past hurts that drag us down;
- study how our view of God determines how we react in life situations, especially when we're under stress;
- learn how to forgive persons who cause us deep emotional wounds;
- learn how being around persons who stand by us when we express our hopes, fears, hurts, and anger can make God's forgiveness and acceptance real to us.

What you'll study each day

Moving to Maturity	Renewing Your View of God	The Depths of God's Love	Dealing with Emotional Scars	Forgiving at a Deeper Level
DAY 1	DAY 2	DAY 3	DAY 4	DAY 5

Memory verse

A key verse to memorize this week

bearing with one another, and forgiving each other, whoever has a complaint against anyone; just as the Lord forgave you, so also should you.
–Colossians 3:13

WordWatch

Words to help you understand this week's lessons

parable–n. a story drawn from nature or human circumstances in order to teach a spiritual lesson. (*Example: Jesus taught through* **parables**.)

forgiveness–v. the act of ceasing to feel resentment against (an offender) . . . the act of granting relief from payment of a debt. (*Example: We must learn* **forgiveness** *of others in the same way Christ forgave us.*)

Moving to Maturity

When Jesus lifted His eyes at Calvary and cried, "It is finished!" (John 19:30). He told us that the provision for people's reconciliation with God was complete. Nothing more needed to be done, because the Word of life had been spoken to all people. People needed only to hear the Word, to let God help them accept it, and to place their hope and trust in Christ.

Why do we wrestle day after day with the same temptations, the same failings, and the same stumbling blocks?

But if the redemption we enjoy is complete, why do we fail to see how it has changed our lives? Why do we wrestle day after day with the same temptations, the same failings, and the same distractions we always have fought? Why can't we break free and move on toward maturity? Why do we fail to grow in our faith?

Why We Don't Grow

parable–n. a narrative drawn from nature or human circumstances in order to teach a spiritual lesson (Vine's)

Christ used a short story called a **parable** (see definition at left) when He needed to illustrate a point. In a story called the parable of the sower in Mark 4:3-20, Christ illustrated the reasons we fail to produce fruit.

Read Mark 4:13-20, a portion of the parable, below.

The Parable of the Sower

And He said to them, "Do you not understand this parable? And how will you understand all the parables? The sower sows the word. And these are the ones who are beside the road where the word is sown; and when they hear, immediately Satan comes and takes away the word which has been sown in them. And in a similar way these are the ones on whom seed was sown on the rocky places, who, when they hear the word, immediately receive it with joy; and they have no firm root in themselves, but are only temporary; then, when affliction or persecution arises because of the word, immediately they fall away. And others are the ones on whom seed was sown among the thorns; these are the ones who have heard the word, and the worries of the world, and the deceitfulness of riches, and the desires for other things enter in and choke the word, and it becomes unfruitful. And those are the ones on whom seed was sown on the good soil; and they hear the word and accept it, and bear fruit, thirty, sixty, and a hundredfold."

–Mark 4:13-20

✎ **Study the parable and answer the following questions.**

❏ Yes ❏ No Do all seeds produce a crop?
❏ Yes ❏ No Do all people respond to God's Word?
❏ Yes ❏ No Does Satan take away the Word?
❏ Yes ❏ No Does trouble or persecution come because of the Word?
❏ Yes ❏ No Do worries, deceitfulness, and desires make us unfruitful?
❏ Yes ❏ No Can we hear the Word, accept it, and then produce a crop?

Whether a crop grows depends on whether the soil is fertile, whether the climate is good, and whether weeds exist. The reasons Christ gave in the parable for a lack of fruit in the believer's life are Satan's taking away the Word of God, persecution, and the worries of the world. For most of us, focusing on the worries of the world represents one of the main reasons we don't grow as Christians. Jesus described it this way:

> And others are the ones on whom seed was sown among the thorns; these are the ones who have heard the word, and the worries of the world, and the deceitfulness of riches and the desires for other things enter in and choke the word, and it becomes unfruitful.
>
> –Mark 4:18-19

 What are some of the worries of the world that you focus on that keep you from growing? List two of them here.

_____ _____

And those are the ones on whom seed was sown on the good soil, and they hear the word and accept it, and bear fruit, thirty, sixty, and a hundredfold.
–Mark 4:20

In the context of honesty, affirmation, and patience, we can focus on the forgiveness God gives us, and we can reject the deception and worldly desires that choke out the Word of life. Look at the Scripture in the left margin to see what Mark said about people who hear the Word and accept it. We can base our lives on God's Word and allow Him to reproduce His character within us by the power of His Spirit.

Reigning over the Events of Our Lives

Grace and peace be multiplied to you in the knowledge of God and of Jesus our Lord; seeing that His divine power has granted to us everything pertaining to life and godliness, through the true knowledge of Him who called us by His own glory and excellence. For by these He has granted to us His precious and magnificent promises, in order that by them you might become partakers of the divine nature, having escaped the corruption that is in the world by lust.
–2 Peter 1:2-4

 Read 2 Peter 1:2-4, which appears in the left margin. Describe here what it means to you that God has given us everything we need for life and godliness.

_____

_____

The moment we trust Christ, we receive everything pertaining to life and godliness, as 2 Peter 1:2-4 indicates. Immediately, we become His sons and daughters, with all the provisions He graciously has given us. As we allow Him to reign over the events of our lives, He transforms our values, attitudes, and behavior so that we are able to glorify Him more and more.

 Think about a time something good happened to you and you immediately remembered to thank God for it. How did it make you feel to give God the credit rather than taking all the credit for yourself?

Put on the new self, which in the likeness of God has been created in righteousness and holiness of the truth.
–Ephesians 4:24

Of course, we still are chained to a mortal body but we are reborn in righteousness and holiness of the truth, as Ephesians 4:24 describes at left. We have within us Christ, who has authority over Satan. Christ has triumphed over Satan by the power of His blood to pay for sin and by the power of His

When He had disarmed the rules and authorities, He made a public display of them, having triumphed over them through Him.

–Colossians 2:15

resurrection to give new life. See Colossians 2:15 at left. Now that we are redeemed, our rightful purpose to rule in life will be denied only if we continue to allow Satan to deceive us. If we fail to recognize our true position of sonship and fail to exercise our new power and authority, we will remain trapped in the world's system. Satan's lies and schemes are designed to keep us from experiencing these wonderful truths.

Our Constant Motivation

To overcome Satan's lies and to begin to enjoy freedom from false beliefs, we need to understand clearly what Christ has done for us through His death on the cross. The more fully we understand what Christ's sacrifice means for us, the more we can experience the freedom, motivation, and power God intends for us.

> God's Word is the source of truth—the truth about Christ, the cross, and redemption—and we should anticipate that God will speak to us through it.

Now for this very reason also, applying all diligence, in your faith supply moral excellence, and in your moral excellence, knowledge; and in your knowledge, self-control, and in your self-control, perseverance, and in your perseverance, godliness; and in your godliness, brotherly kindness, and in your brotherly kindness, love. For if these qualities are yours and are increasing, they render you neither useless nor unfruitful in the true knowledge of our Lord Jesus Christ. For he who lacks these qualities is blind or short-sighted, having forgotten his purification from his former sins.

–2 Peter 1:5-9

The apostle Peter wrote in 2 Peter 1:5-9 (at left) that the cross is not just the beginning of the Christian life but also is our constant motivation to grow spiritually and to live for Christ.

✎ List three things that hinder your emotional and spiritual growth:

_____

_____

_____

✎ Read 2 Peter 1:5-9 at left. List below the qualities that will make you effective and productive in your knowledge of our Lord Jesus Christ.

_____   _____

_____   _____

_____   _____

_____   _____

This passage clearly teaches that we don't grow because we fail to understand or remember what Christ's death on the cross for the forgiveness of our sins means. The cross is central to our motivation and development.

➡ Memorize Colossians 3:13 at left. It will help you remember what Christ's forgiveness means.

✎ Based on this verse, who is our model for forgiving?

bearing with one another, and forgiving each other, whoever has a complaint against anyone; just as the Lord forgave you, so also should you.

–Colossians 3:13

_____

Our Need for Encouragement

The principles in this book can be life-changing, but we can apply them most easily in an environment in which people encourage us to be honest about our hurt, anger, joys, and hopes. Most of us are not very perceptive about ourselves, and we need other people who can see us objectively and who can affirm us as we continue to understand these matters.

Jason deals with past hurts

Do you know someone like Jason? Jason grew up in a troubled home with parents who abused him verbally and physically. As an adult, he always felt full of shame and had a difficult time accepting Christ's forgiveness. Terri and Brian, a couple in his Sunday School class, affirmed Jason as he told them about his past hurts. As Jason saw God use Terri and Brian to stand by him and accept him even with blots on his past, he began to understand God's forgiveness and acceptance in a way he never had before.

➡ **In the left margin name someone who has encouraged you. Stop and thank God for this individual you just named and for this person's role in your development.**

It also is important to realize that working through these principles once often is not enough. Many whom I have counseled and many who have read this material in its previous edition report that they have experienced dramatic growth only as they have applied these truths at an increasingly deeper level of their lives.

> Name one person who has encouraged you to be honest about your hurts, anger, joys, and hopes.
>
> _____

SUMMARY STATEMENTS

- In the context of honesty, affirmation, and patience, we can focus on the forgiveness we have received, and we can reject the deception and worldly desires that choke out the Word of life.
- God's Word is the source of truth—the truth about Christ, the cross, and redemption—and we should pray that God will speak to us through it.
- We don't grow because we fail to remember what Christ's forgiveness means. The cross is central to our motivation and development.

DAY 2

Renewing Your View of God

The most tragic result of the fall was the fact that human beings became alienated from their Creator. Sin separates people from God's love and security.

Apart from the redeeming work of Christ, people are unable to enjoy a close relationship with the Father as Adam and Eve did before the fall. In fact, people hide from God, as Adam and Eve did. Genesis 3:8 describes this when it says, "And they heard the sound of the Lord God walking in the garden in the cool of the day, and the man and his wife hid themselves from the presence of the Lord God among the trees of the garden."

As a result of hiding from God, people see a distorted view of God. Satan's deception and the world's influence cause this to happen.

Where Do We Get These Ideas?

How do you view God? How accurate are your beliefs about His character? Do you know Him in a close way as He has revealed Himself? Or are your perceptions of Him founded on reason, experience, the human and sometimes faulty examples of parental modeling, and the ideas of others?

✎ In the chart below put a check in the column under the word that indicates the degree to which you feel the adjective in the left column describes your view of God. Answer honestly.

HOW I VIEW GOD	Always	Often	Sometimes	Seldom	Never
Loving					
Faithful					
Sovereign					
Friend					
Compassionate					
All-powerful					
Just					
Wise					

✎ Now go back to the "How I View God" chart. Circle the adjective that most quickly comes to mind when you think about your view of God.

One of the best ways to determine your view of the Lord is to examine your actions. Jesus stressed the relationship between people's actions and beliefs.

✎ In the blanks below write how you normally would respond to the situations listed. Then write how you would respond if you were convinced that God is completely loving, powerful, and wise (your believing response).

What do my actions say?

• Someone has stolen your car.

Normal response:

_____

Believing response:

_____

- **Another firm has bought out the company where you work. Each day someone in your department loses his or her job. You very likely could be next.**

  Normal response:

  _____

  Believing response:

  _____

- **Someone else has just started dating your boyfriend or girlfriend.**

  Normal response:

  _____

  Believing response:

  _____

Trusting Him in all things

Most people say that they know that God is all-powerful, but they won't trust Him to take care of the major events in their lives.

Our actions truly and accurately reflect what we actually believe.

✎ **Check each statement below that describes how you respond to stress in your life.**

  ❏ I tend to trust God more when I'm under stress.
  ❏ I tend to forget about God's power when I'm under stress.
  ❏ I respond as if God has deserted me when life is difficult.
  ❏ I sometimes feel God hates me when I'm feeling stressed.
  ❏ It's easy for me to talk about God's love when things aren't going right in my life..

How we react during stress

Stressful situations can produce questions in our minds about the character of God. Many of us freely talk about God's love when life is going well.

However, when life is difficult, we often grumble and respond as if God has deserted us or as though He hates us.

Keep in mind the statement below.

> It is critical that we accurately know the Lord and walk with Him in the midst of our circumstances. This requires that we base our knowledge of God on an unshifting foundation, His Word, and that we allow Him to speak through His Word to us.

Sometimes our natural thoughts (such as, "Surely God wouldn't allow anyone to go to hell") and circumstances (such as, "How can God be good if this happened?") shape our view of God.

 From the list below check the factors that have helped to shape your present view of God. Mark whether each has had a positive or negative impact on your concept.

	Effect	
	Positive	Negative
❑ Opinions of parents	❑	❑
❑ Opinions of spouse	❑	❑
❑ Opinion of peers	❑	❑
❑ Beliefs of God's nature	❑	❑

that the God of our Lord Jesus Christ, the Father of glory, may give to you a spirit of wisdom and of revelation in the knowledge of Him. I pray that the eyes of your heart may be enlightened, so that you may know what is the hope of His calling, what are the riches of the glory of His inheritance of the saints, and what is the surpassing greatness of His power toward us who believe.
–Ephesians 1:17-19

Read Ephesians 1:17-19 in the left margin. In these verses Paul expressed his prayer for the Ephesians. He asked that the eyes of the Ephesians' hearts be enlightened. Read verses 17-18 and fill in the key words in the verse in the blanks.

Paul asked God to give the Ephesians a spirit of _____ and of _____ in the knowledge of Him. He also asked that the eyes of their heart be _____ , so that they may know what is the hope of His calling, what are the riches of the glory of His _____ in the saints, and what is the surpassing greatness of His _____ toward those who believe.

What difference would it make in your life if the "eyes of your heart" were enlightened so that you could view God more accurately?

_____

_____

A distorted look at the Father

Jim's father was an alcoholic and neglected his children. Jim, a teenager, was active in his church but had a hard time praying because he viewed someone with the name of Father as unconcerned about needs. When Jim was an adult, God used Jim's Sunday School teacher to help "enlighten the eyes" of Jim's heart so Jim could see God accurately as loving and caring.

➥ **Think about a time when something bad happened that caused you to have a distorted view of God. Stop and pray. Ask God to help you understand why that event impacted you negatively and to "enlighten the eyes" of your heart so you might view Him more accurately.**

SUMMARY STATEMENTS

• People say they know God is all-powerful, but they won't trust Him to take care of their major life events. Our actions reflect what we actually believe.
• .We can base our knowledge of God on His Word, and we can allow Him to speak through His Word to us.

The Depths of God's Love

✎ To continue our study of our view of God, read John 1:17-18; 14:8-10, both of which appear in the margin at left. As God speaks to us through these Scriptures, we learn two ways we know the truth about God's character. List those two ways here:

1. _____

2. _____

For the law was given through Moses; grace and truth were realized through Jesus Christ. No man has seen God at any time; the only begotten God, who is in the bosom of the Father, He has explained Him.

–John 1:17-18

Philip said to Him, "Lord, show us the Father, and it is enough for us." Jesus said to him, "Have I been so long with you, and yet you have no come to know Me, Philip? He who has seen me has seen the Father; how do you say, 'Show us the Father'?"

–John 14:8-10

Jesus is the perfect representation of the Father on earth. God's Word and God's Son reveal God's character.

✎ **Christ perfectly reveals the Father to us. Match the following Scriptures with the truths these passages teach about Christ.**

_____ John 4:39 A. He laid down His life for me.
_____ John 10:11 B. My Father loves me as He loves Jesus.
_____ John 14:2-3 C. He knows me.
_____ John 15:13-16 D. He wants me to be with Him for all eternity.
_____ John 17:23 E. Christ is the Good Shepherd.

I never will be unloved again!

What an unbelievable privilege to be wanted by the Almighty God!

Read these selected verses from Psalm 103 below.

Praise Him for who He is

3 Who pardons all your iniquities; Who heals all your diseases;
4 Who redeems your life from the pit; Who crowns you with lovingkindness and compassion;
5 Who satisfies your years with good things, So that your youth is renewed like the eagle.
6 The Lord performs righteous deeds, And judgments for all who are oppressed.
8 The Lord is compassionate and gracious, Slow to anger and abounding in lovingkindness,
9 He will not always strive with us; Nor will He keep His anger forever.
10 He has not dealt with us according to our sins, Nor rewarded us according to our iniquities.
11 For as high as the heavens are above the earth, So great is His lovingkindness toward those who fear Him.
12 As far as the east is from the west, So far has He removed our transgressions from us.
13 Just as a father has compassion on his children, So the Lord has compassion on those who fear Him.
17 But the lovingkindness of the Lord is from everlasting to everlasting on those who fear Him, And His righteousness to children's children,
19 The Lord has established His throne in the heavens; And His sovereignty rules over all.

Now complete the chart below, based on what you read in Psalm 103. I have completed the first line for you.

GOD'S CHARACTERISTICS AND HOW THEY AFFECT ME		
	My Heavenly Father is...	As a result, I...
v. 3	*forgiving*	*am forgiven of all sin*
v. 3		
v. 4		
v. 5		
v. 6		
v. 8		
v. 9		
v. 10		
v. 11		
v. 12		
v. 13		
v. 17		
v. 19		

For example: Verse 3 reminds me that my Father has forgiven me of all my sins. God Himself has removed my transgressions as far as the east is from the west. As a result, I can be free from condemnation. No one can accuse me if God has removed my transgressions. My Father loves me—as much as the heavens are above the earth. When I begin to feel discouraged or when others reject me, I can remember the depth of God's love for me. I never will be unloved again!

I never will be unloved again!

> When Jesus therefore saw His mother, and the disciple whom He loved standing nearby, He said to His mother, "Woman, behold your son!"
>
> –John 19:26

 By reading about those who surrounded Christ on earth, we can learn about how Christ's love for us should make us feel. Read John 19:26 at left. In this verse Christ, as He hung on the cross, commissioned the disciple John to take care of His mother. How did John, who wrote this passage, refer to himself?

John called himself the _____ whom Jesus _____ .

Do you think of yourself as the disciple Jesus loves?   ❏ Yes ❏ No

Why or why not? _____

But seek first His kingdom and His righteousness; and all these things shall be added to you. Therefore do not be anxious for tomorrow; for tomorrow will care for itself. Each day has enough trouble of its own.

–Matthew 6:33

And my God shall supply all your needs according to His riches in glory in Christ Jesus.

–Philippians 4:19

This is just as true of you! Try introducing yourself this week to a Christian friend by saying, "I'm the disciple Jesus loves!" or, "I'm the believer who has all my needs provided for." (See Matthew 6:33 and Philippians 4:19 at left for examples of what Christ has done for you.)

 Try writing in the blank below a statement about yourself and Christ's love for you like the one John the disciple made about himself.

I'm _____

You, of course, can use common sense in determining to whom you make such statements, but it is important to begin verbalizing scriptural truths. Verbalizing God's Word will reinforce it in your mind and will enable you more readily to replace false beliefs with His truth.

Praise Him for who He is

➡ **Look at your answers to the questions for today. Take some time to reflect on God's love and power. Praise Him for who He is and thank Him specifically for what He has done for you. Tell Him how grateful you are. Tell Him why you are grateful. Review your study of Psalm 103.**

➡ **Read these verses from Psalm 145 below. Notice the characteristics of God and His activities in our lives.**

3 Great is the Lord, and highly to be praised; And His greatness is unsearchable.
4 One generation shall praise Thy works to another, And shall declare Thy mighty acts.
5 On the glorious splendor of Thy majesty, And on Thy wonderful works, I will meditate.
8 The Lord is gracious and merciful; Slow to anger and great in lovingkindness.
9 The Lord is good to all, And His mercies are over all His works.
14 The Lord sustains all who fall, And raises up all who are bowed down.
17 The Lord is righteous in all His ways, And kind in all His deeds.
18 The Lord is near to all who call upon Him, To all who call upon Him in truth.

 In the blanks below write which four descriptions of God in this psalm make the most difference in your life. (Answers could be: great, gracious, sustaining, and so on.)

_____   _____

_____   _____

Develop the praise habit!

Develop a habit of praising God and of focusing on what Scripture says is true of Him. Memorizing Scripture and allowing God to work through that Scripture to make a difference in your life will help you renew your mind and will give you a true and proper knowledge of God.

> Knowing God is the most critical issue in all of life.

J.I. Packer writes in his book *Knowing God*, "Knowing about God is crucially important for the living of our lives. As it would be cruel to an Amazonian tribesman to fly him to London, put him down without explanation in Trafalgar Square and leave him, as one who knows nothing of English or England, to fend for himself, so we are cruel to ourselves if we try to live in this world without knowing about the God whose world it is and who runs it."[1]

Satan's message: God won't accept someone like you

It is critical that we accurately know the one true God. We will follow only the One whom we know and trust. Satan deceives us by distorting God's character. Satan gives us messages such as: *If you follow and obey God, you'll be miserable. God doesn't love you because you did this. God won't accept someone like you.*

God's message: love

By deceiving us about God's love and power, Satan robs us of the desire to love, obey, and honor Him.

SUMMARY STATEMENTS

- Jesus is the perfect representation of the Father on earth. God's Word and God's Son reveal God's character.
- It is an unbelievable privilege to be wanted by the Almighty God!
- When we begin to feel discouraged or when others reject us, we can remember the depth of God's love. We never will be unloved again!
- Knowing God is the most critical issue in all of life.

DAY 4

Dealing with Emotional Scars

As you begin to be honest about your emotions and to reject what seems to contradict God's Word and replace it with God's truths, you can realize how much the lies of the enemy have influenced you. Many of our beliefs are lies!

We live in a fallen world with fallen individuals. As a result, much of what we've learned about ourselves and the world (our belief system) is distorted.

The world is not becoming closer to the truth but is straying farther from it.

Sadly, the world is not becoming closer and closer to the truth but is straying farther from it. The results are tragic.

Many individuals have been reared in broken homes without one or both parents. Others have gone through traumatic events in their lives. Some have grown up in home environments that drove them to perform and that rejected them when they failed.

Do you know any persons like the ones listed below, or have any of their experiences happened to you?

- Bill's parents never told him they loved him.
- Teresa's dad left when she was 5 years old.
- Ginger's aunt consistently told her she was ugly and asked Ginger why she wasn't beautiful like her sister.
- Peter's girlfriend was pregnant at age 16.
- Regina's teacher told her she'd never make it.
- Justin's father told him he never would be successful.
- Employers rejected Julie three times in her job search.

Search me, O God, and know my heart; Try me and know my anxious thoughts; And see if there be any hurtful way in me, And lead me in the everlasting way.
–Psalm 139:23-24

➡ **Find a quiet place where you won't be disturbed and ask God to reveal any particular events in your past that significantly affect the way you view yourself today. Use as your prayer Psalm 139:23-24, which appears in the left margin. Simply ask God to point out specific instances in your life. It may help if you limit this to a specific fear (failure, rejection, punishment, shame). For example: "Father, show me a particular event in my life in which I experienced rejection."**

Events like the ones you thought about (and countless others) dramatically affect our belief system.

> The incredibly good news is: "If any man is in Christ, he is a new creature. The old things passed away; behold, new things have come."
> –2 Corinthians 5:17

We can't relive the past, but we can deal with damaging experiences so they don't continue to influence our self-worth.

Can we do anything about our past? Yes and no. Obviously, we can't go back and relive it. We never can escape its negative circumstances. However, we can deal with previous poor choices and damaging experiences so that they don't continue to influence our self-worth.

How do we deal with painful events of the past? Recovering from past wounds is not a 1-2-3-step process. Closing the chapter and relinquishing memories of hurtful experiences require the powerful enlightenment of the Holy Spirit and our cooperation with Him. The following may serve as a helpful guide to you during this process.

Seeing the past with a new eye

✎ **Briefly describe one of the past events that came to your mind in the above exercise.**

_____

_____

Now honestly describe how you felt about the event then.

_____

_____

Next describe how you feel about the event now.

_____

_____

➡ At this point you may want to talk to your prayer partner or to a trusted friend about your feelings before you continue this process.

✎ Now list all the persons who contributed to this distressing situation.

_____   _____

_____   _____

And be kind to one another, tender-hearted, forgiving each other, just as God in Christ also has forgiven you.
—Ephesians 4:32

And we know that God causes all things to work together for good to those who love God, to those who are called according to His purpose.
—Romans 8:28

And as for you, you meant evil against me, but God meant it for good in order to bring about this present result.
—Genesis 50:20

Read Ephesians 4:32 (this and the next two verses appear in the left margin). Forgive these persons just as God in Christ has forgiven you.

Read Romans 8:28. Thank God that He can use this situation, even though distressing, for good in your life.

Remember Joseph's words in Genesis 50:20: " 'You meant evil against me, but God meant it for good.' "

✎ Now list the four false beliefs below. (You probably can list them totally from memory by now.) Check the false belief that influenced your thoughts and behavior in the distressing situation you have described.

1. _____

2. _____

3. _____

4. _____

➡ Confess having believed Satan's deception; then reject each lie and replace it with its corresponding truth. Say these truths aloud from memory if possible.

Use these to reject Satan's lies

A REFRESHER ON GOD'S TRUTHS

"There is therefore now no condemnation for those who are in Christ Jesus" (Romans 8:1). You are free from condemnation!

"Therefore, if any man is in Christ, he is a new creature; the old things passed away: behold, new things have come" (2 Corinthians 5:17). The old has gone, and you are a new creature.

➡ Other incidents may exist in your life that God wants to bring to your memory. Right now you may not remember them at all, but in time and with God's help, they likely will come to mind. Pray that God will choose the best time to reveal these to you and ask Him to help you be objective and honest about the pain of your past.

Recovering from hurt requires:
• **The Holy Spirit's insight**
• **Willingness**
• **Patience**
• **Persistence**
• **Time**
• **Application of God's Word**

We can use the above principles as guidelines in the process of turning loose of past painful events. Painful memories don't vanish simply because we decide we want to be rid of them. Recovering from the anguish of hurtful events requires the Holy Spirit's grace and insight, combined with willingness, patience, persistence, time, and our application of God's Word. The truths given here and as God reveals them to us through Scripture will influence our lives only to the degree that we recognize our need for these truths.

As we pursue comfort and happiness, many of us have managed to bury past instances of neglect, rejection, embarrassment, abuse, and failure. We either deny the impact these distressing instances have had on our lives, or we escape through alcohol, drugs, sex, or unhealthy emotional attachments.

Margaret's story

Margaret, a recovering alcoholic with two years of sobriety, couldn't understand why she so often was angry at men. When she was a child, her father neglected her emotionally. Since adolescence, she felt that male peers had rejected her. For years her alcoholism had numbed her from the pain of these hurtful memories. Once she regained her sobriety, she worked through a 12-step program. In the process she decided to forgive the men who rejected her. This was a good start, but Margaret stopped too quickly in the process. She failed to recognize that she needed to apply to all areas of life the steps given her for recovery. As she tried to avoid the sin of constantly harboring resentment, she denied her negative feelings about her father, rather than allowing the Lord to help her work through them.

If merely thinking about a past event causes you to have a strong emotional reaction, this event likely has affected your self-esteem. It takes a while for deeply rooted beliefs about ourselves to disappear. You may find it emotionally painful to focus on God's truths and to reject past beliefs. But that pain will be far less intense than what you will feel if false beliefs rule your life.

➡ Use the outline you followed earlier to deal with any past events God has laid on your heart. Move away from thinking about the event and realizing your feelings. Move to forgiving persons involved to rejecting Satan's lies and believing God's truths.

If you got in touch with some painful memories during this lesson, you may want to study another LIFE Support course, *Making Peace with Your Past*. For this study to be most effective, you can participate in a support group.

SUMMARY STATEMENTS

• We can't go back and relive the past, but we can deal with damaging experiences so they don't continue to influence our self-worth.
• Focusing on past hurts will be far less painful than allowing false beliefs to continue to rule your life.

Forgiving at a Deeper Level

forgiveness–n. the act of ceasing to feel resentment against (an offender)...the granting of relief from payment of a debt (Webster's)

As hurts from our past continue to surface, we often need to begin learning how to forgive at a deeper level.

 Read the definition of *forgiveness* in the left margin. Then in these blanks write what *forgiveness* means to you.

_____

_____

Forgiveness always is a decision, and usually it's a difficult one. Forgiveness and understanding are next of kin, but they're not the same.

Read this illustration to see if it helps you understand what genuine forgiveness means:

Can we forgive like this?

THE BORROWED CAR

Let's say I just purchased a new car. You ask me if you can borrow it for a day. I loan the car to you. You have the misfortune of wrecking it during the first hour it's in your care.

Perhaps the accident occurred in understandable circumstances. Maybe it was pouring rain, the streets were slick, and someone cut in front of you. That's understandable. But "understandable" isn't going to pay the repair cost for my car.

That's the difference. Forgiveness is counting the cost and releasing others from the debt they owe. If I really release you from this debt, I'll resist the urge to remind you about my car. I won't look at you and wink each time the word *car* is mentioned in conversation.

I won't tell you that I've been turning up the radio to avoid hearing the clanky noises my car now makes. Nor will I say, "It's OK, but don't ask to borrow my car again!"

The wisest decision may be for me not to loan you my car again, depending on your driving record. But if I am to forgive you, I must release you from even the guilt of the penalty you would have owed me.

If I genuinely forgive you, I'll also refrain from walking to my car blindfolded so I won't have to see the damage. Forgiveness counts the cost and then releases the offender from the penalty that is owed.

But if you do not forgive men, then your Father will not forgive your transgressions.

–Matthew 6:15

And whenever you stand praying, forgive, if you have anything against anyone; so that your Father also who is in heaven may forgive you your transgressions.

–Mark 11:25

And be kind to one another, tender-hearted, forgiving each other, just as God in Christ also has forgiven you.

–Ephesians 4:32

And when you were dead in your transgressions and the uncircumcision of your flesh, He made you alive together with Him, having forgiven us all our transgressions, having canceled out the certificate of debt consisting of decrees against us and which was hostile to us; and He has taken it out of the way, having nailed it to the cross.

–Colossians 2:13-14

For it was the Father's good pleasure for all the fulness to dwell in Him, and through Him to reconcile all things to Himself, having made peace through the blood of His cross; through Him, I say, whether things on earth or things in heaven. And although you were formerly alienated and hostile in mind, engaged in evil deeds, yet He has now reconciled you in His fleshly body through death, in order to present you before Him holy and blameless and beyond reproach.

–Colossians 1:19-22

Three things involved in forgiveness:
1. An injury
2. A debt resulting from it
3. Cancellation of the debt

✎ **Read the following Scriptures: Matthew 6:15; Mark 11:25; Ephesians 4:32. All appear in the left margin. After reading these Scriptures, check three reasons the Bible gives to show why we should forgive.**

- ❑ 1. An unforgiving spirit hurts us.
- ❑ 2. We will profit financially if we forgive.
- ❑ 3. God commands us to forgive others through Jesus Christ.
- ❑ 4. God has forgiven us through Jesus Christ.
- ❑ 5. People will accept us if we forgive them.
- ❑ 6. Forgiving will cause us to perform better.

✎ **Read Colossians 2:13-14 (in the left margin) and answer this question: How has God extended forgiveness to you through Christ?**

_____

_____

✎ **Read Colossians 1:19-22 (in the left margin) and answer this question: What does it mean to you to know that you are a friend of God?**

_____

_____

> God has extended forgiveness to us through His Son's saving work on the cross. We are reconciled to God through the blood of Jesus.

✎ **Check the statements below that show what effect our reconciliation to God has in our lives.**

- ❑ Christ has avenged the righteous wrath of God for our sins.
- ❑ We are not justified in God's sight.
- ❑ We are justified in God's sight and are fully pleasing to Him despite our sin.
- ❑ We are reconciled to our Creator through the sacrifice of His blood.
- ❑ We can enjoy intimate fellowship with Him.

In his book *Forgiveness* Charles Stanley writes that three elements are essential to the process of forgiving: an injury, a debt resulting from the injury, and a cancellation of the debt.[2] The act of forgiving requires that we look honestly at our injury, how it has affected us in the past, and how it may continue to affect us in the future.

➡ **Pray for God's direction as you complete the next portion of the chart. You will focus on the persons whose names you wrote down on day 4 who you feel have wronged you. Ask God for an open heart and mind.**

✎ **Look back at day 4. Study the list of persons who wronged you. Use the chart on the next page as an example to follow on a separate sheet of** paper on which you'll have more room to write. Write in column 1 the persons who have offended or harmed you. In column 2 write what each person did to harm you. In column 3 write what would be necessary for you to do to release each person for the penalty he or she owes you. (Answer specifically for each person.) This is most difficult to do. Listen for God's leadership.

FORGIVING OTHERS CHART					
Persons who offended me	What each did	What releasing each requires	Date forgiven, how expressed	Results You	Them
1.					
2.					
3.					
4.					

As we deal with the hurt, anger, and grief we have experienced because of an injury, we determine how much we feel we are owed because of it. At this point we may be tempted to indulge in self-pity, hatred, bitterness, and depression. We also may want to seek revenge against the one who has harmed us.

Understanding how deep His forgiveness is gives us the compassion, mercy, and motivation to forgive others.

Until we can truly understand how great our own sin is and how much grief it brings to God and others, we neither can fully appreciate nor fully experience how much it cost Christ to forgive us. Understanding how deep His forgiveness is toward us provides us with the compassion, mercy, and motivation to forgive others.

 Pray daily about the persons you listed above. As the healing process begins, complete column 4 by writing the date you forgave the person and how you expressed forgiveness.

Remember that forgiveness does not mean overlooking an injury or denying its painful consequences in our lives. We never can experience healing from our wounds by neglect. Just as an untreated bodily wound would harm our physical health, failing to treat injuries others cause results in even more damage to our emotional, spiritual, relational, and mental well-being.

 Just as failure to treat injuries others inflict will cause even more damage, positive effects will result in our lives as we forgive others. As you forgive persons watch for the results of your forgiveness. Complete the first part of column 5 by showing the results in your life.

If we are willing to forgive others, that willingness assures us that God is working in our lives through His Holy Spirit and that we are, indeed, recipients of His generous mercy and forgiveness. We can love and be grateful to the Lord more as we become reconciled to a previous offender and therefore grasp how important it is that we are reconciled to God through

Christ. We can be freed from a preoccupation with a past event and can be able to focus on present matters that deserve our attention. We can experience the benefits of peace with others, enabling God to meet our needs for companionship and intimacy and giving Him an opportunity to free us from the destructive effects of prolonged anger, self-pity, resentment, and depression.

 In the last column in the chart on page 178 write the effect of your forgiveness on the person.

We have no guarantees that obeying God will cause others to respond to us positively. However, if others realize they've hurt us and if they see we're willing to forgive them, it's possible they may show their gratitude. It may give them a sense of joy as they experience Christ's love through us. They may feel more comfortable in our presence; but if they are Christians, they may be more highly motivated to continue serving the Lord. If they are not believers, God may use our forgiveness as a way to bring them to a trusting relationship with Him.

> But if you do not forgive men, then your Father will not forgive your transgressions.
> –Matthew 6:15

 Read Matthew 6:15 in the margin at left. What are the consequences of an unwillingness to forgive people?

_____

_____

When you don't forgive, you:
- **Are consumed with the event**
- **May avoid the person**
- **Miss being with the person**
- **May become depressed**

If you choose to withhold forgiveness from others, you likely will become resentful. This will carry over into all of your relationships, including your relationship with God. You may become absorbed in thinking about the person who has harmed you, how this has hurt you, and how you can get even. Or you may avoid this person. As a result, you may miss the benefits that might accompany companionship with him or her. If your anger is prolonged and intense, it may result in severe depression or even in physical problems.

 List the negative effects of unforgiveness on the person you can't forgive.

_____

_____

Unforgiveness harms others by:
- **Alienation from you**
- **Deep anxiety about you**
- **Confusion about your behavior**

If the person who has injured you is unaware of the harm he or she has caused you, he or she likely may be confused by your behavior. Besides feeling alienated from you, this person may experience deep anxiety about you and your relationship.

> Bless those who persecute you, bless and curse not.
> –Romans 12:14

Read Romans 12:14 in the margin at left. Write what it says about how you will treat someone who has harmed you.

_____

_____

We never may be able to forget completely what another person did to harm us. It may not be possible to wipe the incident out of our minds completely. However, if we truly forgive, the memory of the offense will not cloud how we perceive that individual.

Harvey's boss, Derrick, fired him two days after assuring Harvey that he had a bright future with the company. Harvey had left a secure job he had held for 10 years to take the position with Derrick's company. He had uprooted his family and left behind many friends. Now he was unemployed. The next several years were nightmares for Harvey as he struggled to find new employment and to support his family. Harvey wondered if he ever could forgive Derrick. Gradually, however, after much prayer and allowing God to speak to him through His Word, Harvey found that he was able to forgive his cruel former boss. Of course he never forgot the incident, but Harvey was able to distinguish between the individual and his harmful behavior.

When we forgive, we:
- **Think compassionate thoughts**
- **Bless rather than insult**
- **See person apart from action**

Eventually, when we forgive, our thoughts about the person who harmed us increasingly can be characterized by love and compassion; and we can extend a blessing rather than an insult to him or her.

➡️ **It's time for a quick refresher course on your memory work on the affirmation "My Identity in Christ." Review the entire affirmation and repeat it again from memory.**

✎ **Review this week's lessons. Pray and ask God to identify one positive statement that had an impact on your understanding of who you are.**

Write that statement in your own words.

_____

_____

Rewrite your thoughts as a prayer of thankfulness to God.

_____

_____

You probably gained many insights as you worked through this week's lessons. Which insight stands out to you? Write it here.

_____

_____

Notes
[1] J. I. Packer, *Knowing God* (Downer Grove: InterVarsity Press, 1973), 14.
[2] Charles Stanley, *Forgiveness* (Nashville: Oliver-Nelson Books, 1987), 16.

OUR SOURCE OF CHANGE

Case in point

RIGHT DEEDS, WRONG REASONS

Cindy volunteered in her community above and beyond the call of duty. She helped senior adults with crafts activities two days a week, served meals to homeless people on Saturdays, and chaired the fund-raising campaign for the hospital's burns unit. Cindy exhausted herself helping other people. But Cindy was a nonbeliever. She openly told others that her world had no place for God or anything about Him. She said she did these good deeds only to help humanity. (Read more about Cindy's story on page 183.) What does Cindy need in her life?

What you'll learn this week

This week you'll—

- learn why the Heavenly Father sent us the Holy Spirit and how He motivates us to growth;
- see how the Holy Spirit shows us our sins and shows us how we base our self-worth on false beliefs;
- learn how the Holy Spirit can help us to right our wrongs with other people;
- learn how the Holy Spirit can help us avoid being preoccupied with ourselves and our worries;
- study how the Holy Spirit gives us special people in our lives to model Christ to us.

What you'll study each day

The Holy Spirit's Character, Role	The Holy Spirit's Conviction	Confession	Obstacles to His Presence	More Obstacles
DAY 1	DAY 2	DAY 3	DAY 4	DAY 5

Memory verse

A key verse to memorize this week

I will ask the Father, and He will give you another Helper, that He may be with you forever.

–John 14:16

WordWatch

Words to help you understand this week's lessons

spiritual fruit–n. the characteristics of Christ as they are reproduced in His followers. (*Example: The love of Christ produces in us **spiritual fruit**.*)

abide–v. to live, grow, and gain your sustenance from. (*Example: The power of God lives in every believer who **abides** in Him.*)

convict–v. to convince of error or sinfulness. (*Example: The Holy Spirit **convicts** us of ungodliness.*)

confess–v. to admit oneself guilty of what one is accused, as a result of inward conviction (*Example: I **confessed** my sins to God.*)

The Holy Spirit's Character, Role

The truths we have examined in this book can impact greatly our every goal and relationship, but now we need to understand how to put them into practice in our lives. How can we begin to experience positive change? Jesus answered this question in John 13—16, the last time He instructed His disciples personally. He told them that He soon would be put to death but that they would not be left alone. Read in the left margin one of the comforting statements He told them, in John 14:16-17.

And I will ask the Father, and He will give you another Helper, that He may be with you forever; that is the Spirit of truth, whom the world cannot receive, because it does not behold Him or know Him, but you know Him because He abides with you, and will be in you.
–John 14:16-17

That Helper He speaks about in the Scripture is the Holy Spirit, who came some 50 days later to direct and to give power to the believers at Pentecost. That same Holy Spirit lives in each believer today. The Holy Spirit serves as our instructor, counselor, and source of spiritual power as we live for Christ's glory and honor.

But the Helper, the Holy Spirit, whom the Father will send in My name, He will teach you all things, and bring to your remembrance all that I said to you.
–John 14:26

Who is the Holy Spirit, and why did He come? The Holy Spirit, the third Person of the Trinity, is God and has all the characteristics of God. His primary purpose is to glorify Christ, bring attention to Him, and help you remember him (see the verse at left.) Christ said, " 'He shall glorify Me; for He shall take of Mine, and shall disclose it to you' " (John 16:14). The Holy Spirit is our teacher. He guides us into the truth of the Scriptures. By His power that the love of Christ flows through us and produces **spiritual fruit** (see definition at left) in us. The New Testament describes this spiritual fruit in these ways:

spiritual fruit–n. the characteristics of Christ as they are reproduced in His followers

---

WAYS WE DISPLAY SPIRITUAL FRUIT

Intimate friendship with Christ (John 15:12)
Love for one another (John 15:12)
Peace and joy in the midst of difficulties (John 14:27; 15:11)
Steadfastness (Ephesians 5:18-21)
Evangelism and discipleship (Matthew 28:18-20)

Why Do We Need the Holy Spirit?

Why is it necessary for us to have the Holy Spirit? Why do we need Him?

✎ **For this answer read John 14:16-17 in the left margin above. Mark the following statements as *T* (true) or *F* (false).**

_____ Christ realized that you never could live the Christian life in your own effort.

_____ Your sinful nature in some way clouds your understanding and ability to apply God's truths.

_____ You need a Helper who will be with you forever and who will live in you.

_____ The Holy Spirit's role as your Helper is to enable you to understand and to apply biblical truth.

Not a self-improvement program

I am the true vine, and My Father is the vine dresser. **Abide** in Me, and I in you. As the branch cannot bear fruit of itself, unless it abides in the vine, so neither can you unless you abide in Me. I am the vine, you are the branches; he who abide in Me, and I in him, he bears much fruit; for apart from Me you can do nothing.
    –John 15:1, 4-5

abide–v. to live, grow, and gain your sustenance from

As we all know, the Christian life is not easy. It is not simply a self-improvement program. True, at times we may be able to change some of our habits, such as stopping the blame game and the performance trap, through our own discipline and determination, but Christianity is not merely self-effort. We need some special help. In the Christian life we rely on Christ as our resource for direction, encouragement, and strength. In one of the most widely known metaphors of the Bible, Christ described the Christian life in John 15: 1, 4-5 (see the Scripture at left). He used the illustration of a branch and a vine. A definition of one of the key words in the verse appears under the Scripture.

Did you read correctly? Did the verse really say "Apart from Me you can do nothing"? Did it really mean *nothing?* That's right—nothing. Although we may do other things that take a lot of work and use much energy at great personal cost, only things that we do for Christ's glory in the power of His Spirit have eternal value. The very power of God that was evident when God raised Christ from the dead (Ephesians 1:19-21) is available to every believer who abides in Him, who desires that He be honored, and who trusts that His Spirit will produce fruit in his or her life.

✎ **Read John 15:1,4-5 above. Describe below how you feel when you realize you can do nothing apart from Jesus.**

_____

_____

Why did Cindy volunteer?

Cindy volunteered in her community above and beyond the call of duty. She helped senior adults with crafts activities two days a week; she served meals to homeless people on Saturdays; and she chaired the fund-raising campaign for the hospital's burns unit. Cindy exhausted herself helping other people. But Cindy was a nonbeliever. She openly told others that she had no place for God in her life. She said she did these good deeds only to help humanity.

✎ **Think about a time when you did a good deed only for personal gain. Write about it here. Then stop and pray, asking God to help you do good deeds only for His glory.**

_____

_____

The Foundation of Growth

Just as the cross of Christ is the basis of our relationship with God, it also is the foundation of our spiritual growth. Christ's death is the supreme demonstration of God's love, power, and wisdom. The more we understand and apply the truths of justification, propitiation, reconciliation, and regeneration, the more our lives will reflect His character.

> Nothing is more motivating, brings more comfort, makes us want to honor Christ more, or gives us more compassion for others than Christ's sacrifice, which has rescued us from eternal condemnation.

Spiritual growth is not magic. It comes as we apply Christ's love and forgiveness in our daily circumstances. It happens as we reflect on the way Christ has accepted us unconditionally.

It happens as we choose to respond to situations and people in light of His sovereign purpose and His kindness toward us.

As we read in the previous chapter, the apostle Peter stated very clearly that our forgiveness, bought by the death of Christ, is the foundation of spiritual growth.

Read 2 Peter 1:5-9 at left to see why we need spiritual growth.

• •

Now for this very reason also, applying all diligence, in your faith supply moral excellence, and in your moral excellence, knowledge; and in your knowledge, self-control, and in your self-control, perseverance, and in your perseverance, godliness; and in your godliness, brotherly kindness, and in your brotherly kindness, love. For if these qualities are yours and are increasing, they render you neither useless nor unfruitful in the true knowledge of our Lord Jesus Christ. For he who lacks these qualities is blind or short-sighted, having forgotten his purification from his former sins.

2 Peter 1:5-9

If we forget about forgiveness, we will not grow spiritually. We won't understand how Christ accepts us unconditionally, and we won't understand all He has done for us.

Jay's coworker gossiped about him at work. Jay confronted his coworker and told him that this gossip hurt him. The coworker asked Jay to forgive him but Jay continued to be bitter and resentful.

Jay was an active church member but since this incident occurred at work Jay felt he was getting little out of his Bible study. His lack of forgiveness kept him from growing spiritually like he should be doing.

A quick way to stop growing

✎ **Describe a time when you've been bitter and as a result have failed to forgive someone. How did that attitude keep you from growing spiritually?**

_____

_____

_____

✎ **To review, see if you can list below the four false beliefs.**

1. _____

_____

2. _____

_____

3. _____

_____

4. _____

_____

✎ Listed below are the four truths from God's Word. Write the truth or quote it aloud from memory. Look at the inside back cover if you need help.

Justification: _____

Propitiation: _____

Reconciliation: _____

Regeneration: _____

SUMMARY STATEMENTS

* Although we may do other things that take a lot of work and use much energy, only things that we do for Christ's glory have worth in His eyes.
* The more we understand and apply the truths of justification, propitiation, reconciliation, and regeneration, the more our lives will reflect His character.
* If we forget about forgiveness, we will not grow spiritually. We won't understand how Christ accepts us unconditionally, and we won't understand all He has done for us.

DAY 2

convict–v. to convince of error or sinfulness (Webster's)

The Holy Spirit's Conviction

The work of the Holy Spirit to **convict** you (see the left margin for definition) is God's way of showing you that your thoughts and/or actions go against your new nature in Christ. As we have seen, our ungodly thoughts, painful emotions, and disobedient actions usually begin in our false belief system.

The Holy Spirit convicts us of ungodliness in order to—

* expose the wrongdoing;
* expose the fact that ungodliness is based in false beliefs;
* reestablish God's truth as the root of our thoughts and actions;
* draw us back into a life of love and service for Christ.

✎ Write in your own words what the conviction of the Holy Spirit means to you and how you see it working in your life.

_____

_____

The Holy Spirit's conviction means that He shows us our sins as they relate to false beliefs so that we can be drawn to the truths of God's Word and to His love for us as persons.

Some Common Mistakes

The following represent some common mistakes we make when the Holy Spirit convicts us of sin.

Trying to understand on our own

Leaning on our own understanding. The Lord has given the Holy Spirit to convict us of sin. The Holy Spirit needs no help in discovering what sins He wants to reveal to us.

A mature believer knows that the Father does not deal all at one time with every sin His children have committed. We might go for a long period of time before the Holy Spirit puts His finger on something we should or should not be doing. Our Heavenly Father knows we would be discouraged if we realized how far from the mark our performance is, so He begins to shape that performance by revealing to us a few sins at a time. The important issue is not that we realize all the sins we commit but that we respond to those He wishes to show us.

The Holy Spirit's work of conviction begins as He reveals our obviously sinful acts to us—stealing or lying, for instance. Then, as we mature, His conviction more often focuses on sins of omission than commission—more on what we do not do than what we do. Avoid leaning on your own or any other person's understanding about what is sin in your life. Study the Scriptures to see what God reveals that He wants for you and listen to the conviction of the Holy Spirit.

 Stop at this point and pray, asking the Holy Spirit to help you recognize the sins that He wants to reveal to you and not simply to rely on your own ideas about what might be sinful in your life.

Sins, not guilty feelings

Confusing guilt with conviction. You commit enough sins without having to worry about thoughts and actions that aren't sins at all. Take your thoughts and deeds before the Lord to see what He thinks of them. Ask Him to show you which are guilt feelings and which actually are sins.

Not a condemnation

Turning conviction into condemnation. God has declared you to be righteous, holy, and blameless. Christ bore all the condemnation you deserved at the cross. Therefore, the Holy Spirit's conviction of sin in your life is not a condemnation of you. His purpose is to turn you from the sin back to God's ways for abundant living.

A wrong set of standards

Not recognizing the root of sins. Ungodly thoughts and actions usually reflect the false beliefs you use to evaluate yourself. One of the Holy Spirit's goals in pointing out your sin is for you to see that you are basing your self-worth on false beliefs.

 Describe which of the above mistakes you make most often. How does making this mistake affect you?

_____

_____

Use these points of conviction to identify false beliefs, reject them, and replace them with God's truths.

✎ Put a check by the false belief and God's truth as you quote aloud the statement of each.

False Beliefs	God's Truths
❑ The Performance Trap	❑ Justification
❑ Approval Addict	❑ Reconciliation
❑ The Blame Game	❑ Propitiation
❑ Shame	❑ Regeneration

➥ Stop and pray, asking God to help you understand why you make the frequent mistake you listed in the exercise at the bottom of the previous page. Ask Him to help you respond in the proper way when the Holy Spirit convicts you of sin.

SUMMARY STATEMENTS

- The work of the Holy Spirit to convict you is God's way of showing you that your thoughts and/or actions go against your new nature in Christ.
- Avoid leaning on your own or any other person's understanding about what is sin in your life.
- Christ bore all the condemnation you deserved at the cross. Therefore, the Holy Spirit's conviction of sin in your life is not a condemnation of you.

DAY 3

If we confess our sins, He is faithful and righteous to forgive us our sins and cleanse us from all unrighteousness.
—1 John 1:9

confess–v.to admit oneself guilty of what one is accused of, as a result of inward conviction (Vine's)

Confession

The Holy Spirit convicts us of sins so that we will be brought to a point of confession, repentance, and forgiveness. Read what the verse in the margin at left says will happen if we **confess** (see definition at left) our sins.

Confession means *to agree with*. Confession is not dragging from our memory all the sins we've ever committed and telling them to God. Confession is agreeing with God about the specific sin of which we are convicted.

We agree with God about sin in three ways:

1. **Agreement**—I sinned when I (name a certain sin). The lie, or false belief, I was believing about myself when I sinned was (name the false belief).

2. **Claiming forgiveness**—I am forgiven through Christ's death on the cross.

3. **Repentance**—I am deeply loved, completely forgiven, fully pleasing, totally accepted, and absolutely complete in Christ. I now choose to act in a way that honors Him, which means I will (name what you will do differently).

Not just feeling sorry

repent–v. to change one's mind or purpose for the better (Vine's)

Our confession does not make us forgiven. We have forgiveness because Christ died to pay for our sins. Confession is a way for us to *experience* our forgiveness, not a means for us to *obtain* it. We can confess with an attitude of repentance—turning away from sin and turning to God. To **repent** (see definition at left) doesn't mean feeling sorry just because we got caught. True confession causes us to reject sin because it grieves the Lord. Confession allows us to know forgiveness and to enjoy fellowship with God.

✎ **Write in the blanks below what *confession* means to you.**

Confession means _____

_____.

Here is an example of a proper confession of sin:

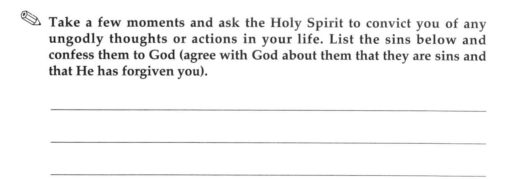

Telling It All to God

Dear Father,

The Holy Spirit has pointed out to me that I sinned when I (name specific thoughts and actions). I was believing the lie (name specific false belief) when I sinned. Thank You that I am completely forgiven and that You choose not to remember my sin. I know that You have decided and declared me to be deeply loved, completely forgiven, fully pleasing, totally accepted, and—absolutely complete in Christ.

Amen.

✎ **Take a few moments and ask the Holy Spirit to convict you of any ungodly thoughts or actions in your life. List the sins below and confess them to God (agree with God about them that they are sins and that He has forgiven you).**

_____

_____

_____

Understanding More About Confession

The following points will give you some added insights about confession.

Against Thee, Thee only, I have sinned, And done what is evil in Thy sight.
　　　　　　　　　–Psalm 51:4a

Why have you despised the word of the Lord by doing evil in His sight?
　　　　　　　　　–2 Samuel 12:9

• **All sin is against God.** Notice that David recognized this in Psalm 51:4, shown at left. He committed adultery with Bathsheba and had her husband murdered to cover up his sin. Although his sin had affected others, David recognized that when he sinned, he primarily did so against God. Now read in the second verse at left what the prophet Nathan said in confronting David about this sin. Notice that the focus is on God, not on David or on others.

When we have the truth of God's Word to guide us, and we still choose to sin, God says we are *despising* Him. Few of us openly would tell God that we have no use for His Word or, worse, that we despise Him; yet that actually is what we do when we sin against Him. Perhaps if before choosing to sin, we would say to God, "I despise You and Your Word," we would be more enlightened about how sin grieves our Heavenly Father.

• **Confession recognizes the full scope of sin.** Correct confession requires that we not only recognize a specific act as sinful but that we also understand that the ungodly thoughts and false beliefs which generated the ungodliness are sinful as well. The excuses we might use to justify our sin are part of the ungodly thoughts that cause us to act in an ungodly manner. Narrowly defining sin as only a wrong action is misleading. Deal with the root of the action: the false belief.

• **Confession involves accepting our forgiveness in Christ.** All too often, Christians construct a penance cycle that they believe they must put themselves through before they can feel forgiven. Once convicted of a sin, they might plead with God for forgiveness and then feel depressed for a couple of days to show that they are really sorry and deserve to be forgiven.

This cycle is typical of "works-righteousness." The Lord Jesus died on the cross for our sins and has declared us justified. We cannot earn our forgiveness by punishing ourselves. Confession simply is an application of the forgiveness we already have. Accepting our forgiveness allows us to move on in fellowship with the Lord and to serve Him joyfully. God does not put us on the shelf and declare us permanently unusable because of our sin. Even after Peter denied Christ, he experienced forgiveness. God used Peter powerfully as a leader of the church.

Used powerfully by God

• **True confession involves repentance.** Repentance means turning away from sin and turning instead to God. When we truly repent, our attitude about sin changes. In fact, because repentance involves recognizing how serious our sin is, our sin should grieve us as much as it does God.

restitution–n. restoring something to its rightful owner, a making good of or giving an equivalent for some injury (Webster's)

• **True confession may involve restitution.** (See definition at left.) In confession, it may be necessary to make right a wrong. You may need to confess your sin to an individual to ask for her forgiveness. You may need to pay back something you stole or to replace something you broke.

If you therefore are presenting your offering at the altar, and there remember that your brother has something against you, leave your offering there before the altar, and go your way; first be reconciled to your brother, and then come and present your offering.
–Matthew 5:23-24

Christ taught us in the verse at left that we should be reconciled to one another before we can move on.

✎ **Think about someone to whom you need to make right a wrong so you can move on with life. In the blanks below write how you plan to ask this person for forgiveness.**

_____

_____

_____

➥ **Stop and pray, asking God to give you the courage to say the words you wrote above and the courage to talk with the individual.**

DAY 4

Obstacles to His Presence

At least five obstacles that stem from a misunderstanding of Christ's love and forgiveness often prevent us from experiencing His presence and power in the fullest way possible. These obstacles are:

✔ 1. We have wrong motives.
✔ 2. Our approach to the Christian life is too mechanical or regimented.
✔ 3. We are too mystical.
   4. We lack knowledge about the availability of Christ's love and power.
   5. We are harboring sin, which blocks our fellowship with Christ.

Let's take a closer look at these obstacles. We'll address the first three (the ones checked above) here and the last two in day 5.

Wrong Motives

Where do we go wrong?

Determining where we go wrong in our motivation often is difficult. We usually have a variety of motives for what we pursue, and we probably do nothing with completely pure motives. However, we can examine some of the reasons we may follow Christ before we can consider whether our motivations might hinder our walk with Him.

Many of us tend to approach Christian living as a self-improvement program. We may desire spiritual growth, or we may have one or more fairly serious problems from which we desperately want to be delivered. Although certainly nothing is wrong with spiritual growth or with desiring to be rid of a constantly present problem, why are we motivated to achieve goals like these?

Perhaps we desire success or others' approval. Perhaps we fear that God really can't accept us until we have spiritually matured or until our problem is removed. Perhaps we just want to feel better without having to struggle through the process of making major changes in our attitudes and behavior.

Motivations such as these may be mixed with a genuine desire to honor the Lord, but it's also possible that deep within us is a primary desire to glorify ourselves. When self-improvement, rather than Christ, becomes the center of our focus, our focus is displaced.

Which is the best motive?

 Which of the following is the most appropriate motive for Christian (Christlike) living?

❏ 1. I want to honor Christ and express my love by obeying Him.
❏ 2. I want to improve myself so I will be acceptable to God and have others' approval.

It is important to understand that fruitfulness and growth are the *results* of focusing on Christ and of desiring to honor Him. When growth and change are our primary goals, we tend to be preoccupied with ourselves instead of with Christ. We constantly may ask ourselves questions like, *Am I growing? Am I getting any better? Am I more like Christ today? What am I learning?* This preoccupation with self-improvement in many ways parallels our culture's self-help and personal-enhancement movement. Personal development certainly is not wrong, but it is misleading. It can be very disappointing if we make it our major goal. If it is our goal at all, it should be secondary.

> My grace is sufficient for you, for power is perfected in weakness.
> —2 Corinthians 12:9

As we grasp the unconditional love, grace, and power of God, then honoring Christ increasingly can be our consuming passion. God wants us to have a healthy self-awareness and to analyze our lives periodically, but He does not want us to be preoccupied with ourselves. The only One worthy of our preoccupation is Christ, our sovereign Lord, who told the apostle Paul about His sufficient grace (see the verse at left). If, through affirming Christian relationships, the power of God's Word, His Spirit, and time, we can begin to realize that Christ fully meets our needs for security, gradually we can take our attention and affections off ourselves and place them on Him. Only then can we begin to adopt Paul's intense desire to honor Christ in the manner we read about in the second verse at left.

> Therefore also we have as our ambition . . . to be pleasing to Him.
> —2 Corinthians 5:9

 Describe here a time in which having wrong motives has kept you from experiencing Christ's love and forgiveness and serving Him effectively.

Too Mechanical

Some of us are too mechanical in our approach to the Christian life. Although we rigorously may schedule and discipline our lives in an effort to conform to what we believe is a biblical life-style, our lives may show little of the freshness, joy, and spontaneity of Christ.

The organized man's story

One man organized his life into hourly segments, each designated to accomplish some particular "biblical purpose." True, he was organized and accomplished some good things, but he was miserable. This man trusted in himself, instead of the Holy Spirit, to produce a life that pleased God.

> And one of them, a lawyer, asked Him a question, testing Him, "Teacher, which is the great commandment in the Law?" And he said to him, "You shall love the Lord your God with all your heart, and with all your soul, and with all your mind. This is the great and foremost commandment. The second is like it, You shall love your neighbor as yourself."
> —Matthew 22:35-38

Eventually, this man joined a church Bible study considering the subject of God's grace. A man leading the group met with him regularly. The super-organized man asked many questions. Slowly, he began to realize that Christ's foremost commandment is to love Him and others, as the verse at left shows, and that joy, peace, and kindness are much more important to God than is sticking to strict rules (for which Jesus scolded the Pharisees). Over the next few months, as the man continued in this affirming relationship, he gained a new outlook, which led to a new life-style of love and joy. This man still is an organized person, but being organized no longer dominates his life.

Though we may not be as extreme as this man is, many of us have certain Christian activities (such as church attendance, tithing, Bible studies, and so forth) that we feel we must do in order to be "good Christians." These activities themselves obviously are not wrong, but a performance-oriented perspective *is* wrong. Christ wants us to receive our joy and acceptance from Him instead of merely following rules or schedules. He is the Lord; He alone is our source of security, joy, and meaning.

Being a 'good' Christian

✎ **List below four things you feel you need to do in order to be a "good Christian."**

1. _____   3. _____

2. _____   4. _____

Go back and place beside each one a *P* if you do this to bring glory to your performance and a *G* if you do this to bring glory to God.

Too Mystical

A third obstacle to abiding in Christ is that we become too mystical or that we depend on supernatural feelings to dictate our relationship with God. Depending on feelings leads to two problems. The first occurs when we wait for feelings to motivate us, and the other occurs when we see virtually every emotion as a sign from God. Let's examine these.

Some of us won't get out of bed until the Lord "tells" us to. We may not want to share Christ with others until we feel that God is prompting us. What we may forget is that Christianity primarily is faith in action. Our emotions are not the most reliable source of motivation. The Holy Spirit sometimes prompts us through impressions, but He already has given us through the Scriptures most of what He wants us to do, and He speaks to us through them.

Rather than waiting for a "holy zap" to get us going, we can believe the truth of God's Word, let God speak to us through it, and then act for His glory. Must we wait until we feel like loving other Christians, praying, studying the Scriptures, or sharing our faith? No. We can follow the examples Hebrews 11 recounts of the men and women who acted on their faith in God, often in spite of their feelings. True, these people often prayed for God's direction, but they always acted on His truth.

Must we wait until we feel like loving other Christians, praying, studying the Scriptures, or sharing our faith?

The second problem with depending on our feelings occurs when we believe that our emotions represent a primary means of God's communication with us and therefore are signs from God indicating His leading. This may cause us to make statements about God's will (for ourselves and others) that are based on little more than how we feel. As in the first extreme, the Scriptures and what God says to us through them may take a back seat as we sometimes justify foolish and even immoral acts by this false "leading from the Lord."

Commit your works to the Lord, and your plans will be established.
–Proverbs 16:3

We can follow the direction of the verse from Proverbs at left. Though God through the Scriptures encourages us to be real and honest about our emotions, He never tells us to live by our emotions. God's Word, the Bible, represents the only reliable guide for our lives. Our feelings may reinforce these truths, but they also may reflect Satan's lies that God doesn't love us, that the fun of a particular sin is more satisfying than is following God, or that God never will answer our prayers. God's speaking to us through the truths of His Word, not our feelings, is our authority.

 Write below why we should not rely on our feelings to dictate our relationship to God.

_____

_____

 Stop and pray, asking God to help you rely on His Word as He speaks to you through it about the correct way for you to act.

SUMMARY STATEMENTS

- God wants us to have a healthy self-awareness and to analyze our lives periodically, but He does not want us to be preoccupied with ourselves.
- Christ wants us to receive our joy and acceptance from Him instead of merely following rules or schedules.
- God's speaking to us through the truths of His Word, not our feelings, is our authority.

DAY 5

More Obstacles

In day 4 we addressed the first three of the five obstacles listed here that often prevent us from experiencing His presence and power in the fullest way possible. Today we'll do the last two (the ones with check marks).

1. We have wrong motives.
2. Our approach to the Christian life is too mechanical or regimented.
3. We are too mystical.
 4. We lack knowledge about the availability of Christ's love and power.
5. We are harboring sin, which blocks our fellowship with Christ.

Lack of Knowledge

Many of us find ourselves walking slowly or hesitantly with God because we do not realize the nature and depth of the love and power available to us in Christ.

We haven't yet fully comprehended the magnificent truths of the Scriptures as God speaks to us through them.

✎ **Fill in the blanks below to show what the Scriptures tell you about yourself, based on the affirmation you memorized. I have filled in the first one for you. The Scriptures tell you that—**

- *I am deeply loved*

- _____

- _____

- _____

- _____

Rich and don't know it

We may be like the West Texas sheep rancher who lived in poverty even though vast resources of oil were under his property. He was fabulously rich but didn't even know it! Since its discovery many years ago, this particular oil field has proven to be one of the richest and most productive in the world. Likewise, we have incredible resources available to us through the Holy Spirit. Here are some of those resources—some of the ways the Holy Spirit enables us to experience the reality of Christ's love and power—and Scriptures you can look up to tell you more about those resources.

POWERFUL RESOURCES

The Holy Spirit—

- Uses other believers to model to us the character of Christ over a period of time (John 13:34-35; 1 John 4:7,12).
- Reveals sin in our lives so that we can confess it and prevent our fellowship with God from being hindered (1 John 1:9).
- Helps us choose to honor Christ in our circumstances and relationships (2 Corinthians 5:9).
- Enables us to endure as we follow Christ (Romans 5:1-5)
- Produces spiritual fruit in our lives (John 15:1-8; Galatians 5:22-23).

Christ's character in others

✎ **List below the names of individuals who model Christ's character to you. Beside their names describe how this person models this character to you.**

1. _____

2. _____

 Now choose another one of the powerful resources of the Holy Spirit from the list. Stop and pray, thanking God for a specific way that resource has been a reality in your life recently.

Harboring Sin

Willful sin is a fifth obstacle that clouds our fellowship with God. Indeed, sin may be pleasurable for a moment; but inevitably, its destructive nature reveals itself in many ways: broken relationships, poor self-esteem, and a poor witness for Christ. Whether we commit the obvious sin of immorality or the more subtle sin of pride, we can learn to deal decisively with all sin, for our benefit and for Christ's glory.

Whether our sin is obvious or subtle, we can learn to deal with all sin decisively, for our benefit and for Christ's glory.

Christ's death paid for all of our sins; they are completely forgiven. Comprehending His love and forgiveness encourages us to admit that we have sinned and to claim forgiveness for any and every sin as soon as we become aware of it. Again, this prevents our fellowship with Christ from being hindered and enables us to continue experiencing His love and power.

Read in the margin at left what the apostle Paul wrote about the characteristics of the Holy Spirit that we should have. As we respond to the love of Christ and trust His Spirit to fill us, these characteristics can become increasingly evident in our lives. In the box at left list the two characteristics that you feel you want to set as the first goals to achieve.

The fruit of the Spirit is love, joy, peace, patience, kindness, goodness, faithfulness, gentleness, self-control.
–Galatians 5:22-23

As we are filled with the Holy Spirit, something happens to our purpose (we strive to bring honor to Christ instead of to ourselves) and to our resources (we trust in His love and power to accomplish results, instead of trusting in our own wisdom and abilities).

Although over the years we mature in our relationship with the Lord, we can begin to experience His love, strength, and purpose from the moment we put Him at the center of our lives.

> **The above verse tells about the fruit of the Spirit. Name two that you want to set as goals to achieve first.**
>
> _____
>
> _____

✎ **Describe below how you have experienced new purpose and resources as a result of the Holy Spirit in your life.**

1. _____

2. _____

✎ **Which of the five obstacles to experiencing God's love and forgiveness do you think you encounter the most often? Write here why you think that obstacle trips you up.**

_____

_____

_____

Taking Steps

Are you depending on God's Spirit to teach you, change you, and use you in the lives of others?

If so, continue trusting Him! If not, review the five obstacles to following Christ listed for you again on the next page.

Truths that can set you free

✎ Read the list and check the obstacles you commit to work on first in order to have a closer relationship with Christ.

❏ 1. We have wrong motives.
❏ 2. Our approach to the Christian life is too mechanical or regimented.
❏ 3. We are too mystical.
❏ 4. We lack knowledge about the availability of Christ's love and power.
❏ 5. We harbor sin, which blocks our fellowship with Christ.

➡ **As you reflect, do you have any sins you need to confess regarding these obstacles? Stop now and pray, confessing those sins to God and asking for forgiveness.**

As you learned, *confession* means to agree with God that you have sinned and that Christ has forgiven you completely. It also means to repent—to turn from your sins to a life of love and obedience to God. As you experience more of God's grace, take time to reflect on His love and power. Trust Him to guide you by His Word, fill you with His Spirit, and enable you to live for Him and use you in others' lives. Abiding in Christ does not mean you are free from problems; but it can provide a powerful relationship with the One who is the source of wisdom, love to encourage you, and strength to endure.

Trust Him to enable you to live for Him and use you in others' lives.

✎ Quote from memory the following. Check the box as you complete each.

❏ Four false beliefs
❏ Four truths of God's Word
❏ "My Identity in Christ" Affirmation

✎ Review this week's lessons. Pray and ask God to identify one positive statement that had an impact on your understanding of who you are.

Write that statement in your own words.

_____

_____

Rewrite your thoughts as a prayer of thankfulness to God.

_____

_____

_____

You probably gained many insights as you worked through this week's lessons. Which insight stands out to you? Write it here.

_____

_____

_____

RENEWING OUR MINDS

> ### PLAGUED WITH GUILT
>
> Lisa and Brad, a married couple, rose quickly in their careers and soon received large salaries. They bought expensive cars and other luxury items. In their process of living high, they dropped all of their Christian friends and started drinking heavily. Then Brad lost his job. Sobered by this turn of events, Brad and Lisa realized that they had lost track of their commitment to Christ in the midst of their materialistic lifestyle. They began to be plagued with guilt. (Read more about their story on pages 200-201.) What do Lisa and Brad need in their lives?

This week you'll–

- learn that persons who accept Christ are free from the eternal condemnation their sins deserve;
- study about how we can stop feeling guilty about a sin after we have repented of and accepted Christ's forgiveness for that sin;
- see how our thoughts affect how we behave;
- learn that we can take responsibility for how we react to disturbing situations in life;
- learn how to use strategies like self-talk to overcome false beliefs in our lives.

Guilt: A Constant Burden	More About the Process	Under-standing Our Behavior	A New Way to React to Hurt	The Weapons of Repentance
DAY 1	DAY 2	DAY 3	DAY 4	DAY 5

A key verse to memorize this week

There is therefore now no condemnation for those who are in Christ Jesus.
  –Romans 8:1

Words to help you understand this week's lessons

paraclete–n. advocate, helper, counselor, supporter (*Example: The Holy Spirit is a paraclete to lift us up and encourage us.*)

renew–v. to transform, alter the content of, renovate (*Example: Changes in your behavior take place when you renew your mind.*)

Guilt: A Constant Burden

No feeling produces pain, fear, and alienation quite like the feeling of guilt. Many of us experience it as a constant burden. We feel that a particular sin in the past never will stop haunting us. We feel that our sins are so bad that they have doomed us forever. We feel we are unable to move on with life because something in our past keeps dragging us down. We condemn ourselves over and over again. The good news is that guilt need not be a way of life for us.

Guilt need not be a way of life for us.

Let's look at the process that surrounds our feelings of guilt and look at how we can change that process as God speaks to us through His Word.

Yes, You Can Be Free!

condemnation–n. a sentence pronounced, a verdict, the decision resulting from an investigation (Vine's)

To begin with, people who accept Christ are free from eternal **condemnation** (see definition at left) for their sins. Romans 8:1, which appears at left, makes this perfectly clear.

There is therefore now no condemnation for those who are in Christ Jesus.
–Romans 8:1

I met for several months with a troubled Christian friend and discussed with him the important truth of this verse in Romans. Once as I talked with him, his eyes filled with tears and he said, "I can't believe that all this burden I have been carrying is unnecessary. I can't believe I can be free from these tormenting feelings of condemnation." This man was beginning to understand what happened when he accepted Christ—that he was freed from eternal condemnation. Sometimes we believe that despite our salvation, we still are doomed for our sins. We can be free from that wrong idea.

God has been trying to tell us that truth in Romans for centuries, but few of us have listened. We feel that because of our sins we deserve to be condemned. We fail to realize that Christ has freed us from the condemnation our sins deserve. When we trust Christ, He gives us a once-and-for-all relationship of freedom from condemnation.

 Describe your thoughts as you read the past three paragraphs? For instance, you might respond, "Yes, that's true. I feel the same way," or "I don't believe that at all."

_____

_____

The first thing, then, that we need in this process of understanding about what guilt does to us is to remember the words in the box below.

> Our condemnation is removed only through Christ. He accepted the penalty for our sins and suffered the full punishment for all sin. Because of His substitution we are free from our sentence of spiritual death.

The Destructiveness of Guilt

How does what we just studied relate to guilt and to the destructive effects it has on our lives?

To begin with, even after we've trusted Christ and are freed from eternal condemnation, we still sin. First John 1:8-10 at left tells us about this. We miss the mark; we make mistakes; we turn from God's ways. What happens at that point? Should we then feel guilty about what we've done?

The Bible indicates that God intends for us to feel *something* when we sin, and we don't stop feeling that *something* just because we accept Christ. It's not God's intention that just because we accept Christ, we can go on sinning and sinning without our sins ever bothering us.

Here's what happens: When we sin, something brings us to a point at which we **confess** those sins. (We also studied this term in unit 10.) The definition at left says that a person confesses sin by admitting himself guilty of what He is accused. This comes about through **conviction** (see second definition at left)— the work of the Holy Spirit in our lives to get us to agree with God about the wrong we've done. We feel what we're feeling because the Holy Spirit is convicting us of sin.

However, God wants us to feel a godly sorrow, or grief, for our sins. He does not want us to experience guilt that eats away at us and destroys our self-esteem. Second Corinthians 7:9-10 at left describes this kind of sorrow. It says that sorrow brings us to the point of repentance.

Once we confess our sin, repent, and accept Christ's forgiveness, we may continue to have regret and remorse, but we can be assured the Christ has forgiven us completely. Because of this forgiveness we need condemn ourselves no more.

What Guilt Does to Us

When people allow guilt to burden them even after God forgives them, they can find themselves harmed emotionally. This kind of lingering guilt causes a loss of self-respect. It causes the human spirit to wither, and it eats away at our personal significance and self-esteem. It causes us to condemn ourselves.

Guilt plays on our fears of failure and rejection; therefore, it never can ultimately build, encourage, or inspire us in our desire to live for Christ.

✎ **Write on the lines below about a time when guilt had a destructive effect on your life.**

_____

_____

_____

Unfortunately, some people tell us that even after God has forgiven us of a particular sin, we still are guilty. And sadly, we hear this statement in

---

If we say that we have no sin, we are deceiving ourselves, and the truth is not in us. If we confess our sins, He is faithful and righteous to forgive us our sins and to cleanse us from all unrighteousness. If we say that we have not sinned, we make Him a liar, and His word is not in us.

–1 John 1:8-10

confess–v. to declare by way of admitting oneself guilty of what one is accused of, the result of inward conviction (Vine's)

conviction–n. the act of convincing a person of error (Webster's)

I now rejoice, not that you were made sorrowful, but that you were made sorrowful to the point of repentance; for you were made sorrowful according to the will of God, in order that you might not suffer loss in anything through us. For the sorrow that is according to the will of God produces a repentance without regret, leading to salvation; but the sorrow of the world produces death.
–2 Corinthians 7:9-10

What guilt does:
• **Destroys self-respect**
• **Withers the human spirit**
• **Eats away at significance**
• **Enhances fear of failure**

Describe a time when you felt that someone tried to make you feel guilty to motivate you to do something.

_____

_____

_____

_____

churches—places that loudly and clearly should proclaim God's forgiveness. Sometimes people may try to make us feel guilty in order to motivate us to respond in certain ways. Guilt, however, is not a healthy motivator for us. In the margin box at left, briefly describe a time when you felt that someone tried to make you feel guilty to motivate you to do something.

Perhaps some people think that if they don't use guilt motivation, people won't respond. Because guilt motivation is so deeply ingrained in us, it will take time for us to develop more healthy motivations—the proper motivations that can come from God. That kind of motivation can come from within ourselves because of the grace God has granted us. Be patient with yourself as you learn to develop healthy motivations.

 Put a check in the box by each true statement below.

❏ As a child of God, I still sin at times.
❏ God never refuses to hear when we repent from sin.
❏ The Father never condemns me, for I am in Jesus Christ.
❏ As a child of God, the Father rejects me at times because of my sinfulness.
❏ By the mercies of God a time never will exist when my Father will reject me because of my sinfulness.
❏ I want to do right because of the inner motivation that comes from the grace God has granted me.

Even though as children of God we all sin, the Father through Jesus Christ has freed us from condemnation. God never refuses to hear us when we repent from sin. He always holds the door open for us to accept Him, thus freeing us from condemnation.

> Once we accept Christ, He always stands ready to forgive us when we turn from His ways.

Recognize the Lies

Focus on Christ's forgiveness

Learn to identify the results of guilt in your thoughts. Then focus instead on the unconditional love and forgiveness of Christ. His love is powerful, and He is worthy of our intense zeal to obey and honor Him.

Christians are subject to grief, or sorrow, over our sins. The Bible frequently speaks of the Holy Spirit's work to convict believers of sin. He directs and encourages our spiritual progress by revealing our sins in contrast to the holiness and purity of Christ. The purpose of conviction is to return us to God's way for our lives. The Holy Spirit's conviction of us is not intended to produce pangs of guilt long after we've been forgiven of our sins. Conviction is the Holy Spirit's way of showing the error of our performance in light of God's standard and truth. His motivation is love, correction, and protection.

Lisa and Brad's story

Lisa and Brad, a married couple, rose quickly in their careers and soon received large salaries, which they spent as quickly as they received their paychecks. They bought expensive cars and other luxury items. In their process of living high, they dropped all of their Christian friends and started drinking heavily.

Then almost as quickly as they rose to success, Brad lost his job. Sobered by this turn of events, Brad and Lisa realized that they had lost track of their commitment to Christ in the midst of their materialistic life-style. The Holy Spirit convicted them by showing them the error of their ways. They felt grief for turning from God's direction. Lisa and Brad prayed that God would forgive them for losing their focus on Him.

As they turned back to Him, they felt sorry for what they did but also felt a sense of relief at being forgiven.

After we repent and feel God's forgiveness for a sin, no reasons exist for feelings of guilt to be part of our lives.

Godly sorrow that comes about through conviction enables us to realize the beauty of God's forgiveness and to experience His love and power. After we repent and feel God's forgiveness for a sin, no reasons exist from God's perspective for feelings of guilt to be part of our lives. We can be assured of His forgiveness.

✎ **Describe here a time when conviction caused you to experience godly sorrow for a sin.**

_____

_____

_____

_____

➡ **Thank God for convicting you and for what you learned from that experience. If you never have experienced conviction, ask God to help you understand the beauty of His forgiveness that conviction can bring.**

SUMMARY STATEMENTS

- Persons who accept Christ are free from eternal condemnation.
- God wants us to feel a godly sorrow, or grief, for our sins. He does not want us to experience guilt that eats away at us and destroys our self-esteem.
- Godly sorrow, or grief, for our sins brings us to the point of repentance.
- Once we confess our sin, repent, and accept Christ's forgiveness, we may continue to have regret and remorse, but we can be assured the Christ has forgiven us completely.
- When people allow guilt to burden them even after God forgives them, they can find themselves harmed emotionally. This kind of lingering guilt causes a loss of self-respect.
- Conviction is the Holy Spirit's way of showing the error of our performance in light of God's standard and truth.
- Because guilt motivation is so deeply ingrained in us, it will take time to develop more healthy motivations. Be patient with yourself.

More About the Process

Here are some more statements about conviction, how it occurs in our lives, and its effects on us.

CONVICTION

Basic Focus––Conviction focuses on behavior: This act is unworthy of Christ and is destructive.

Primary Concern––Conviction deals with the loss of our moment-by-moment communication with God: This act is destructive to me and interferes with my walk with God.

Primary Fear—Conviction produces a fear of the destructiveness of the act itself: This behavior is destructive to me and to others, and it robs me of what God intends for me.

Agent—The agent of conviction is the Holy Spirit . . . but if by the Spirit you are putting to death the deeds of the body, you will live (Romans 8:13).

Behavioral Results—Conviction leads to repentance, the turning from sin to Christ: Lord, I agree with You that my sin is wrong and destructive. What do You want me to do?

Interpersonal Result—The interpersonal result of conviction is restoration, a desire to remedy the harm done to others: Father, what would You have me do to right this wrong and to restore the relationship with the one I have offended?

Personal Results—Conviction ends in comfort, the realization of forgiveness: Thank You, Lord, that I am completely forgiven and totally accepted by You.

Remedy—The remedy for conviction is confession, agreeing with God that our sin is wrong, that Christ has forgiven us, and that our attitude and actions will change. The outgrowth of conviction is repentance, which is turning away from the sin and returning to God.

Thank You, Lord

✎ **Now look back at the purpose of conviction and write your own understanding of it. Then stop to pray, turning your statement into a prayer of thanksgiving and confession to God.**

_____

_____

_____

We Need to Be Convinced

paraclete–n. advocate, helper, counselor, supporter (Mercer)

Although Christians no longer are subject to condemnation, we cannot be free from its destructive power until we learn that we no longer have to fear judgment. The Holy Spirit wants us to be convinced that we are totally secure—because of Christ. The Holy Spirit is the **paraclete** (see definition in margin at left) to lift us up and encourage us. As a part of the Holy Spirit's ministry, He faithfully makes us aware of any of our behaviors that do not reflect the characteristics of Christ. He helps us understand both our righteousness before God and the failures in our performance. From these observations we can conclude that conviction leads us to confession and repentance and to a new ability to realize God's grace and forgiveness. Write about your feelings about this in the margin box.

> **Write how you feel as you have come to realize that God never will condemn or reject you.**

How, Then, Do We Deal with Guilt?

Knowing this, how can we deal with feelings of guilt? First, we can study here a little more about how guilt affects us.

GUILT

Basic Focus––Guilt focuses on self-condemnation: I am unworthy.

Primary Concern––Guilt deals with the sinner's loss of self-esteem and wounded self-pride: What will others think of me?

Primary Fear––Guilt produces a fear of punishment: Now I'm going to get it!

Behavioral Results––Guilt leads to depression and more sin: I am just a low-down, dirty, rotten sinner; or to rebellion: I don't care; I'm going to do whatever I want to do.

Interpersonal Results––The interpersonal result of guilt is alienation, a feeling of shame that drives one away from the person wronged: I never can face him again.

Personal Results––Guilt ends in depression, bitterness, and self-pity: I'm just no good.

Remedy––The remedy for guilt is to remember that if you have repented of your sin, Christ has forgiven you and remembers your sin no more.

 Look back in the box at the statements about guilt and check any that you might have experienced.

To deal with feelings of guilt, we first can affirm that Christ has forgiven us. As believers, we are not condemned when we sin, but that sin is harmful and dishonors God. We can confess our sin to God, claim the forgiveness we already have in Christ, and then move on in joy and freedom to honor Him. The following prayer expresses this attitude.

Confessing our sin to God

CLAIMING OUR FORGIVENESS

Father,

I know that I am deeply loved by You, that I am fully pleasing to You, and that I am totally accepted in Your sight. You have made me complete and have given me the righteousness of Christ, even though my performance often falls short. Lord, I confess my sins to you. (List them. Be specific.) I agree with You that these are wrong. Please forgive me. Thank You for Your grace and forgiveness. Do I need to return anything, repay anyone, or apologize to anyone? I will do it, with your leading.

Thank You.

 Stop for a few moments and ask the Holy Spirit to convict you of any unforgiven sin. Use the prayer above to deal with sins He has revealed to you. Thank God for His love and acceptance of you.

Make the prayer you just prayed a daily experience. Allow it always to be present in your thoughts and heart.

It is important to affirm our righteousness in Christ as well as to confess our sins. God does not need to be reminded of our right standing in Him, but we can be reminded of that right standing. We can make this prayer a daily experience. We can allow it always to be present in our thoughts and hearts.

As we yield to the gentle urging of God-given conviction, confess our sins, and affirm our true relationship with Him, He gradually will shape and mold us in such a way that we will increasingly honor the One who died and rose again on their [our] behalf (2 Corinthians 5:15, emphasis added). We may not experience joy and freedom immediately, especially if we have developed the painful habit of condemning ourselves over and over again as a way of dealing with sin. Loving friends who listen to us and encourage us can be examples of God's forgiveness to us.

As we become more honest about our feelings through these affirming relationships, we can experience more and more the freedom, forgiveness, and freshness of God's grace.

SUMMARY STATEMENTS

- The Holy Spirit helps us understand both our righteousness before God and the failures in our performance.
- As we become more honest about our feelings through affirming relationships, we increasingly can experience the freedom, forgiveness, and freshness of God's grace.

Understanding Our Behavior

For as he thinks within himself, so he is.
–Proverbs 23:7

A very clear statement in the Bible tells how your life functions. We find this statement in Proverbs 23:7 (look in the left margin). This verse represents the biblical viewpoint of psychology as it describes how a person's emotions and behavior flow from the mind. Our thoughts are like a gushing spring of fresh water that rises from the earth and then flows off as a stream of emotions and behavior. Our emotions and behavior never just happen; they always begin in our thought processes. At the beginning, thought occurs, and from thought comes emotion. Sometimes emotions seem to have lives of their own. However, a previous, split-second mental judgment causes every emotion you experience.

Emotions, in turn, energize behavior. The linkage between thought, emotion, and behavior operates like a chain reaction. The direction of our human responses moves from thinking to feeling to behavior in that order. Although your surface problem appears to be the need to handle your harmful emotions and your harmful behavior, the fact is that your constant harmful emotions and behavior do not magically exist in their own right. Most of your emotions and behavior stem directly from your thoughts.

The thoughts that you deeply believe will determine how you feel about and behave in situations you encounter.

You can change your thinking in order to change your behavior. We are not saying that every thought that passes through your mind will trigger an emotion. The Bible doesn't say, "As he thinks, so he is." What the passage says is, "As he thinks *within himself* so is he." The qualifying phrase *within himself* refers to a particular kind of thought: a biased, strongly evaluative, deep-felt kind of thinking. What you think *within yourself* refers to what you believe deep inside you. The thoughts that you deeply believe will determine how you feel about and behave in situations you encounter. Complete the margin box at left.

Write here about a time when what you believed deep inside determined how you felt and behaved in a situation you encountered.

_____

_____

_____

_____

_____

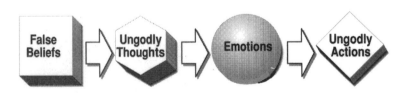

A newspaper reporter interviewed a town's oldest citizen on his 90th birthday. When the reporter asked this elderly Christian gentleman why he thought he had lived so long, the man gave a one-word answer, "Serenity." People who knew him well agreed completely with the answer their friend gave. They never had known him to lose his deep sense of inner calm, which he attributed to his relationship with Christ. As it turned out, this man lived until he was only a few months away from turning 100. What he thought within himself affected his overall outlook until he went to be with the Lord.

The Behavior Sequence

Our behavior sequence, then, begins with thinking, which produces emotions and behavior. What you think determines how you feel. "The more I thought about it, the madder I got" is the way we state it. So the human-behavior sequence flows in the direction described on the next page.

When we keep reminding ourselves of false beliefs, they show up in the way we behave.

Your beliefs (value system) stir your emotions, and emotions trigger behavior. Behavior, then, tends to reinforce your belief in a cyclical fashion. For example, to believe you are inferior can make you feel inferior. To feel inferior, in turn, can cause you to behave in manner reflecting your sense of inferiority (for example, withdrawal to hide, or aggressiveness to defend yourself.) And this behavior merely reinforces the belief that you are inferior. When we keep subconsciously reminding ourselves of these false beliefs, they become ingrained in our thinking process and show up in the way we behave.

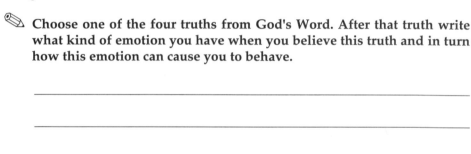

Therefore, your thinking process almost always precedes your emotions, or perpetuates your emotions, or both. The directional flow of a habitual behavioral sequence begins with beliefs, which produce emotions, which energize behavior in that order.

✎ **Choose one of the four truths from God's Word. After that truth write what kind of emotion you have when you believe this truth and in turn how this emotion can cause you to behave.**

_____

_____

_____

SUMMARY STATEMENTS

- When we keep reminding ourselves of false beliefs, they show up in the way we behave.
- The thoughts that you deeply believe determine how you feel about and behave in situations you encounter.

A New Way to React to Hurt

Since thoughts (beliefs or values) cause emotions and emotions trigger behavior, then false beliefs naturally can cause painful emotions and painful emotions can trigger destructive behavior. You can trace 90 percent of all your painful emotions to the four false beliefs. The reason most things affect you negatively is because you take them personally. The reasons you take them personally are found in the four false beliefs about your worth as a person!

Our Wrong Reactions to Situations

We constantly react as if situations cause feelings and as if a situation itself can cause an emotion and behavior.

We contend that all your painful emotions and painful behavior have their origin in false beliefs. However, most people feel differently about this; in fact, they take the opposite viewpoint. We constantly react as if situations cause feelings and as if a situation itself can cause an emotion and behavior, apart from our beliefs.

Blaming it on the boss

Let's say, for example, that your boss criticizes you for having some incorrect figures on a report. When you arrive home from work that evening, you notice that your eight-year-old son is jumping on the living room sofa. Instead of discussing the matter calmly with your child, you scream at him in rage.

Later, when you realize that you responded in anger, you blame your anger on the situation with your boss. You say that your boss's criticism of you is the reason you responded inappropriately to your son.

However, just the opposite is true. The false belief that you had about yourself growing from the incident with your boss—*I must meet certain standards to feel good about myself*—caused you to fear failure and therefore caused you to take the ungodly action of scolding your son angrily.

✎ **Think of a time when you responded wrongly as the father in the above illustration did. Think about how you blamed a situation rather than the false belief you had about yourself. Describe that incident here.**

Changing response patterns

_____

_____

_____

_____

One of the greatest marks of personal maturity is evident when you're willing to accept the full responsibility for your emotional and behavioral reactions in all the disturbing situations of life.

You can consider yourself really mature when you once-and-for-all accept the fact that situations do not cause harmful emotions and behavior; your false beliefs about the situations cause your self-destructive reactions.

Dear Lord, I confess . . .

✎ **Take a few moments and spend time in prayer with your Heavenly Father, who deeply loves you. Come to an understanding deep within your heart that your harmful behavior is the result of one or more of the four false beliefs that control your thinking. Write below your prayer of confession to the Lord.**

_____

_____

_____

_____

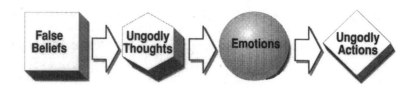

A habit is formed

When similar situations endlessly repeat themselves so that your false beliefs produce harmful emotions and harmful behavior, a habit is formed. And situations, practiced over a long period of time, become conditioned reflexes. That is, harmful emotions become almost completely under the cue control of external situations. Therefore, when situations become habitual enough to establish conditioned reflexes, a cycle results in which problem situations serve as layers of negative reinforcement to perpetuate your low self-esteem.

To gain a higher self-worth, change your response pattern to situations that keep your self-esteem low. You can respond to these situations in a way that conforms to the truths of God's Word, not to the false belief patterns of this world.

 By now you likely have memorized the four false beliefs and the four truths from God's Word. Try saying them aloud from memory. Check each as you recite it correctly. If you cannot do this without help, stop and take a few moments to place them in your heart for safe keeping.

FALSE BELIEFS	GOD'S TRUTHS
❑ Fear of failure	❑ Justification
❑ Fear of rejection	❑ Reconciliation
❑ Fear of punishment	❑ Propitiation
❑ Feelings of shame	❑ Regeneration

And do not be conformed to this world, but be transformed by the renewing of your mind, that you may prove what the will of God is, that which is good and acceptable and perfect.

–Romans 12:2

As we pointed out, thinking is the source of our emotions and behavior. Therefore, to change your mental perspective is to begin to change the way you feel and the way you act. Many books and theories exist on how to change people, but the one Book that really counts states that changes in your behavior take place by the renewing of your mind. See what that Book—the Bible, God's Word—says about this in Romans 12:2, in the left margin.

To renew a mind requires more than merely to inform it. To renew a mind is to transform it, to alter its content, to renovate it. The Greek word translated *renew* is *anakainosis,* and it means *to restore thought content in error.*

What we renew in our minds are misconceptions, or a distorted belief system, which we have called false beliefs. To renew your mind is to gain enough insight to recognize your false beliefs and to replace your incorrect thinking with God's truth. Millions suffer from a wide range of mental and emotional disorders because of false beliefs about themselves, about God, and about the world around them.

 Write in your own words your understanding of the word *renewing,* **found in Romans 12:2.**

DAY 5

For the weapons of war are not of the flesh, but divinely powerful for the destruction of fortresses. We are destroying speculations and every lofty thing raised up against the knowledge of God, and we are taking every thought captive to the obedience of Christ.
—2 Corinthians 10:4-5

Weapons of Repentance

The passage of Scripture in the left margin speaks about arguments and thoughts that set themselves up against the knowledge of God. We can take these thoughts captive and make them obedient to Christ. Some of these thoughts we can take captive are the deeply held false beliefs about ourselves that have been part of our belief system for many years. Expose these false beliefs and oppose them. Consider them to be enemies of everything that is best for us. Learning to recognize your false beliefs is critically important, but recognizing them by itself does not necessarily change you. You literally can declare war on these false beliefs and resist them.

In the Corinthian Statement, the passage of Scripture at left, Paul described this activity as a type of mental warfare: "The weapons of our warfare are . . . divinely powerful for the destruction of fortresses." Paul referred to certain weapons of warfare by which we can destroy strongholds (or fortresses) of false beliefs in our mind. Don't confuse these weapons with the armor of the Christian, as Ephesians 6 discusses. The armor of the Christian is for defense; weapons are for offense. Armor protects you from attacks outside ourselves; weapons overcome fortresses within ourselves.

The weapons of 2 Corinthians 10:4-5 refer to weapons of mental warfare by which you storm the fortresses of your mind.

 List on the next page some examples of attacks outside yourself that affect your life. Then list some examples of fortresses within yourself that you need to overcome. For example, one person might list attacks outside as a schedule conflict that keeps her from attending a Bible study. A fortress within could be lack of forgiveness toward a friend who told a lie about you.

Attacks outside: _____

_____

Fortresses within: _____

_____

I now rejoice, not that you were made sorrowful, but that you were made sorrowful to the point of repentance; for you were made sorrowful according to the will of God, in order that you might not suffer loss in anything through us. For the sorrow that is according to the will of God produces a repentance without regret, leading to salvation, but the sorrow of the world produces death.
—2 Corinthians 7:9-10

The tactical method of our mental warfare is to repent. The verse at left tells about the kind of repentance God has in mind for us. The original Greek word here translated repentance is *metanoia*, meaning *to change your mind*. (We first studied about this in unit 10.) To repent is to change your thoughts, purpose, and views about a matter; it is to have another mind about a thing. To repent of your false beliefs is to feel sorry about your deception, to recognize your false beliefs as untrue, to reject them, and to replace your false beliefs with a truth from God's Word.

Three Weapons of Repentance

We can use three weapons of repentance. They are contrition, rejection, and confession.

Seeing through God's eyes

Contrition—An important element in the nature of repentance is contrition, or godly sorrow. To repent is to feel sorry about about a wrong in your life, for you now see it through God's eyes. So a deep sense of grief and regret exists in any true experience of repentance. Indeed, the very nature of repentance requires an attitude of contrition. To repent about a false belief, then, is to experience deep sorrow about the fact that you have believed one of Satan's deceptions that goes against the knowledge of God.

A decided turn from wrong

Rejection—The second mental weapon of repentance is **rejection**. Once you get in touch with what you feel about a situation, and once you trace your emotions back to the false beliefs which cause them, you can reject these false belief assertively. Refuse to live by them. Declare war on them. Seek to wipe them from your mind. Biblical repentance is characterized by a definite turn from one thing and a decided turn to something else.

When you attack your false beliefs, use self-talk. That's right, actually talk to yourself—aloud, if possible. For example, you might express yourself in the manner the statement in the box below illustrates.

> **SELF-TALK**
>
> I admit the fact that I am taking this personally because I wrongly hold the false beliefs that I must be adequate and competent in my performance and that I must have others' approval to feel good about myself. I reject these false beliefs. I refuse to base my worth on my performance and on what others think of it. I will not live by these lies any longer.

No glossing over false beliefs

Focus on your false beliefs again and again until you become highly conscious of them.

Write here an example of self-talk that you could use the next time your false beliefs about a disturbing situation affect your thoughts and emotions.

_____

_____

_____

_____

_____

And they overcame him because of the blood of the Lamb and because of the word of their testimony, and they did not love their life even to death.
–Revelation 12:11

When you use self-talk like the example you just read, do so forcefully and even loudly. If you can't do this aloud, then do it forcefully in your mind. Act as if you really mean it! It is not enough just to recognize your false beliefs. You also can reject them. Too often, after we recognize our false beliefs, we tend to gloss over them and rush on to confess our worth in a given situation. Therefore, the false beliefs remain in our mind, unchallenged and unrejected. They retain their subconscious influence and can cause further wrong reactions at every similar situation in the future.

Your second weapon of repentance, then, is to reject your false beliefs each time they affect you. Focus on your false beliefs again and again, in all types of difficult situations, until you become highly conscious of them. This practice lifts your false beliefs from your subconscious into your conscious awareness. Once you expose your false beliefs so often that you become consciously aware of them, you can confront them more directly, consistently, and forcefully. Soon you can wage a conscious and constant warfare of rejecting your false beliefs. This is what it takes to reverse years of habitual wrong thinking. Practice by completing the margin box at left.

Confession—The third mental weapon of repentance is **confession**. You correct your false beliefs by confessing the truth. Reversing years of false beliefs will be a difficult and long task. Such confession is virtual warfare! Confession is a mental weapon of great spiritual value. As used in the Scriptures, *confession* means *to agree with God*. To confess is to state God's viewpoint about a matter as a statement of your own viewpoint by hope and to keep on doing so until you consistently see it just as God does.

The Book of Revelation speaks of the way by which Satan deceives the whole world and accuses us all of not measuring up. The passage in the left margin below says we can overcome satanic deception by "the word of [our] testimony" (Revelation 12:11)—our confession of the truth. Confession is the ultimate weapon with which you attack the fortresses of your mind and bring every thought into obedience to Christ.

✎ **Review this week's lessons. Pray and ask God to identify one positive statement that had an impact on your understanding of who you are.**

Write that statement in your own words.

_____

_____

Rewrite your thoughts as a prayer of thankfulness to God.

_____

_____

You probably gained many insights as you worked through this week's lessons. Which insight stands out to you? Write it here.

_____

_____

THE TRIP IN

> ## A CAREER DOWN THE TUBE?
>
> John was a chronic alcoholic who completed a substance-abuse treatment program and was involved in Alcoholics Anonymous. He wisely made sobriety his absolute priority. However, business pressures made him so anxious and distracted him to the point he felt he must resign his executive job to stay sober. A promising career was about to go right down the tube! (Read more about John's story on page 222.) What does John need in his life?

What you'll learn this week

This week you'll—

- learn how to take The Trip In by looking inside yourself and by correcting the false beliefs causing your harmful emotions and destructive behavior;
- study how to identify what you are feeling in a situation and learn how to describe that feeling accurately;
- determine how to use a special formula to detect which false belief is causing your painful feeling;
- learn how to use self-talk to reject a false belief and learn how to affirm your personal worth;
- learn the importance of acting as if you believe you are a loved and forgiven child of God

What you'll study each day

Getting Ready for the Journey	Step 1: What Do I Feel?	Step 2: Why Do I Feel It?	Step 3: What Do I Believe?	Step 4: How Will I Act?
DAY 1	DAY 2	DAY 3	DAY 4	DAY 5

Memory verse

A key verse to memorize this week

For if anyone is a hearer of the word and not a doer, he is like a man who looks at his natural face in a mirror, for once he has looked at himself and gone away, he has immediately forgotten what kind of person he was.
—James 1:23-24

WordWatch

A word to help you understand this week's lessons

repress–v. to prevent the natural or normal expression, activity, or development of. (*Example: We may have learned to* ***repress*** *painful emotions.*)

The Trip In–n. a look inside yourself in a special, deliberate way to enable you to correct the false beliefs causing your painful emotions. (*Example: Persons can use* ***The Trip In*** *to identify the emotion they feel in a painful situation and then to determine which false belief causes this painful feeling.*)

DAY
1

For though we walk in the flesh, we do not war according to the flesh, for the weapons of our warfare are not of the flesh, but divinely powerful for the destruction of fortresses. We are destroying speculations and every lofty thing raised up against the knowledge of God, and we are taking every thought captive to the obedience of Christ.
–2 Corinthians 10:3-5

Be transformed by the renewing of your mind, that you may prove what the will of God is, that which is good and acceptable and perfect.
–Romans 12:2

These exercises are big helps!

Getting Ready for the Journey

Believe it or not, desire it or not, understand it or not, we are at war. The Scripture in the margin at left tells a little about this warfare. Most of us don't like to think about spiritual warfare. We hope, like the proverbial ostrich with its head in the sand, that it will pass us by. Just burying our heads doesn't mean that spiritual warfare isn't always present with us, however. It's always close at hand. Our minds become the battlefield for this warfare. Paul instructs us about this in the second Scripture at left.

Satan's goal is to keep our minds as they are so that we won't be transformed. Satan does this by establishing fortresses of deception which produce thoughts that go against the knowledge or understanding of God. Fortresses of deception are belief systems that are reinforced over the years by the thoughts, emotions, and actions they produce. These are self-feeding systems.

For instance, let's look what happens when a person who normally believes she is a failure succeeds at something. When she succeeds, her belief system (her fortress) produces such thoughts as:

• What luck!
• It's about time. Look at all the failure you had to go through just to get one success.
• How unusual for a loser like you to do something right!

If the person fails, her belief system produces such thoughts as:
• I told you you'd fail.
• What a loser you are!
• You can't help it; you just can't do any better.

Whether she succeeds or fails, the result is the same. It merely reinforces her belief that she is a failure.

 Review the list of thoughts you just read about the person who succeeds although she believes she is a failure. Circle any statements that you may have thought about yourself in similar situations.

Establishing a Stronghold of Truth

You can learn to use the following practices to begin through memorization and meditation to establishing a stronghold of truth in your mind. This mind renewal is essential to what the lesson in day 4 explains about rejecting Satan's lies and replacing them with God's truths.

The Truth Card

A simple three-by-five-inch card can be a key factor in helping you base your self-worth on the freeing truths of the Scriptures.

1. To make the Truth Card, use a three-by-five inch card. On the front write the following truths and their corresponding verses from Scripture.
   • I am deeply loved by God (1 John 4:9-10).

- I am completely forgiven and fully pleasing to God (Romans 5:1).
- I am totally accepted by God (Colossians 1:21-22).
- I am a new creation, absolutely complete in Christ (2 Corinthians 5:17).

On the back of the card, write the false beliefs appearing on the back cover.

2. Learn how to use the Truth Card. Carry this card with you continuously. For one month, each time you do a routine activity, like drinking your morning cup of coffee, look at the front side and slowly meditate on each phrase. Thank the Lord for making you into a person with these qualities. By doing this exercise for the next month, you can develop a habit of remembering that you are deeply loved, completely forgiven, fully pleasing, totally accepted, and absolutely complete in Christ.

If you have not already done so, memorize during the next four days the supporting verses listed on the card. Look in your Bible for other verses that support these truths. Memorize these verses. Doing this will establish God's Word as the basis for your beliefs and will let God speak to you through them, as the verse at left instructs you to do. Also memorize the false beliefs. The more familiar you are with these lies, the more likely you are to recognize them in your thoughts. As you recognize them, you can replace them with the truths of God's Word.

The Trip In

Your ability to correct the false beliefs that cause your harmful emotions and destructive behavior will depend on the way in which you learn to look within yourself. You can learn to do this in a special, deliberate way.

You can take The Trip In—a journey in which you can do these things:
1. Select as a starting point an unpleasant situation that has happened to you within the past week. Identify the destructive behavior that accompanied it.
2. Look inside yourself to sift through various feelings until you discover the underlying painful emotion triggering your outward behavior.
3. Move through your emotions to detect the false beliefs causing your painful emotion.
4. After you detect the false beliefs and reject them, affirm the truth about your special worth as a person. Go above and beyond the situation by taking action in line with the loved and forgiven child of God you see yourself to be! These are the four basic steps to be taken for a successful Trip In. During the next few days we will discuss each step in detail.

✎ **Circle the above step that you feel will be the most difficult for you to accomplish. Stop and pray, asking God to help you accomplish it.**

Develop this good habit

Let the word of Christ richly dwell within you, with all wisdom teaching and admonishing one another with psalms and hymns and spiritual songs, singing with thankfulness in your hearts to God.

–Colossians 3:16

Do these things in a Trip In:
- **Identify destructive behavior.**
- **Discover the trigger emotion.**
- **Detect the false beliefs.**
- **Reject the false beliefs.**
- **Affirm the truth about your worth. Act accordingly!**

SUMMARY STATEMENTS

- Satan's goal is to keep us from being transformed. Satan does this by establishing fortresses of deception which produce thoughts that go against the knowledge or understanding of God.
- Taking The Trip In by looking inside yourself in a special, deliberate way can enable you to correct the false beliefs causing your painful emotions and destructive behavior.

Filter through all the painful emotions you're feeling until you detect the one that underlies the others.

A college student's Trip In

Step 1: What Do I Feel?

When a situation in your day-to-day life arises which bothers you, The Trip In provides a process in which you get in touch with what you really feel about the situation. Your first step is to identify the painful emotions causing your destructive behavior in a specific situation.

In any given situation you could experience several painful emotions. The objective is to identify all the painful emotions you're feeling and to filter through them until you detect the one that underlies all the others. Some emotions, such as anger and hatred, are sharp, clearly felt, and easily labeled. But underlying emotions such as fear and shame often are unclear until you focus on them deliberately.

A college student once focused on his feelings about his father. As he took his Trip In, he at first decided he felt *angry* about his father. Then, as he thought some more, he decided that instead of anger, the correct description of how he felt actually might be *resentment*. Although he knew he was getting close, the student tried to probe even more deeply to identify his emotion correctly. He next considered the feeling of being *neglected* as he tried to zero in on the precise emotion. Finally he realized that what he really felt was *abandonment and the fear of being abandoned again*. His father left him feeling totally abandoned; that was the emotion underlying all the others.

Now You Try It

When you look inside yourself to examine the painful emotions you are feeling about a particular situation, do these things:
1. Take time to find a place where you can be uninterrupted.
2. Shut everything else out. Concentrate on how you feel about the situation.
3. Think of the single feeling at the root of your emotional response to the situation. Don't try to analyze the problem. You are trying to get to the underlying emotion prompting your response to the situation.

✎ **As you begin to focus, you might sense a number of emotions. Make note of all you feel. One of the most important techniques for focusing is to ask yourself questions such as the ones below.**

What is the worst thing about this situation? _____

_____

How does it affect me personally? _____

_____

What is the central part of the problem? What is the main thing in it that

makes me feel bad? _____

Describe the worst part of this feeling. _____

_____

Take your time and concentrate. Let the awareness of your feeling come to you naturally; do not force it. Be honest about your emotions. Often you may think you have arrived at the underlying emotion that you feel about your situation before you actually do. The keys to accomplishing this are openness, honesty, and determination. Until you find what really feels right, it can be like hide-and-seek when someone says *Cold, colder, ice cold* if you are moving in the wrong direction or *Warm, warmer, red hot* as you move in the right direction. Take your time. Move through your feelings until you gain an insight of the underlying emotion that you feel.

repress-v. to prevent the natural or normal expression, activity, or development of; to exclude from consciousness (Webster's)

Sometimes we have a hard time identifying our emotions because we may have learned to **repress** (see definition at left) painful emotions. We often do this because we are frightened of confronting them. Some of us have become numb, unable to feel either anger or joy, hurt or love. Sometimes as a defense mechanism we forget painful emotions we've had, or we deny them, claiming that they really didn't hurt. Or, we minimize them, claiming these emotions didn't have much effect on us. Learning to identify our feelings and to be honest about them allows us to use them as a gauge to determine if our response to a situation is based on the truth or a lie.

How Will You Know?

How can you know when you have discovered the emotion that is at the root of what you feel about a situation? The more you take The Trip In, the more easily you can tell when you have arrived at the underlying emotion, because you often experience a feeling of release.

Think about how your mind works when you have a vague sense that you have forgotten something.

Think about how your mind works when you have a vague sense that you have forgotten something. *What did I forget? What was it?* you ask yourself as you probe for the answer. No matter how much you tell yourself that you will not worry about what you've forgotten, the feeling usually keeps nagging at you. Then, suddenly, what you forgot bursts to the surface of your conscious mind. You remember, *I forgot to bring those legal contracts that I promised John.* You hit it, and the realization gives you a sudden sense of relief. This is the key characteristic of identifying the underlying emotion that you feel. It's like exhaling after holding your breath. It's a sort of "That's it! I found it!" feeling. The person at that point then can begin to resolve the hurts that cause the emotion.

A "That's it! I found it!" feeling

Three main benefits exist from zeroing in on the underlying emotion you feel in a bothersome situation. It allows you to be honest about the realities of a situation and your response to it; it allows you to grieve the sense of loss you feel; and it allows you to take responsibility for your choices and behaviors.

✎ **Think of a painful situation that happened to you recently. Try to focus on the underlying emotion you felt. As you focus, study the words listed below that describe how you might have felt. Then see if you can isolate one feeling that seems to represent the underlying emotion you felt. Put a check by that emotion.**

❏ abandoned	❏ forgotten	❏ neglected	❏ afraid
❏ angry	❏ humiliated	❏ ostracized	❏ disgusted
❏ betrayed	❏ ignored	❏ perplexed	❏ resentful
❏ confused	❏ lonely	❏ ridiculed	❏ _____
❏ excluded	❏ misunderstood	❏ unappreciated	

DAY 3

Step 2: Why Do I Feel It?

Once you have discovered the emotions that you feel in a distressing situation, you can venture still deeper within to ask yourself, *Why do I feel this way? What are the false beliefs causing my painful feelings?*

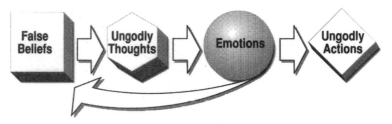

By asking, Why do I feel it? you can go behind your painful emotions to identify the specific false beliefs causing them. To help you detect your false beliefs, think through the following questions about what you are feeling. We refer to this set of questions as "The Why Formula."

THE WHY FORMULA

- Why am I feeling this way? I must be taking this situation personally for it to make me feel this badly.
- What are the specific false beliefs about myself that are causing my painful feelings?

The four false beliefs causing your painful emotions are discussed in earlier chapters. Almost every destructive behavior in your life has one of these four false beliefs as the root cause.

Letting the Formula Work for You

Bill's story

Bill overslept and thus was late to work for an important meeting at which he was to make a presentation. Bill prided himself on being prompt, so this incident embarrassed him terribly. When Bill walked into the meeting his boss chided him, and he became flustered as his coworkers glared at him. One of Bill's coworkers even made a sarcastic remark about his late arrival. Bill felt as if a harsh spotlight focused its white beam directly on him. He felt exposed and humiliated as a result. The rest of the day Bill was so depressed he avoided other responsibilities at work.

Fortunately Bill earlier had learned about taking the Trip In to analyze his destructive behavior. After this embarrassing situation at work Bill remembered to take a Trip In to see why this situation bothered him so much.

First, Bill focused on his emotions. He asked himself, *What do I really feel? What emotions are causing my destructive behavior?* As he began to sift through his emotions, he discovered that he felt anxiety about his boss' chiding and his coworkers' glares. Then he realized that he felt humiliated. Finally, he discovered that the most intense emotion that he felt was that of personal failure. After he discovered this emotion, he completed his Trip In by focusing on the false beliefs causing his painful emotion. He applied "The Why Formula" by asking himself, *Why am I feeling this way? I must be taking this situation personally for it to make me feel this badly. What are the false beliefs which cause me to feel this way?*

As he progressed from the questions in "The Why Formula" to the four false beliefs, Bill detected the false belief causing his reaction to being late to the meeting. Bill recognized how the second false belief influenced him and said to himself, *I have this false belief because I feel I must be adequate and achieve in my performance in order to have self-worth. That is precisely why it depresses me when my boss and others snipe and glare at me when I'm late. Since I believe I have self-worth when I feel I'm prompt and prepared, I set myself up to feel like a failure when I feel that someone criticizes my performance.* In the margin box, you try "The Why Formula" as Bill did.

Note that Bill's proper response was not, *I'm not anxious. I don't feel like a failure,* when in fact, he did feel that way. Denial only compounds our problems; it is not a solution. We can be honest about our feelings.

Instead of blaming his boss and his coworkers, Bill began taking responsibility for his reaction. The real cause of his anxiety was his own false belief. Once Bill began rejecting his false belief and began affirming his worth as a person, he conquered his hypersensitivity to the scolding of his boss and the sarcastic comment and the glares of his colleagues. Bill simply refused to take their scolding, stares, and snipes as a reflection on him!

✎ **Look back through the story of Bill and the embarrassing meeting. Underline statements about Bill's feelings that remind you of similar painful feelings you had in uncomfortable situations. Ask yourself, "To what false beliefs can I trace my painful emotions?" Then stop and pray that God will help you learn to make "The Why Formula" second nature in your life to help you overcome your painful feelings.**

Sifting through Bill's emotions—
- anxiety
- humiliation
- personal failure

Apply The Why Formula to the negative situation you listed in day 2. Write your answers below.

_____

_____

_____

_____

Instead of blaming his boss, his coworkers and even the friend who picked him up late, Bill began taking responsibility for his reaction.

SUMMARY STATEMENTS

- By asking, *Why do I feel it?* you can go behind your painful emotions to identify the specific false beliefs causing them.
- Denial only compounds our problems; it is not a solution. We can be honest about our feelings.

Bill was determined to stop his pattern of believing lies about himself and his situation.

Bill needed a mind change

Step 3: What Do I Believe?

Once you really get in touch with what you feel about a situation and trace your emotions back to the false beliefs causing them, you can begin consciously and boldly to reject your false beliefs. Recognizing those beliefs does not necessarily change you unless you literally declare war on them. Refuse to live by those false beliefs! Seek to remove them from your mind!

For example Bill saw that he held to the false belief that he must achieve in his performance to feel good about himself as a person. Bill declared war on his false belief. Bill was determined to stop his pattern of believing lies about himself and his situation. Bill rejected his false belief as he declared to himself, *I admit the fact that I am taking this personally because I wrongly hold to the false belief that I must be adequate and achieve in my performance to feel good about myself as a person. I reject this false belief. I refuse to base my self-worth on my performance. I will not live by this lie any longer.* (Note how decisively, verbally, and forcefully Bill rejected his false belief.)

 You have selected a painful situation in your life, and using the principles of the Trip In, you have discovered the emotion that you feel and have found the controlling false belief. Now write a forceful rejection of that false belief. Then, to practice this process, say your forceful rejection out loud.

_____

_____

You not only can learn to detect your false beliefs; you can learn to reject them. When we first begin to recognize our false beliefs; we gloss over them and rush to affirm our worth in a given situation. The false beliefs remain in our mind, unchallenged and unchanged. They keep their unconscious influence and can cause more destructive reactions in similar situations in the future.

For example, some people might have told Bill his problem was that he wrongfully avoided his responsibilities at work later that day. They also might have said he was wrong to harbor resentment toward his boss and coworkers. They would advise him to confess his wrongdoing and resentment, to pray, and to change his behavior. Such advice is effective as far as it goes. If Bill confessed a wrong attitude about his boss and coworkers and aired his resentment, he might feel some immediate relief and feel somewhat better about himself—at least he would accept the responsibility for his actions.

However, if this is all Bill does, he still likely will harbor the unconscious false belief that really caused his harmful emotions and behavior in the first place. Bill would change his attitude only temporarily; then he probably would fall back into the same behavior pattern again and probably would feel even more guilty for his failure. Bill needed a mind change about his specific false belief. Bill began to reject that false belief and refused to live on the basis of it.

Step 3 in your Trip In, then, is to reject your false beliefs each time they affect you. Use self-talk. For example, if you are seeking to renew your mind by rejecting the third false belief, say something like the following: *I reject this false*

> Write an example of self-talk you could use to reject a false belief you might have had about yourself.

_____

_____

_____

_____

belief. I am not going to base my worth on what other people think about me any longer. My day of being a people-pleaser is over, once and for all. I am through! Try this exercise for yourself in the margin box. Practice makes perfect!

Let every disturbing situation be an opportunity to focus on a false belief that affects you. Focus on your false beliefs again and again, in various types of problem situations, until you become highly conscious of them. This lifts your false beliefs from your unconscious into your conscious awareness! This way you can confront those false beliefs more directly, consistently, and forcefully.

Correcting by Affirming

However, rejection alone still is not enough to rid your mind of false beliefs. You not only can reject them but also correct them by affirming the truth about your worth as a person. To correct false beliefs about yourself, affirm the truth about your self-worth. You do this by rejecting your false beliefs about specific situations. Furthermore, you reject all the false beliefs about your personal worth when you say the affirmation "My Identity in Christ," provided on page 224 of this book. You reject your false belief and then correct it by repeating your affirmation. Remind yourself of your identity in Christ so that eventually you can believe it with assurance and deep conviction.

 Repeat from memory the affirmation "My Identity in Christ." Then write below about a typical, predictable situation in your life in which you will commit to using the affirmation to reject false beliefs.

_____

_____

Really celebrate!

Make it a celebration each time you affirm your personal worth. You can tell yourself, *How marvelous it is to know I am a new creation of infinite worth! I really can believe this, so I don't have to feel like a person of low self-worth. I can regret this painful situation but don't have to overreact to it.* Make certain that each time you take a Trip In, you follow through and take all four steps so that every Trip In always ends in a celebration of your identity in Christ.

People often have a mental block against taking this kind of inner look because, deep inside, they fear what they see will make them feel even worse about themselves. But you can keep that from happening if during your Trip In you reject your false self-concept and celebrate your worth as a person!

You will find that the task of reversing years of false beliefs about yourself and of affirming a different self-concept is a long one. Here are several things to keep in mind about how to affirm your worth:

How to affirm your worth

1. Merely affirming your identity in Christ does not mean your mind instantly agrees with what you are affirming. Affirming is a way by which you get a truth into your belief or value system. Repeat your affirmation insistently, over and over, until you can accept the affirmation as truth deep inside you.

2. Remember that you are affirming a new truth. You can satisfy your mind about the undeniable basis for believing you are a loved and forgiven child of God. Be convinced of the truth you are affirming.

3. Affirm the truth of your identity in Christ about specific false beliefs as they relate to a particular situation in your life.

4. Take the time to think through the truth of the affirmation about your worth as a loved and forgiven child of God until you really sense the full meaning of your affirmation. Consciously realizing the logic in the truth it contains, not mechanically uttering this affirmation, can correct your false beliefs.

 In the steps you just read, go back and underline the portion you feel represents the biggest challenge for you. Stop and pray, asking God to help you with that challenge.

SUMMARY STATEMENTS

- Once you really get in touch with what you feel about a situation and trace your emotions back to the false beliefs causing them, you can begin consciously and boldly to reject your false beliefs.
- To correct false beliefs about yourself, affirm the truth about your identity in Christ.

DAY
5

For if anyone is a hearer of the word and not a doer, he is like a man who looks at his natural face in a mirror, for once he has looked at himself and gone away, he has immediately forgotten what kind of person he was.

–James 1:23-24

Step 4: How Will I Act?

You truly can know you have affirmed a truth into your belief system when you find you act in the way most in line with what you believe. You can act and think and live like the loved and forgiven child of God you see yourself to be. Read the verse at left about hearing about and doing godly actions. The fourth step in your Trip In is to act in a way befitting the loved and forgiven child of God you affirm yourself to be. As we said earlier, the sequence of a Trip In is to: (1) determine the source of the destructive behavior; (2) discover the harmful emotions; (3) detect and reject the false belief; and (4) take action befitting the loved and forgiven child of God you are.

If Bill in our earlier example truly believed in his identity in Christ and acted in a way befitting the person of worth he believed himself to be, he might continue to feel the hurt but would forgive his boss for his wounding words. Hopefully Bill's boss would understand about Bill's being late, but if not, Bill still could choose to focus on his identity in Christ and to make good choices in his relationships and in his work that day.

Think how you would act in a certain situation if you really believed your identity in Christ. Take that action! As you act in line with that identity in Christ you believe yourself to have, your action in response to distressing situations can reinforce your faith in the person of worth you are! The moment you act is the moment when life change occurs.

Act like a loved child of God

 Think about the painful situation you described in step 2. Now describe on the next page how you would act in that situation if you truly believed you were a loved and forgiven child of God.

The Holy Spirit Helps

Such actions never come easy. At times it may seem as though you have no assistance. But later you can look back on the situation and realize the Holy Spirit worked on your behalf as you took your positive and willful action. He enables you to do things you can't begin to explain in human terms!

John's story

John was a chronic alcoholic who completed a substance-abuse treatment program and was involved in Alcoholics Anonymous. He wisely made sobriety his absolute priority. However, business pressures made him anxious and distracted him. He soon felt he must resign his executive job to stay sober. A promising career was about to go right down the tube! But John learned to take the Trip In. He began to recognize how much he suffered from the second false belief—he had to be adequate, successful, and achieving to feel self-worth.

In time, John began to see he could do nothing to make himself one degree more valuable as a person. He began consistently to exercise his will to live in accordance with his high self-concept. John reasoned that he did not need to fear failure in his business or in anything else since he was a loved and forgiven child of God.

John reasoned he did not need to fear failure in his business or in anything else since he was a person of worth.

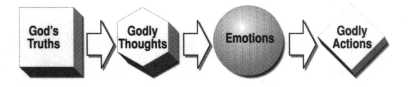

John chose to stay in his career. Rather than give in to his painful emotions and resign from his job, the Holy Spirit helped him act consistently with a belief in his self-worth. When John separated his personal worth from his job performance, he began to enjoy his job once again. Quiet confidence came as John began to act and live out what he believed about himself.

When you act like a loved and forgiven child of God you may—
- **admit mistakes**
- **correct errors**
- **make amends**
- **set goals**
- **disclose thoughts and feelings**
- **attempt new tasks**

Acting in line with the loved and forgiven child of God you are may lead you to admit mistakes, make amends, and correct errors whenever possible. It might release you to set goals. To act in light of your self-worth may free you to disclose thoughts and feelings without worry about pleasing others. You may attempt tasks that fear of failure might have kept you from trying.

✎ **Write the truths about yourself you have discovered as you rejected your false beliefs in day 4. Ask the Father to help you act in a way befitting a loved and forgiven child of God.**

What you do in such situations indeed *is* your choice. You can choose to let your feelings control you, or you can choose to act in light of your identity in Christ! As you begin to act in light of your identity in Christ in various situations, your action can reinforce your belief. You can establish a positive cycle, and you can change your entire life-style. You eventually can find it easier to believe yourself to be the person of worth that you really are.

The Next Step

Hopefully you have learned in *Search for Significance* how to use your emotions to identify your beliefs, so you can reject Satan's lies and replace them with God's truths. But do not expect perfection! You have built your existing belief system over a period of many years. Sometimes replacing lies with the truth may seem easy, while at other times it may be frustrating.

The enemy of our souls does not want us to be freed from his lies. Expect spiritual battles, uneasy feelings, and some discouragement. The enemy wants to confuse you and to muddle your thinking. Be patient and persistent. As you apply these principles, the time interval between your painful emotions and your ability to replace lies with God's truths can become shorter and shorter. Then teach these truths to others. Teaching is the best way to learn because we pay more attention and study more diligently when we communicate scriptural truths to someone else.

Develop a godly tenacity and keep following Christ. You may make mistakes; you may encounter others' disapproval; you may blame someone; you may fail to apply these truths; and you occasionally may dishonor the Lord. But realize that you are deeply loved, completely forgiven, fully pleasing, totally accepted, and absolutely complete because Christ died for you and was raised from the dead to give you new life! You are free to "proclaim the excellencies of Him who has called you out of darkness into His marvelous light" (1 Peter 2:9). The Lord is for you! He gives you wisdom, strength, and encouragement—so keep at it!

✎ **Review this week's lessons. Pray and ask God to identify one positive statement that had an impact on your understanding of who you are.**

Write that statement in your own words.

_____

_____

Rewrite your thoughts as a prayer of thankfulness to God.

_____

_____

You probably gained many insights as you worked through this week's lessons. Which insight stands out to you? Write it here.

_____

_____

Apply what you've learned by—
- **understanding the false beliefs**
- **rejecting lies and replacing them with God's truths**
- **preparing yourself for spiritual battles**
- **being patient and persistent**
- **teaching these truths to others**
- **continuing to follow Christ**

MY IDENTITY IN CHRIST

Because of Christ's redemption,
I am a new creation of infinite worth.

I am deeply loved,
I am completely forgiven,
I am fully pleasing,
I am totally accepted by God.
I am absolutely complete in Christ.

When my performance
reflects my new identity in Christ,
that reflection is dynamically unique.

There has never been another person like me
in the history of mankind,
nor will there ever be.
God has made me an original,
one of a kind, really somebody!